A NEW SEX ETHICS
and
MARRIAGE STRUCTURE

A NEW SEX ETHICS

and

MARRIAGE STRUCTURE

discussed by Adam and Eve

BY

MARION BASSETT

PHILOSOPHICAL LIBRARY

New York

Library of Congress Catalog Card No. 60-53155
Printed in the United States of America

Dedicated to all the Eves and Adams

who read this book

with open and understanding minds

CONTENTS

CONTENTS

PREFACE

When Charles Darwin demonstrated the process of evolution in living matter and the fact that human beings developed from lower animals during many millions of years, most people were upset at having their theories and myths found to be wrong in many respects. Yet we are far better off recognizing the truth and having a basis for learning more about ourselves and nature than we would be if we still held the former theories about human creation given in the Bible. People generally felt that to accept evolution they were denying the existence of a God. But many scientists hold that we can conceive of God as in part this great power of creation revealed in evolution.

We recognize that there is a corresponding evolutionary process in our thinking. For instance, our ideas regarding government and ethics have gradually developed over the ages. We have come to believe that a monarchy with absolute power held by a king is an inferior form of government; less apt to bring progress than a representative form with power in the hands of the people. And we have come to disapprove of sacrificing boys and girls on altars in religious ceremonies.

In this evolution of our attitudes toward human relations and government there is an area where progress has been very slow. This is the area of relations between men and women. The basic attitudes presented in the Bible representing thought from about 2000 B.C. to 400 A.D. are still held by a majority of persons today. These attitudes are presented in the story of God's creating Adam and later Eve from his rib to keep him company and to serve him. The theories that the male is definitely superior to the female; that he should be her "head," leading her in all matters; that the woman's function in childbirth indicates that she is less favored by God, are still embodied in our laws and institutions today. For instance, our laws make the man the legal head of the family no matter what his character may be. The man still owns his wife sexually; she must serve him as the legal concept of "wifely duty" indicates. She is forbidden any sexual relations unless she goes under the control of one particular man. Then he may abandon her if she once has relations with another.

Can we continue to hold the theory of male superiority while we are discarding the theories of innate race superiority? We have felt the evil effects of the Hitler doctrine of German superiority and are now seeing the results of the false doctrine of innate white superiority.

Yet many intelligent people have not yet let in the light of rational thought or scientific knowledge in the relations between the sexes. To look into this will doubtless shock many of my readers. But just as Darwin's great demonstration of evolution of the human being has allowed us to vision a hidden truth and to make further progress, I believe that understanding the evolution of the attitudes of Biblical times, and their slight change since then, will give us insight and allow us to make further progress in the relationship between men and women.

What materials should be drawn upon? Certainly we must cut through the boundary lines between academic disciplines, which method C. Wright Mills claims to be the most promising in considering many social problems today. Therefore I present studies in the psychology of sub-human primates, primitive man, human psychology, early myths and laws, and the marriage and divorce laws of today. It is impossible to give details in all these areas without extending this discussion into several volumes. Necessarily I present the general views of scientists in these various fields. When I, for instance, give a particular example of a primitive ceremony or some psychological tests with monkeys, I do not claim these alone prove sweeping conclusions.

Rather they are given to illustrate and to make more vivid the scientists' general views in these matters.

We are disturbed over the divorce rate and are persuading people in churches and colleges to fit into our marriage institution. It is time we stop to study this institution itself, to determine whether it may contain serious faults and not be adapted to present needs or present democratic ideals.

Marion Bassett

Rather they are given to illustrate and to make more vivid the scientists' general views in these matters.

We are disturbed over the divorce rate and are persuading people in churches and colleges to fit into our marriage institution. It is time we stop to study this institution itself, to determine whether it may contain serious faults and not be adapted to present needs or present democratic ideals.

Marion Bassett

To Dr. Robert L. Dickinson, my good friend, I acknowledge a great debt. He went over several of these chapters and encouraged me to complete the book. Much of it was written since his death, but he would say, "Speak out. Oh! how we need women's thoughts on sex and marriage — they have the wombs of the race. Men do most of the writing."

He was a genius who went to fundamentals, then thought originally and independently about them, discarding in the process much of man's erroneous thinking. For instance, he sensed people's hunger to know more about human reproduction, discarded the views that they best be kept in ignorance, and became the courageous pioneer in sex enlightenment. He wrote articles and books, talked to doctors and laymen, and prepared the series of sculptures showing prenatal growth and the birth process which were exhibited at the 1939 New York World's Fair, and attracted thousands who often waited in line for hours to pass by them. Pictures of these models are now used everywhere.

He became convinced that mothers' health and well-being should receive more attention and established The National Committee on Maternal Health. He was also the first doctor of our country to see the importance of birth control and willing to give time fighting for the cause.

As a leading doctor, artist and humanitarian he treated the subject of sex with an artist's touch and his generous interest extended to the poor as well as the fortunate. He promoted the theory that physical well-being and emotional health were interdependent, long before psychosomatic medicine was generally adopted.

A founder of the American College of Surgeons and the American Gynecological Society of which he was the first president, he is regarded as the dean of American obstetricians and gynecologists of his day. He and I started a discussion group called the "Conference on Socio-sexual Relations" which met off and on for two years. Most of its members and others formed the American Association of Marriage Counselors.

How did he happen to live to be almost ninety years old with a beautifully functioning mind; an erect, energetic body and a warm, sparkling spirit to the end? Partly because he loved nature spending days exploring the country for his illustrations of the "New York Walk Book"; also because he loved people to whom he gave freely of his time during his last twenty years; and lastly, because he was interested in that life-giving, fascinating subject of sex.

As his pupil, I have tried to write this book as an artist, a humanitarian and an independent scientist seeking the truth.

MARION BASSETT

xiv

A NEW SEX ETHICS
and
MARRIAGE STRUCTURE

CHAPTER 1

Letter to Adam

Dear Adam,

You know all too well how much I adore you when you are loving! You know how dependent I am upon you, absolutely, for my romantic life—that part of living which brightens all existence. Without you my life would be barren, barren of the deep richness and variations of our unity, barren of the exhilarations, the soaring into the unknown, the constant inspiration from the joining of our feelings and our minds—and barren of those little beings who carry our lives into the future. Our children need you as their father —your help to me is basic while I give vitality to their prenatal growth, their birth and rearing. They need your strong arms under them offering security and they look to you to learn the ways of men.

How can you know what I think unless I frankly tell you? Of course you can guess but guesses are often filled with wishful thinking. The woman with whom you enjoy that thrilling mutual love, or that calm, settled companionship founded on years of friendly living together, cannot tell you some of her thoughts if that relationship is to continue. She must treat this feeling on your part like a tender flower, nourishing it each day. Yet all love is a mixture of admiration, toleration and even dislike of some of the other's qualities. Since you and she both tend to bury these dissatisfactions a good airing may be helpful. So I here attempt to express some of Eve's. Since I am only an abstraction to you, Adam, no glorious tie will be broken if I am outspoken and this frankness may help you look more searchingly into your lover's life and establish your relationship on a firmer basis.

It is a truism that if the marriage relationship is successful we both are inspired persons, filled with vitality, hope and kindness. On the other hand, if man and wife do not understand, help and encourage each other as we are buffeted around by the outside world we can lose all *joie de vivre*.

Yet how little analysis there has been of the factors which break us apart or carry us on high. Analysis of any relationship implies viewing one's self critically and against a background of beings, all struggling for self-fulfillment. But just as a doctor's physical examination, followed by certain improved habits, may not be pleasant, in the long run one enjoys better health if he pauses at times for such a study.

A man and woman joined by love form the complete living being. Each of the pair reacts to the condition of the other as directly as the leaves of a tree react to the health of its roots. The circular response of the man to the woman's thoughts and feelings, and hers to the man's all know who have lived deeply together. Your true satisfaction with life, Adam, therefore rests upon mine. The relationships between men and women will continue, *n'est-ce pas?* The question is, what kind shall they be?

Have you discovered yet the quixotic nature of happiness? The more persistently you seek it the more it often hangs just beyond your reach. Still more illusive is sexual pleasure. It is found for a period with your wife, then often seems to wither away. It may then be found with another, only to wither again. You may then reach for still more freedom and variety, only to discover that a fleeting, physical relief is found—no deep satisfaction of mind and spirit. In desperation for the perfect lover and the pinnacle of pleasure you may turn to full freedom, not even waiting for real friendship before taking a sexual partner. You may revel in change and variation, then wonder why your partners don't show more affection and response to your attentions. They of course see and feel you as you really are, not at all in love but only experimenting. They cannot possibly respond where there is no warm tenderness and deep personal feeling to rouse them. Contentment with moderation that

2

allows real consideration for your mate and possible children, whether within or without marriage, may be the key to the greatest and most lasting sexual happiness. Can a pattern be developed which includes this along with some variation in partners? We are all truly baffled — but we should consider it. Deep sexual pleasure cannot be disassociated from other aspects of human relations, cannot be sought and gained alone, but only along with other satisfactions, such as that one is helping his mate and that one is standing by his children.

Now that man can travel faster than sound, send missiles to the moon and explode life-annihilating bombs we can talk of the need of planning human preservation without being ridiculed. We are forced to think basically and courageously. In such thinking we should consider the relations between men and women, as to whether the present customs and laws which determine their lives in and out of marriage are leading to the race's survival and its health. It is a vast subject upon which one enters in fear and trembling. The common attitude is to joke about the difficulties between the sexes and let the problems pass with a good laugh.

Yet, Adam, instead of something amusing the relation between the sexes may be at the core of forces leading to continuation or destruction of humankind. Our present condition, developed and led by men, is caught in an impasse over power to destroy, an impasse between competing nations. Some scientists believe that it necessarily leads to extensive destruction and a return to more primitive conditions. Insufficient drives of certain kinds necessary to break this impasse seem to be lacking. We need drives centered on the preservation of life, on the nurture of all this globe's human beings, on the condition of children, always emphasizing the future. Where will we find these needed drives?

I say we will find them in our women — in these lowly creatures, the mothers. In this half of the human race whose members have thus far not been free to develop their minds and abilities, but rather been made to fit into man's culture. They have been led to become mainly attractive sexual prizes in order to live a complete life with a mate — to develop submissiveness and patient performance of the mechanics of food preparation and cleanliness.

When men write of women they inevitably treat of her appearance, of her attractive youth or older age, of the emphasis she puts upon her clothes, and often imply her light-mindedness and frivolity. Little do these men realize that in doing this they reveal their masculine point of view which regards as prime the sexual appeal of women. There is far, far more to women than this. Their minds often range to far horizons; center on the future of their own and their country's children, considering problems of yet unconceived children; weigh men's thoughts and actions, their demands upon themselves and the consequences of these.

In this period of awesome revolutionary changes does anyone think the relationship between men and women should remain the same as in the dark ages? Dear Adam, only you and I together, while seeking to understand each other, combining our thinking, determined to lift each other's spirits, can move ahead step by step into some pattern which allows us and our children to drink more fully of life's riches.

With my love, your
Eve

4

CHAPTER 2

Sexual Life Not Yet Democratic

Their canoe was drifting out in the center of the small lake. Adam and Eve had left the others at the cocktail party on the campus, had fled from the confusing crisscross conversion of their high-spirited friends. In contrast they were calm as the ripples softly lapped at the sides of the boat and they watched the combinations of shadows, some pitch black, others not so black, but movement could be seen within and blotches of light where the starry sky was not hidden by the trees.

Their group had been throwing back and forth thoughts on marriage — on the outside freedoms in sex life and about "demasculinizing" women who dominate men. Adam's mind was running in that direction, "It's true when our times are written up in history the revolution in sex will be an important part — the great changes in attitudes toward intercourse and the actual behavior both within and without marriage."

"Of course Alfred Kinsey's studies will be mentioned and the other scores of books on sex techniques always entitled 'Sex in Marriage' or such like."

"And, Eve, if the historian is any good, he'll picture the awful contrast — I say awful because it is full of awe — between what actually takes place on the one hand — and on the other, the preaching of the churches, the synagogues, the teaching in the schools and colleges and the laws enforced in courts. That contrast — is as interesting as the breaking over the traces itself."

"You remember we were going to write a book on it all looking at it from our own point of view today, that of a man and woman college teacher."

5

"Oh yes. I'm itching to get it started. Let's resolve, let's swear to this beautiful evening that we'll start it this month!"

"I swear to God we will, Adam. We'll push each other to it."

"I'm bursting with ideas, they're rushing around my head like wild animals in a cage. Even this quiet place doesn't put them to rest."

"Good. That's my state, too. I read along with thousands 'Lady Chatterley's Lover' and my sympathy is with the love-starved wife who finds deep satisfying life with her lover, breaking our ancient laws, our honored and sacred institution. And I see in the film 'Hiroshima, Mon Amour' the moving drama of illicit relations between another man and woman, both married, which bring a marvelous closeness between them, a sharing of our deepest human problems." Eve paused, then went on, "These along with other books and plays presenting similar themes make many people think the thing is solved—we will no longer submit to the rigid restrictions of monogamous marriage.—Yet we're miles away from the solution of combining our surging emotions and sexual desires with the careful nurture of children and the winning of a rewarding life through the years for men and women."

"Yes, we're miles away from a pattern which works. The intellectuals, the teachers, ministers, lawyers, and psychiatrists largely hold up the marriage institution with all its rigid requirements."

"If a mother enclosed in a round of household chores with a husband who is unable to give her any real affection or appreciation flees to the warmth of an affair with another man, they jump to the conclusion that she is a warped person, a case for a psychiatrist. They look at her behavior in relation to the inherited pattern of marriage and are shocked. They don't step outside that frame of reference and consider her actions in relation to the basic needs of all human beings for some reciprocation of regard and affection

6

— and the life-giving powers of sex with love. That would take them into an uncharted sea."

"We'll venture into that sea in our book, won't we Eve? It has been assumed that people, and women in particular, are sinful or neurotic if they don't conform to the restrictions marriage places upon them and happily blossom forth while doing so. — It is time to analyze the marriage institution itself."

"Exactly, to consider how well it fits the needs of individual men and women today—also those of children—and of society in its stumbling for peace."

"The institution is on the skew-jinx," Adam breathed. A long, thin animal which swiftly swam by their canoe to the shore diverted their attention for a while.

Then Eve continued, "The marriage laws were formed before great areas of knowledge now entirely accepted were discovered—such as: knowledge of the human body and its glandular functioning; knowledge of the human mind and of the needs of infants. For instance, they say in effect to women, 'An important part of your job as wife is to please your husband sexually, this is called wifely duty. He may divorce you if you refuse him for a certain period or even if you don't sufficiently please him. It doesn't matter if you have six children already, more than you can care for, or whether your husband's attitude toward you and toward sex are such that you are cold when he approaches you. And you must deny even to yourself any strong feelings toward another man who shows you some warmth and understanding. A good woman doesn't have such feelings. She knows that her role is solely to serve her husband, to hold her family together no matter how difficult. — She also knows that if her husband dies she must go on living contentedly with no male companionship, with no relief in her loneliness through the close embrace.' The laws say all this in their high-sounding words, seemingly convinced that they understand women thoroughly and know just what is good for them.

"I am leading up to what I learned the other day. It is new knowledge to most of us. It is that when women are sexually hungry it is not a matter of their mind, their imagination or evil thinking — it is a physiological fact which medical science can present in physical terms just as it can describe the physiological facts of hunger for food. Likewise when a woman is thoroughly satisfied sexually it is not only an idea in her mind but a physical situation, orgasm, which pervades her whole body and also can be described in physical terms by Dr. William H. Masters and others, and clearly demonstrated."

"Well put. Yet not long ago leading doctors wrote that a virtuous woman experienced no pleasure in sex. They didn't recognize even the possibility of her orgasm. The wife was to serve her husband whenever he desired, having no rising and falling of desire herself but was rather a half-living being in the matter of sex, almost inanimate. And I agree such ideas are embodied in our legislation still on the books."

Sounds of laughter came over the water and drew them back to their friends. As Adam paddled he pleaded, "You write something, Eve, to start us off. Let's meet in my office next Saturday. We'll begin to talk out our book in front of the sound recorder as we have planned."

"What subject should I present first? — I'll write something that's purely a woman's statement."

"Yes that's right. Why don't you write about how well sexual customs have satisfied women?"

"All right. I'll make a stab at it."

It was early September before the students had arrived. Adam Ofenden and Eve Beaupomme, through their study of relations between men and women in the past centuries, as well as the present, had become fascinated with the subject. Both knew marriage and had gained much knowledge from others problems which were brought to them.

They decided to talk frankly and openly before the recording machine, then go over this material deciding just what was safe to put into their book and what should be

8

omitted. (The following chapters, however, are their recorded conversations before they censored them and some sections Eve wrote herself.)

Adam is not a typical man for he has given far more time and thought to this subject than most. He is more like the rare men of the past who have understood some of the handicaps placed upon women and the need for removing them, such as William Lloyd Garrison and Wendell Phillips, who recognized the justice in women's having a voice in the election of persons to govern them. Another was Lester Ward, called our country's first great sociologist, who wrote of the importance of man's greater size and freedom from burdens of reproduction in giving him the dominant social position. One other was the late Robert L. Dickinson, who saw the vital need for allowing women to control the functioning of their own bodies, that is, to determine when they should assume the big task of growing and bearing a child.

Since Adam stands with these, he and Eve find agreement in many areas. They do not, for instance, have to argue whether women are full persons and whether our ideals of democracy should be applied to women or not. They can spend time on the more intricate problems of carrying out these ideals.

Adam waited uneasily in his office at the University this Saturday morning listening for Eve and hoping she would bring the material she had promised to write. She hadn't failed him before. No, she wouldn't this time—here she was with her papers, as lovely as in the canoe the other evening and more awake.

He jumped up to greet her. She with apologies passed him her statement, which he eagerly took and began to read without much ceremony.

The big mystery for men — a woman

Surely a basic need is for men to really understand a woman's feelings and desires, and likewise for her to understand his. The big mystery for men is why a woman acts

9

as she does, and how it feels to be a woman. He can guess, he can imagine, but he never will really know what it feels like to have breasts, to be the woman in intercourse, to discover that oneself is pregnant, and to give birth to a child. If he wins the trust of a woman and asks her to explain these experiences she may try her best but she will be limited to words—clumsy, indefinite words which only vaguely express what she means.

Of course for woman the feelings of men are equally a mystery. She will also never really know how it feels when sexual relations during the prime of one's life are entirely free of any possibility of carrying an unborn child; what it is like to be the man in intercourse and to be unable to have relations unless one really wants them and is ready for them.

Still further, man does not know what it means for women to conform to our social customs. He has not even tried to guess how it is to be prohibited from taking the initiative in expressing one's interest to an attractive man or telling him of her love. Nor has he begun to imagine what a wife's feelings are when she knows he is enjoying a deep relationship with another woman, while she is required to be faithfully centered upon him and their home.

Even the man Sigmund Freud, who concentrated upon the relations between the sexes, admitted he didn't understand women. He confessed to a certain hopelessness concerning his ability to help them, writing that in no phase of his analytic work had he suffered more from the oppressive feeling that all his efforts were in vain.[1] In fact, he did not separate the biological factors, such as her reproductive burdens, from the restrictions placed upon her by the social customs and laws. He regarded both of these sets of factors as making one complex to which she should submit, and recognize her feminine role, as passive dependency. Freud's followers today largely hold the same view, saying woman attains fullest maturity when she learns to accept "her role." But many women know that, although they must accept their biological functions, there is no necessity of their accepting the social restrictions which are wound around them — the double standard of morals; the confinement largely to their homes; economic dependence upon one man after marriage and, in Arabia and other countries, the purdah.

Fortunately the general human craving for sexual satisfaction is now acknowledged but the special nature of women's needs still remains largely unrecognized. Since they are compelled to live within a rigidly imposed set of restrictions they hardly know their own free sexual impulses, and still less do men know these.

No doubt women have been so regarded because men are the subjects, the ones who more extensively and more freely have expressed their thoughts. Women are the objects, the ones about whom observations are made. Everyone takes himself largely for granted and thinks about the strange and interesting ways of others, though his own ways are usually just as strange. Those who do most of the talking and writing, if not challenged, regard their attitudes as correct, and the public tends to adopt them.

Men, the subjects, have expressed in rivers of printed matter their thoughts about women, because women have been the most interesting objects of their environment and the center of their sexual lives. Not their minds nor their education interest men so much as their beautiful bodies, their lovely faces, their voluptuous voices, their dainty but revealing clothes. Men have not meant to belittle other sides of women's nature but their own vital urges have led them to center on these features. And men have struggled to control these women-objects. They have been somewhat wild and unreasonable about it; they want so much and such different things from them. From a wife, for instance, the man wants a hard-working, stay-at-home house-keeping mother who is also a glamour girl. The limitations of reality they recognize to some extent, but they have not yet been forced to come down to earth with their demands.

In practically all writing by men, even in the serious fields of medicine, sociology and most impressively in jurisprudence, men are usually caught in this net of regarding women more or less as objects, or those persons who serve men. This attitude so completely surrounds men that they are hardly conscious of its existence. They, the subjects, view women as those who enchant and torment them, rather than as full persons who also are being enchanted and tormented by men. The man fiction writer almost always presents his women through men's eyes, centering upon her physical beauty and her desire to please her lover or her husband. The woman's relationship to the rest of the world, her opportunity to develop her unique personality, her character as a citizen, her contribution in learning, her part in the struggle for cooperation and peace are almost ignored. Young women are largely regarded as the flowers which men study, then pick, each man plucking the best he can obtain in the competitive game among pickers. The *Miss* or *Mrs.* label shows whether each feminine flower has been chosen or is still free to be taken. Men carry no such label to help women know their status.

Adam glanced up from his reading at Eve who was watching his reaction to her words, nervously waiting his comment. "You've got it down well, with much more punch than I could use. Of course our book would be more popular with many if it included slang, gags and slapstick but we aren't writing for entertainment. We're trying to encourage constructive thought."

Eve beamed, "Yes, I kept questioning to myself whether it should be high temperature or low temperature writing. I decided we had enough in high temperature, dramatic cases, wild jealousy and murders — some careful thought was needed." Adam nodded as he continued reading:

Nature has lavishly endowed each woman — and man —
with sex desire

People *can* live without sexual satisfaction during their lives. People can also live without sight. To say that a person

12

can live without seeing or can live with no sexual pleasure tells only a small part of the truth about life. Those liberated from the outlook of a moralistic past probably agree that a person deprived of sexual satisfactions is a handicapped person, for he lacks a whole range of valuable and revitalizing experience. The experience is largely in the realm of feeling but that does not mean it is any less real or pervading than experience in other realms. This world of feeling is the center of all romance. It offers many almost the only experience in life of unadulterated joy and complete satisfaction. The feelings of full sexual pleasure can no more be conveyed in words to those who are virgins, men or women, than can the sensations of light and shade and color be communicated to one who has never had the power of sight. Ignorance of such an important world as that of sex naturally brings about a certain caution and lack of self-confidence. A vague feeling of frustration together with perhaps a certain glandular sluggishness often affects the woman celibate's nervous stability. She may never through sex feel that life begins anew, that she is reborn. To Freud and his disciples must go much of the credit for awakening us to the damage which many personalities suffer from the non-arousal of latent sex desire or a constant repression of active desire.

Those who have experienced the full delights of love will agree with John Cooper Powys:

> "Liberated by love, at one grand stroke from these superficialities, the mind experiences an incredible relaxation. This relaxation very soon lends itself to a vibrant sensitivity in which impressions are received and values noted of a kind that are fresh, thrilling, original. What love can achieve in a person's life-culture is on a par with the miracle that a heavy dew can work upon a thirsty garden. The juices and the saps of a million frustrated growths bestir themselves within their parched stalks." [2]

The drive for sex satisfaction remains nature's great mystery. Rodin's exquisite piece of sculpture *The Hand of*

God which shows two lovers lying in locked embrace within Divinity's great palm, expresses the same thought. The lovers are helplessly in the grasp of that overpowering demand that they fuse their lives and bring to full completion their consuming desire.

Throughout history men have admitted the urge within themselves for sexual expression. They have commonly allowed themselves not one but many wives; wives and concubines; wives and women captured from the enemy; wives and slave girls; wives and prostitutes. They have insistently and ingeniously assured themselves sexual satisfaction whether at home or away from home. The man-made laws of all countries have dealt leniently with these masculine "necessities" as evidenced by the universal and age-old institution of prostitution. This institution helps the young, unmarried man; the weaker or poorer man who lacks his own woman; the succesful man who can buy variety, and opens a way for them all against even a temporary deprivation. They in one way or another can have their "sex." The picture is quite clear.

Yet parallel with men's recognition of their own impelling sexual needs and the consequent provision for their fulfillment is a great silence about women's sexual needs and how well or ill these have been fulfilled. What do we find to insure women's sexual fulfillment?

"Less than a hundred years ago the English surgeon, Acton, wrote a book which until near the end of the last century was the standard authority on sexual questions, and stated in it that to attribute sexual feelings to women was a 'vile asperation' . . . In another standard medical work, it was laid down that only 'lascivious women' showed any physical signs of pleasure when in the embrace of their husbands." [3]

Men often ignore this urge in women

In the past men as individuals and men as a group have taught that the virtuous woman was one whose only sexual desire was to afford her husband pleasure. The idea of "wifely duty" comes down through history, is written in English common law and that of our country today. It implies that she should be always ready for relations, has no spontaneous desires, as men do, according to her mood or monthly tides of feeling; also that arousal of her interest by his affection and thoughtfulness need not be a prerequisite. [4]

Men have tried to frighten women out of their spontaneous sexual desires. Not only within marriage were women to be submissive and unaroused, but any desired relations outside of marriage were not even to be mentioned. Many a wife in order to be "virtuous" and "pure" has tried not to admit even to herself that the physical relations with her husband have become devoid of any spark of satisfaction, while her blood surges through her body with passion at the very sight of another man she loves.

Yet a physiological need cannot be entirely preached out of existence. We cannot convince a physically tired person that he does not crave sleep, and we cannot convince a sexually starved woman that she does not want satisfaction. Man's chief achievement here has been compelling woman to muffle her desires and frustrations, while often pretending a false contentment. We cannot criticize women for responding as men decreed for the very lives of women have been largely in men's control.

It is significant that in some *few* cultures where women can more freely express themselves, they voice opinions indeed shocking to our society. Among the Tchambuli a widow or a dissatisfied wife chooses her own new husband. The people say in explanation, "Has she no sexual needs? Are women passive sexless creatures, who can be expected to wait upon the dilly-dallying of formal considerations . . . Men, not so urgently sexed, may be expected to submit themselves to the discipline of a due order of prudence." [5]

In a few other primitive cultures men have become convinced that sexual experience is more enjoyable when the woman herself is well pleased and have developed customs which sometimes give her initiative and at other times require her consent before intercourse.[6]

Yet among *most* cultures equally primitive, women's sexual pleasure is ignored. [7] The sexual impulse in its simplest form contains little tenderness or love. "The male and female in their congress merely express a primitive instinct, which has nothing altruistic, kindly or social about it, and Freud states that the sexual impulse must have a cruel acquisitiveness, or else the mate cannot be possessed." [8] Many a primitive man has probably never experienced sexual intercourse with a woman who loved him and was eager for him, and hence he cannot compare such mutual delight with the satisfaction he obtains from his crude and selfish approaches. Apparently not only individuals, but whole tribes of women find their sex life an "abomination" not because of any condition in themselves, but because of the way in which the men manage sexual relations. It is significant that a woman anthropologist, Margaret Mead, was probably the first to present these facts about some primitive women's attitudes. She says of the Manus in New Guinea, "Every woman successfully conveys to her growing daughters her own affective reaction to the wearisome abomination which is sex." [9]

We need neither censure our masculine forebears nor today's primitive men who allot their women small sexual satisfaction. After all, they had no conception of equal opportunities, individual rights, or democracy. Might made right in general and their religion justified those who dominated others. The treatment of the aged and those of other tribes was often all in keeping with this principle.[10]

Men's misjudgment of women's sexuality in the past and present is based partly upon a misinterpretation of the physiological differences between the sexes. It is reasoned that since women are always able to have congress there should be no variation in their sexual desire at different times. Likewise, since they emphasize the physical side, they

16

have imagined that it made little difference to a woman to which man she was mated or when intercourse took place. But actually her readiness for intercourse, resulting largely from her favorable mental attitude toward the man and toward conjugation in general, which cause certain glandular secretions to flow through her body, increasing her circulation and transforming her sexual organs, make all the difference in the world in her enjoyment. If her mate has won her love and she is in the mood at the time, her pleasure may reach the highest point. However, if he has not, intercourse may be an indifferent matter or even painful, as we will later discuss. This is one of the delicate matters wives often are unable to fully convey to their husbands.

Men instead often think that since there is no female process corresponding to the male erection and accumulation of semen, the female desire cannot be varied at different times nor be so definite as his. Likewise today they usually think that some fifteen million women in our country, the single, separated and widowed, are quite happy living in enforced celibacy. And lastly, the man often imagines that since he obtains a degree of satisfaction from the mere physical act even though there is no mutual affection, women should react similarly. These mistaken views have been carried down through the centuries with small effort to verify them since they are in accord with the submissive role allotted women and justify men's "using" them fitfully or not at all, according to their own moods.

Knowledge brings responsibility. Today men understand, or should understand, far more than in the past about women's physiology and psychology. Along with this knowledge men have espoused the principle of equal opportunity for all. The men therefore in our country today who still support theories that women have been happy when required to submit and when forced to be celibate and that women are at present content playing a secondary role in the sexual world, will be judged by history differently from the men of earlier days.

To this day the truth about women's sex desires is unknown. Why? Because in most societies convention has even inhibited women's considering these themselves, much less discussing them. This is true largely even of our most modern customs. Since initiative in sexual matters has been largely denied women, we do not know how much initiative they would enjoy nor men's reaction to their greater spontaneity. A certain concept has most effectively prolonged women's subordination. Calverton says that it illustrates "so well how the male mind — the male mind always of the ruling class, but extending down, in its logic, through vertical organizations such as the church and the state, to the male minds of the lower classes as well — has been able to perpetuate its supremacy without a struggle. The first of these concepts is concerned with the monogamous nature of the female. . . . Woman certainly is not innately or biologically monogamous — no more monogamous than man. . . . Those men who have contended . . . that . . . women have always preferred the monogamous relation have merely tried to build up a rationalization for their own morality. There is not a single consecutive historical argument that can be scientifically submitted in defense of this thesis." [11]

The history of women seems to suport Calverton, for it reveals that she has been kept "faithful to her husband" not entirely through her own volition nor through his gentle persuasion, but by tales of the thundering of celestial gods, a life hereafter in hell, threats of ruin to the entire town or tribe, and even punishment by death if she took one wayward step. Death was a common legal punishment for a misstep by a European wife as late as the 1800's.

Along with these preachments and publishments the husband has generally assumed rights to abandon his wife and to deny her further support when she wandered from the straight and narrow path. Such were the laws of the past. And such are the laws of the present day in our own democracy.

An authority writes, "In the ecclesiastical courts it was clear that alimony was not to be allowed to a wife divorced for her own misconduct . . . In 23 states the statutes are silent as to the effect of the wife's guilt so the ecclesiastical rule seems to apply. Seventeen others achieve the same result by providing that alimony is to be allowed . . . to a party *not* in default . . ." [12] Others forbid an allowance when the wife "commits adultery." In short, all except three states deprive the guilty wife of alimony. We should here remember that most mothers with young children are not in a position to earn nor gain experience for earning, and that family savings are usually retained by the husband. In addition to freeing the husband from obligation to aid in supporting a former wife, 20 states deprive the guilty wife of real estate held by her at time of divorce, [13] while 9 states allow the court to decree to the husband some of her personal property. [14] In fact we have not progressed far toward balanced thinking concerning the unfaithful wife and the unfaithful husband. In many respects the attitude of 2000 B.C. rules today. At that time however the one-sided arrangement was not camouflaged by a pretended equality, but boldly presented in its unbalanced form in written laws: "If a man be with the wife of another man at her wish there shall be no penalty for him. As for the woman, her husband shall punish her as he pleases." [15]

True, the husband can be divorced today for committing adultery, if this can be *proved by the wife*. But since his movements and association with women can easily be covered under the guise of business and his expenses need not be revealed to his wife, this is most difficult for her to prove. And even if adultery should be determined and he were divorced, he would take with him his earning power and probably most the family savings. Then our customs regarding the spouses' relative ages allow the man to seek a new wife among the single women from his own age to a generation younger. These advantages usually place him in a position attractive to a new bride. Divorce is thus often not a hardship for the husband, but instead frequently a release for another honeymoon.

How can we know the sexual needs of a woman when we force her to live according to one restricted pattern and when even within marriage she must play a role which often suppresses her spontaneous desire? It may be safe to say that the custom is still such that if the wife's own sexual needs should happen to coincide with those of her husband's for her, then the pleasure of the virtuous woman could be shown. But if she desires him when he is away or when he is not in the mood (perhaps because he has had another woman) she, if wise, does not express her wishes. Of course, the husband is physically unable to have sexual intercourse without a certain degree of desire. He cannot be "used" as a woman can. If the attitude of the old saying, "Women were created for the comfort of men" could be discarded, men would greatly increase mutually desirous intercourse. At present in our country many a wife has sexual relations when she is indifferent and goes without when she is filled with desire. There are also the deep-lying feelings toward sex implanted in her girlhood in the effort to preserve her virginity which often interfere with the wife's real liberation in the marriage relationship. We are now, however, in the process of change among more enlightened people toward a new pattern of sex in marriage.

In the long history of silenced women we find some occasions when women of nobility were allowed to express themselves and even to live with some sexual freedom. One of these was in twelfth century France when certain noblewomen were allowed to enjoy troubadours and others as lovers in additions to their husbands. Since their husbands were often absent on crusades and skirmishes, sometimes for years, and since these women held wealth and power, they were granted this freedom. They themselves laid down bounds of propriety. For instance, Queen Eleanor of Aquitaine held courts of love, where questions on actual or imaginary situations were discussed with great insight and sensitivity. The following are some of their maxims on love:

"What the lover takes from his beloved against her will has no relish.

No one should be deprived of love without abundant reason.

It is unseemly to love those whom one would be ashamed to marry.

A true lover does not wish to enjoy the love of another than his beloved.

A new love drives away the old." [16]

A certain Viscountess of Norbonne acting as judge in one of these courts said: "The wealthy woman is deservedly praised if she seeks as a lover a poor man to whose aid, after his wealth is gone, her own riches can come . . . But if a woman be weighed down by the meanness of poverty, she receives a wealthy lover more readily." [17] She was referring to lovers and not husbands, for the marriage of these women was arranged by their parents.

In another statement she said, "Assuredly any woman's attitude is condemned as shameless who seeks to be loved and yet herself refuses to love." [18] (This could apply to men as well.)

Women's sentiments expressed in these courts of love, when pillaging and barbarities of all kinds were common, indicate their native interest and sense of balance about relationships between the sexes.

Ermengard stated in a decision "in marriage the wife has no choice about dispensing her favors, since the husband has a right to demand her presence in his bed. In a lady's association with a lover, however, she has the privilege of granting or withholding her ultimate favors as she desires. And the character of the love that results from these two relationships differ so fundamentally and in so many aspects that no comparison is possible." [19]

In these courts the psychological needs of women and delicate weighing of justice played an important part. The crude crust of patriarchy did not overlay their thought. The

21

arbitrators recognized women as human beings with the same fundamental needs as men.

Reasons for women's frigidity

All American studies reveal a surprising lack among women of full sexual satisfaction in marriage. In one of the studies, one-third of normal married women were found never or rarely to have experienced an intense climax, or orgasm. They either were repulsed by some phases of the sex experience or were simply giving what their husbands expected. Another third enjoyed sexual relations but generally experienced no orgasm; while only approximately one-third were well adjusted, usually had an orgasm and considered the act a most satisfying experience. The wives studied were under 35. [20] Inclusion of older couples would have doubtless lowered the percentage of those well satisfied. About the same proportion of married women were found by Dickinson and Beam and Hamilton [21] never to experience through orgasm a full degree of satisfaction.

In recent years it has become recognized that women in general do not experience orgasm as frequently as men and that this may be an innate biological difference since it also is found to be so among mammals in general. [22] Many women seem to enjoy relations to a high degree without reaching a climax. If we, therefore, don't judge wives' satisfactions by their experiencing orgasm or not, but rather by whether they enjoy the experience, we still find that about one quarter of all wives fail to receive satisfaction from sexual relations. These roughly six million wives, one out of four, either prefer that their husbands do not approach them, or desire relations but are left frustrated.[23]

Extended frigidity or lack of sex enjoyment among many American women is probably due mainly to our culture and not to their biological constitution. Anthropological studies showing the influence of customs as well as increased capacity for orgasm under skilled treatment [24] indicate that it is not mainly physiological.

The major cause of our sexually unsatisfied womanhood is probably the combination of two factors: (1) the general sex-negating attitude of American culture impressed particularly upon women, and (2) the male dominâtion characteristic of human society in general. Many scientific workers are courageously attacking the first factor; few have seen the crucial importance of changing the second.

It is significant that the artists, past and present, who portray the beauty and inspiration of sex-love usually do not present married love. In poetry, literature and drama it is the couple before marriage, or the lovers "under the rose" who are generally pictured. Most popular songs are about pre-marriage love and the dreams of later life. Few recent novels describe romantic love with varied and exciting episodes throughout the life of a husband and wife. There is, of course, high romance often in the early years of marriage but in marriage as a whole some of the elements of spontaneity and continued free choice of each other as mates are usually lacking, and it is these elements which artists want.

We live in a strange dichotomy. Our society in one breath holds married love as the ideal and with another recognizes the frequent failure of marriage to provide the sought-for happiness and the high divorce rate. We try to fit our young people into the ancient family pattern without stopping to see whether it needs analysis and improvement.

Many doctors are impressed with the number of married couples who have given up all sexual intercourse with each other. Probably at least, all separations and divorces are preceded by such a period. One case told by the wife involved typifies many. We should notice that it combines economic and personality problems and long working hours by the wife:

> "I struggled for years to keep the flame of our love alive, while my three children were young and my husband was tired and irritable. I helped him in his business in addition to my housework. He would say or do something that would knock out of me the last

23

shred of passion and love I had for him. After a time by pulling together all my resources I would be able to forgive and forget and to love him again. But then there would be another blow, a scolding because I didn't do more although I was exhausted at the end of each day — and all love would be quenched again. It was a series of heartbreaks. Sometimes I cried for two days at a time over the hopelessness of keeping our mutual love or of simply pleasing him. Combined with his uncontrolled and erratic treatment, practically all of the family savings were lost in speculation periodically and other difficult problems presented. After some years of this the spring from which the feelings of love are born seemed to run dry. The only way I could maintain my spirit to keep on living was to give up trying to re-kindle again and again my desire for him and instead to let my life run along in a smooth cool, non-emotional, non-sexual way, trying to please him but not being disappointed if I could not feel toward him what I had formerly. My satisfactions from sexual relations were greatly reduced. He of course noticed this. He then felt hurt that things had changed and felt justified to seek sex companionship with other women outside of marriage. As I became conscious of this our sexual pleasures were reduced still more. Finally we went along several years with all sexual desire for each other quite dead. He would have told a psychologist if he had talked to one that I had become frigid. Actually however I was only frigid toward him. I enjoyed considerable erotic pleasure while dancing with some other men and was more excited at holding hands with some than having full intercourse with my husband. The home was maintained for the sake of the children when eventually my husband found a woman some fifteen years younger than himself who would marry him. Then one day he explained to me in an attitude of self-righteousness, 'We are living a lie.' He gradually cut down the funds allowed to run the home and asked me to get a divorce. I expect to live out my life alone for I was 46 years old when we finally separated.

"What could I have done to prevent this? I could not will myself to love him when he constantly killed it. Nor could I will myself to enjoy him sexually for that

24

is not subject to will power. Nor could I get strength from any source to do more work than I was doing."

For every marriage which breaks there are perhaps several times more which are being tolerated though there is sexual misery in the marriage, or none at all, because it is far easier to muddle along than to separate. A home for children with both a mother and a father is maintained which also furnishes the comforts of shelter, meals and association with old friends. Of course, besides these less fortunate marriages there are many more which work out quite happily through the years, because the good character of *both* parties demands of them far more than our laws and customs require. Combined with such character are usually good fortune in health and finances and freedom from unusually extensive burdens. When such couples have their dark hours, one and then the other musters strength and understanding to pull both out into better times.

As Adam finished he sat in thought then burst out with "Excellent, perfect, just the thing to start the ball rolling."

CHAPTER 2

1. "Analysis, Terminable and Interminable," *International Journal of Psychoanalysis*, XVIII, 1937.
2. John Cowper Powys, *The Meaning of Culture*, W. W. Norton & Co., 1929, p. 138.
3. Havelock Ellis, "Woman's Sexual Nature," *Woman's Coming of Age*, ed. by S. D. Schmalhausen and V. F. Calverton, Horace Liveright, Inc., 1931, pp. 231-232. Ellis referred to William Acton, *The Functions and Disorders of the Reproductive Organs*, Lindsay and Blakiston, Philadelphia, 1875.
4. A husband in some states today may divorce on the ground of desertion, which may mean desertion "from bed." More important, refusal by the wife is likely to lead to divorce obtained on other grounds.
   The Catholic Church carries forward the idea of "wifely duty"

in the following words: "Christian law permits continence in matrimony when *both* parties consent." Pope Pius XI, Encyclical on Christian Marriage, New York Times, January 9, 1931, (italics are mine). That is, if the wife has no desire for sexual relations this does not justify her refusal according to this Encyclical.

5. Margaret Mead, *Sex and Temperment in Three Primitive Societies,* William Morrow & Co., 1935 (Reprinted in *From the South Seas,* William Morrow & Co., 1939) p. 259.
    Among the Panikocch "a grown-up girl may take a husband for herself. Among the Garo the initiative is with the girl. L.T. Hobhouse, G.C. Wheeler & M. Ginsberg, *The Material Culture and Social Institutions of the Simpler Peoples,* Chapman Hall, Ltd., London, 1930, p. 144.

6. The Arapesh allow the woman to be equally spontaneous with the man in many sexual matters and require gentle, unaggressive attitudes from all. Margaret Mead, *Sex and Temperament,* op. cit., p. 140.
    Among the Trobriand Islanders love-making has some of the romantic features of our culture. Bronislaw Malinowski, *The Sexual Life of Savages in Northwestern Melanesia,* Horace Liveright, Inc., 1926.

7. Margaret Mead, *Growing Up in New Guinea, William Morrow* & Co., 1930 (Reprinted in *From the South Seas,* op. cit., 1939) pp. 64, 166.

8. Abraham Myerson, *Social Psychology,* Prentice-Hall, Inc., 1934, p. 518.

9. Margaret Mead, *Growing Up in New Guinea,* op. cit. "Most women welcome children because it gives their husbands a new interest and diverts their unwelcome attention from themselves," p. 165. "Her husband regards her as fit for forced intercourse, childbearing, and housework." p. 159.

10. Robert Lowie has pointed out that the "status" of woman in a given society involves a kind of rating on at least four separate scales: (1) her physical and mental treatment by man, (2) her legal status, (3) her opportunity for public activity, and (4) the character and extent of her labors. As a subdivision of the first should be added the concern for woman's sexual satisfaction. In some of the tribes woman is well off in one or more of these respects and poorly off in others. *Primitive Society,* Boni and Liveright, Inc., 1925, p. 186.
    L. T. Hobhouse, *Morals in Evolution,* Chapman and Hall, Ltd., 8th ed., 1925, pp. 171-178.

11. V. F. Calverton "Are Women Monogamous?" *Women's Coming of Age,* op. cit., pp. 478-480.

12. Chester G. Vernier, *American Family Laws,* Stanford University Press., California, 1931-1938. Vol. II, pp. 266-268. Italics are mine.

13. Courts of other states are given power to distribute her real estate. Ibid., p. 224.

14. Ibid., pp. 232-250.
15. Part of the Assyrian Code 2000 B.C.-H. L. Mencken, *A New Dictionary of Quotations*, Alfred A. Knopf, 1942.
    L. T. Tobhouse, *Morals in Evolution*, op. cit. Ch. IV.
16. Melrich V. Rosenberg, *Eleanor of Aquitaine*, Houghton Mifflin Co., 1939, p. 230.
17. Ibid., p. 214.
18. Ibid., p. 215
19. Ermengard was given the right by Louise VII to act as a magistrate in her domains. Ibid., p. 203.
20. Carney Landis, *et al*, *Sex in Development*, Paul B. Hoeber, Inc., 1940, pp. 91, 302.
21. Robert L. Dickinson and Lura Beam, *One Thousand Marriages*, Williams and Wilkins, Baltimore, 1931. Two out of five subjects had never experienced orgasm.
    G. V. Hamilton, *A Research in Marriage*, Albert and Charles Boni, 1929, p. 69. Almost one-half (46 per cent) had inadequately adjusted in this respect and 26 per cent never had an orgasm or were not sure of it.
22. Clellan S. Ford and Frank A. Beach, *Patterns of Sexual Behavior*, Harper & Bros., 1949, pp. 244-249.
23. Abraham Stone, "An Important Problem Confronting Men and Women-Sexual Frigidity", *Pageant* magazine, December, 1949. Remarks are based on a number of studies.
24. Some doctors, for instance, have found that by simple explanations about physiology and technique many women were able to achieve orgasm who had not done so previously.

CHAPTER 3

We Look at the Double Standard

"You lead up to the great stumbling block for successful marriage, Eve. This is the double standard under which our society still largely operates. It is at the root of innumerable laws, customs and problems."

"Yes, it's a subject often avoided when discussing the family as too delicate, too complex — so let us give it first place."

Adam approves a single standard — with variations

"I would say that since the man is allowed only one wife at a time and his affairs before and after marriage are kept under cover we ostensibly live under a single standard. I approve of a single standard — but of course a certain amount of leniency for men should be allowed since his nature demands some freedom and variation in mates," Adam continued. "On the surface we must maintain for our children's and wives' sakes the appearance of a strict and monogamous society. You know, Eve, since the woman carries the unborn child she is the one who may bear evidence of relations outside of marriage. That provides the basis of the double standard."

Eve did not agree but thought a while as to just how to answer. Then she began slowly "Let us consider a situation outside our country so that we may see it with perspective. There may be a society in South America where women wear tightly fitting dresses and the men loose capes or ponchos. Let us imagine a few of each sex at times went shop lifting in the vegetable and poultry market of their village. The men hid their stolen goods neatly under their ponchos but the women often were 'caught with the goods.'

The attitude in this society might well develop that it is nowhere nearly as serious for men to go shoplifting as for women and a double standard on shoplifting result. Even their gods were called in to sanctify the double standard and impress it upon the women. Men pretended not to shoplift but they certainly did at times and neatly got away with it.

"The logic of your reasoning to support the double standard on sexual behavior, that women may carry evidence of their actions and therefore must be more restricted, is exactly the same as that of these simple people for their double standard on shoplifting."

Adam didn't answer. He was buried in thought, Then he ventured, "There is a similarity, I admit."

Eve took his hand to show her friendship while she went further. "You say that respected women must walk a straight and narrow path, because if they don't, they may 'get caught with the goods,' to make a comparison with this South American group, while men approving the strict pattern for themselves can step aside from its restrictions and never carry any clear evidence of their action. If we are frank, isn't your theory that men like to *pretend* they obey the same pattern as their wives while they cherish the advantage of being able to break away without being discovered?"

"Well, that's part of it. I hate to admit it. But there are other factors."

"Yes, let's consider them all. It seems to me that many men don't want to face the situation. They are perplexed and run away from any analysis. Have you read that part of James Boswell's diary in *London Journey* which was recently published? Boswell in his amazing frankness tells not only of his experiences but also of his reactions." Eve passed the book to Adam with certain passages marked.

Adam ran through some of Boswell's accounts of relations with prostitutes and then read to himself a description of how on the night of the King's birthday Boswell dressed like a blackguard, carried an old oaken stick and went into the park. There he made an agreement with a "little profligate wretch" for sixpence and tells how he "abused her in blackguard style." [1]

Later in the diary Adam reads about the servant girl, Peggy Doig, the mother of Boswell's illegitimate son who died when fifteen months old. She is in London. "I have seen her and advised her not to fall into such a scrape again. I really don't know how to talk on such a subject, when I consider that I led her into the scrape." [2]

Another description he scanned told of going into the park and "performing concubinage with a strong plump . . . girl." The next day he "went to Temple Church and heard a very good sermon . . . This with music and the good building put me into a very devout frame and after service my mind was left in a pleasing, calm state." [3]

"What a man to write all that," Adam breathed. "He sees no inconsistency between using a prostitute, then gaining 'a pleasing, calm state' from a church service. It does make one think. He admits being perplexed about his feelings toward the mother of his illegitimate child."

"If we only had similar frank diaries by most men we'd be able to know the real situation," Eve said as Adam smiled. "I don't think it's a healthy state of affairs to have one standard ostensibly held by society while a lot of deception is carried on.—The fact that men don't get caught with evidence of their side-stepping doesn't really justify a freer standard for them. That reasoning, and the other side, that since women may show the results of breaking from the supposed behavior of society they must be more careful, is all based on a great hypocrisy and the matter of who can be more hypocritical. It claims the men may, and therefore we should accept different behavior from them. But it just doesn't go with a society that stands for truth, for honesty, for sincere human relations, a society which supports churches and sends its children to Sunday schools. — One may think the effects of these two standards are minor influences in our social life. But I hold that they ramify through all areas."

"Well, I'm open minded about it, Eve. I really only expressed a common attitude. It would be good to dig into the situation."

"It is time it was frankly pulled apart and exposed under a bright light and a microscope as scientists do in laboratories. That is the way new knowledge has been gained in physics and chemistry. Scientists constantly reconsider past beliefs and old attitudes and constantly discard many of them. Some ceased to honor the old idea that an atom could not be split and that is why they stepped into a vast new world of knowledge.

"Our human relations must also be studied if we are to make progress," Eve continued. "If we close our eyes and cling to the old folklore and unsound attitudes still supporting some of our ways we are heading for more tragic times ahead. If certain ideas about social behavior work against people's well-being they should be discarded. New attitudes must take their place even though we hesitate to embrace them because they are strangers.

"People have found it difficult to build new patterns for life. The process is filled with fear. The good old ways always offer us a false sense of security. Yet as we read history we realize that those before us were forced to work out new patterns of life to go with new knowledge and new conditions. Their lives would have been in greater danger if they had clung to old customs after electricity, new continents, new medical knowledge had been discovered. The same is true today. We are safer if we study today's folklore and develop new and appropriate attitudes than if we fearfully hold to the ways of our ancestors."

A knock at the door interrupted them. Adam's cousin, John de Dios, entered. They invited him to join their discussion. After telling him their subject and their views they asked for his.

He was a confident, outspoken fellow so he declared forthrightly, "I believe in a double standard and in its entire

31

acceptance. No pretense of a single standard, no hypocrisy about it. Children should expect their fathers to have affairs with other women and wives should adjust to them. — I therefore do not base my reasoning on the fact that men can get away with breaking a single standard because they don't become pregnant. I base my reasoning on the fact that women become attached to their babies, want to care for them and bring them into their homes — where another man than the child's father may raise them. Men don't have these mother instincts. There's no chance they will bring illegitimate children into the homes of their wives. Nature gave men this advantage which allows their sexual freedom. And men have used it through history."

Adam's cousin openly supports the double standard

Adam could see that Eve was holding on to herself and figuring how to be tactful in her reply. She had heard such arguments before. "That's a good clear statement, John, of what many think. Let's stop to analyze it. — Every baby starts its life by the joining of a reproductive cell from a man with one from a woman. His body just as much as hers enters into the conception of new life. Likewise, his actions, just as much as hers, lead to the starting of this new child. By no twisting of logic can he claim that the new life is more the result of her actions than of his. And also by no reasoning can he hold that when the child is born it is more her responsibility to care for. The child in all truth is the product of the two, is flesh of their flesh, and carries the inheritance of both into the next generation. Men know all this but don't want to apply it.

"If the man is equally mature he will want his child to have opportunities for growth, just as much as the mother does, and he'll want to assume his full half-share of providing these. Of course, however, if he does not regard himself as an equally mature and responsible person as the woman, he can put his head in the sand and ignore his illegitimate child. Remember though, he can logically uphold the double standard only if he believes the man is a less responsible person and approves of his remaining so.

"That is, a man has a choice of these two attitudes. He can consider himself a person as responsible as the woman, in which case he would acknowledge his child 'under the rose,' support it as his own, either in his own home or in another's. If he holds this to be the course for a respected and honored man — then he would be as careful as a woman not to start a child whom he didn't want to raise. The caution of both man and woman would be the same and we'd have a single standard regarding sexual relations.

"On the other hand, the man may hold himself as a less responsible person than a woman, one who doesn't recognize the value of human life as she does. Therefore, he is not so concerned about possible conception and the life of his own child. Then, and only then, can he approve man's greater sexual liberties and the two different standards."

John thought for a while, then turned to a way out and said with spirit. "Well, Eve, we are willing to be regarded as less responsible persons than women. We just are — we want to continue to be so — nature made us this way. We want the double standard, our own freedom, but not that for our wives!"

Eve calmly replied, "How about our laws and customs which assume men are wiser, more responsible than women, and therefore men become the officers of companies, heads of most churches and projects of all kinds, hold the important government positions, make the laws for all and are the legal heads of our families? Should all this be changed?"

John looked a little sheepish. He wanted men to hold all these prerogatives based on their greater virtue, and also wanted the double standard which can be based only upon their lesser virtue — their valuing human life less than the women do. He couldn't think of a good reply.

Eve broke the silence. "There is still another pattern which could be followed. A society could approve a single standard, and both men and women would be equally unconcerned about possible conception out of marriage and equally indifferent to the well-being of any illegitimate children. Such a society might well practice infanticide, killing or exposing such babies or selling them as prostitutes or slaves, as has been done."

"That would be of course a society gone to seed, degenerate, chaotic — out of the question! We rely on women not to let it go this way," John vigorously replied.

"Perhaps men give women far too heavy a job through the double standard which assumes men should not do their part in caring for all their children."

John calmed down and said quietly, "But, Eve, let's be frank, you know it is far more difficult for a man than a woman to walk the narrow path and always to be concerned with consequences."

"You think so, but, remember, you don't know how great women's urges are to step aside. You like to imagine they aren't so strong as yours. What ground have you for such a belief? True, men have held it. Adam and I the other day looked at the medical book by Acton which says women have no sexual feelings or urges. But we know better now. Most intelligent men today recognize that women are full human beings physically and psychologically with hungers as strong as men's for delicious food and delicious experiences."

"I always thought myself an intelligent man."

"Excuse me, John! I should have said a man who has kept up on recent thinking and writing in this field. Of course most don't. They often think this a subject which should not be written about. — There is an excellent study by Ford and Beach which brings some light on the matter. It shows that among many human societies where pressure is not placed on women to suppress and conceal their interests they show as much desire for sexual satisfactions as the men, and in some societies even more. [4] Likewise, we are coming to the realization that when women have not been trained to fear and avoid sexual experience in youth and

34

are treated lovingly by their mates their enjoyment is likely to be fully as great as men's. Thus, approval of a double standard on the ground that the man has greater difficulty in controlling himself than the woman does not hold."

Eve saw that he was not hurt by what she was saying. Instead he was intrigued by the new ideas of women being innately more desirous of a complete, full life than society allowed them — even the old maids and the widows. He glimpsed a pattern that might be more fun for all than this double standard. He urged her to tell more of her thoughts.

"You have never guessed how far-reaching are the effects of this one-sided arrangement. Even most women have not stopped to recognize this, John. You men create two classes of women in order to meet your wishes for strictly controlled wives and also women who will be free for your affairs outside of marriage.

"We could say that woman's two dominant needs give men great power over her. One is her need for a sexual life, the other her need for assistance in raising children. Men have, in their subconscious and unplanned urge to control her, used both these needs. They have said in effect through their laws to the women, 'If you want me to be a responsible father then you must acknowledge my complete sexual ownership of you. On the other hand, if you take any freedom in sex, then you will not have a responsible father for your child.' That is, they divide women according to their sexual actions into wives and those of a lower caste, the 'sinful' and the 'fallen'. Men's feelings about this 'sinful' group are ambivalent. When they are talking in the company of wives or married couples they scorn this lower caste, but when men alone are talking they often admit how much they love their present mistresses or friends 'under the rose'. But the laws place these latter women in a precarious position. They can be arrested if prostitution is established, they are given practically no assistance through the courts in winning proper assistance from the father if one has a child. The father may help her due to a kind impulse but our laws actually seldom force him to carry his half share. Because she is considered 'sinful' she has almost no basic rights as we shall later note. — Corresponding to these two groups of women what do we find among men?"

John hesitated, then Adam said, "Just one group, yes. They are not divided according to whether they take some freedom or not. Men's varied behavior does not so much concern others. In fact, most all are expected to show their masculine nature by stepping aside sometime in their lives."

"And our laws protect them amazingly, even as the customers of prostitutes."

"Yes, when that house of prostitution was raided by the police last week all the men customers were freed and the women arrested," Adam observed.

"Actually this double standard which makes women 'sinful' for the same action which is considered natural for a man has a vicious influence. It extends its effects through all phases of all women's lives hanging the 'sword of Damocles' over all their heads. It provides grounds for hubsands' unreasonable criticism of wives often based on suspicion alone. It also provides a ready method for anyone who wants to hurt a woman. He or she need only start a rumor. It places every woman who is in a relatively weak position, through her low economic position or simply her single state, where she can be badly injured. The effects, in short, force her to be cautious and fearful, which means less courage and self-confidence in many ways. Her insecurity, if she has a suspicious husband, often affects her self-confident poise necessary to wisely handle her children. I have known several cases of this. And simple suspicion by a husband can lead to her divorce, for we know divorces can be obtained without substantial grounds in various special places. The whole tone and tenor of every woman's life is shadowed by this 'sword of Damocles' causing her to walk in kind of a strait jacket. Some may not feel this since they have never imagined a different status.

"She is subject to all of this of course while she is often

frustrated as a celibate single or widowed woman, or married to a husband who no longer loves her. The contrast between her position and that of a man who enjoys his wife and also without much fear tastes some adventure and novelty with other attractive women, you cannot fully realize."

Eve looked at John and found him slumped in his chair. He was a good sport to listen attentively and try to understand. After a few minutes he said, "True we think women lacking in courage to do this and that, over-cautious about appearances and the middle aged ones often with no sparkle. — You know, when we give attention to some young woman and propose a little affair, we forget we're offering to place her in a tough position."

"Yes indeed! I'm glad you see that," Eve said enthusiastically. "Her risks of rumor, of detection — and of pregnancy with her whole life often influenced by such a drastic experience, sometimes, you know, even leading to suicide, place her in a totally different position from the man. — You men often complain of women being too cautious, too strait-laced, yet you have done almost everything you can to make them that way. You have put them in an agonizing position. Here is a lovely young woman who is eager to marry a congenial man, who proposes relations. What is she faced with? She may desire these as much as he, but she knows all these overhanging risks. If she refuses he may drop her for another friend, although he may be just the man for her husband. He would like to marry a virgin, yet he wants his sweetheart to join him now as his full sexual companion! He is asking contradictory things of her, as do those frequently who are in a position of advantage. Besides his contradictory wishes, she is not sure if he wants to marry her. This young woman may be your daughter. Shouldn't we face her perplexities and try to help?"

Since John had two daughters he understood and nodded, yes.

Eve was encouraged to continue, "What an uproar we

would hear if someone suggested to an audience that in bridge the rules be made so that an ace would be the highest card for men and the lowest ranking card for women players. Or that in tennis a man's ball should be counted in when three feet beyond the outer lines of the court but a woman's ball must be within the boundary lines. To slightly change the picture, how about rules that the shorter men, under five feet six inches, must pay income taxes at twice the rate for men over this height? Yet all these weighted, one-sided rules would not effect the player's lives as much as do the warped rules called the double standard of morals."

John and Adam looked at each other with a feeling that there was some sense in what Eve was saying. "This is really interesting," John commented. "I don't know where we're being led, but you don't seem to think, Eve, that, if women are as interested in sexual pleasures as men, *we all* should be put under a rigid, confining single standard. I'm glad I dropped in."

"Nor do you think we all should be granted extensive freedom, for that would bring chaotic conditions," Adam said.

Eve laughed. "You are both right. It's most complex. We can't come to a conclusion yet."

Wives, prostitutes, hetaerae

"As we have mentioned," Eve continued, "today, when one asks, 'What kind of a man is he?' one does not mean, 'What is the pattern of his sexual life?' That is considered to be of his own private concern. Yet 'What kind of a girl is she?' often means just this. Her sex life is the rightful concern of all, which is another indication that she is regarded largely as a sexual person or object. The questioner wants to know to what degree she is free or strict. In our discussion we have brought out that women are placed in two main groups according to their sexual lives: one, those who keep within the prescribed restrictions; the other, those who provide partners for men outside of marriage and who are called all sorts of names — loose woman, prostitute, harlot, whore and many others. Thus, men have their proper wives and also others, whom they must condemn at least to mixed groups, and whom the law also in effect condemns.

"Now something interesting is happening," Eve went on, "and it is most significant. A third group is developing, which could be called the hetaerae, women who are somewhat independent of men and the sexual restrictions placed on them. During one period of the Greek Empire there were women of education and refinement who were economically independent. They did not marry but enjoyed friendships and relations with those they chose. Thornton Wilder's *Woman of Andros*,[5] gives us a vivid picture of the beauty and character of some of the Greek hetaerae. Sappho of immortal lyrics was one among many leading hetaerae who were authors, musicians, philosophers and teachers. Some of their companions with whom they passed long years were Menander, Pericles and Alexander the Great. Their minds were developed, their imaginations stimulated and they had knowledge of their world, so they could make some of the outstanding contributions of their age. In contrast were the wives whose days were filled with household chores and heavy childbearing, whose spirits were often broken. Demosthenes cogently expressed the men's view toward women and their classification according to the sexual use made of them. 'We have courtesans (hetaerae) for pleasure, concubines (palladides) for daily use, and wives to provide us with legitimate children and to grow old faithfully in the interior of the house.'

"At present in western countries I think we now find three similar divisions of women determined by their sexual life: the married; the prostitutes earning a livelihood mainly through prostitution; and those we might call the hetaerae, who are financially independent though unmarried — and who have relations of their own choosing. They may be independent through their earnings, or property. Also among these are young unmarried college women supported by their families who have affairs with college men not for any economic purpose but for the same reason as their bachelor partners. The number of hetaerae is probably increasing.

"Their development is one step away from sexual bondage, either as the sexual possession of a husband or as a sexual servant of the man customer in prostitution. The hetaerae may consent to relations or refuse them; may approve a particular partner and later refuse him. They, in short, are in control of their own bodies."

"That's a striking statement, Eve," Adam interjected.

"Yes, I know it is. Later we should look into it further."

"I'd like to join you in some of your later talks if I may. You've got me thinking," John said as he passed around cigarettes and helped the others light them.

"We'd like to have you, John, I see you have an open and unprejudiced mind—are willing to look under the surface."

"I'm interested in what you were saying about the problems of girls today."

"Yes — their problems are crucial. It looks as though we are in a period of change, feeling our way out of a pattern, perhaps too restrictive — and involving too much hypocrisy. To have a small number of hetaerae who own their own bodies is a significant step but this pattern doesn't include the important factor of children and child-care. That is what offers complications."

"Oh, indeed," Adam murmured.

"During these days girls and women are bearing the brunt of both the confusion of changing attitudes and the double standard. For instance, we mentioned the single girl who knows that to yield to her sweetheart's pleas for relations may cause her to be rejected as his later wife. On the other hand, if she refuses him she may be discarded as his present companion. All, while her parents unmindful of her real problem, are constantly warning, 'Oh, darling, do be careful.' — Later after marriage when her husband leaves her for a lengthy trip he may say, 'Dearest, while I'm gone be a good wife for me.' And then she may hear from a childhood beau, 'Mary, I'm sailing for the front overseas. Have a heart, dear! For old friendship's sake!' These are a few of the contradictory pressures through which women wind their way.

"If the young unmarried woman has relations with her particular friend or friends, many influences lead her into the class of hetaerae. She may become popular, confident and sparkling since her life is complete," Eve went on. "Her men friends, on the other hand, often pick some less popular virgins for their future housekeeping wives. Yet some hetaerae marry, and some properly restrained virgin young women are never asked. Many women try both patterns at different times during their lives endeavoring to discover what men really want. Although some college men are becoming more tolerant toward the non-virgin as a bride, the young men who are casual in their relationships do not want their brides to have followed the same code. [6] That is, the most fair-minded still hold a form of double standard.

"There are many men who have as sex partners wives, hetaerae and perhaps prostitutes within a short space of time. Men may play double or triple roles but few women can play more than one role at once, and few are not handicapped by their 'past.' I say 'handicapped' regardless of what their past is. The conservatively reared and restricted young woman may be limited and handicapped by her experience just as truly as is she who has enjoyed some sexual freedom. A woman must usually choose a limited sex 'policy' and take the disadvantages tied to each pattern while a man can be a sexual opportunist."

"Yes, Eve, that's right. One of my daughters now in high school is a serious-minded and proper little girl. There's only one boy friend who takes her out occasionally. He is rather bashful and serious, too. My other daughter now in college, I often wonder about. She is very popular. During vacation sometimes when she comes at night after a dance her face is radiant beyond description, her hair and dress

41

badly ruffled. I worry about each of them, for as you say each is building a pattern and reputation which will aid or hinder a good marriage. My wife and I discuss it, but come to no conclusions as to just what's the wise course for girls today," John observed between puffs on his cigarette.

"That's it," agreed Eve, "Now let's consider the choice presented women during their years of maturity. Let's see if we can use our imaginations sufficiently to make this real. Here is a turned-about society in which men play women's present roles and women take the men's. Men would have to choose between these two courses, determined by their sex policy:

> A man could take a partner in marriage which would mean:
> a. A home with mate and children.
> b. Fitting himself into a prescribed occupation, that of housekeeping. His housework would provide services for his family, but he and his children would be financially dependent upon his mate who earned outside.
> c. Having some sexual satisfaction with his wife but with her alone. (She, however, might have affairs with a man secretary or other handsome single man, younger than her husband, not restricted to home and children.)

"Now let me think about that," Adam interposed. "The man would be the house-husband. The funds to run the family and for his own clothes he'd receive from his wife."

"Yes, and he'd give extensive time to the children," Eve continued. On the other hand, he could choose a pattern corresponding to that of the single women, which would mean:

> a. No home with a mate, no children.
> b. Freedom to enter other vocations than housekeeping, but probably in a less responsible job and at a lower income than if he were a woman.
> c. All sexual life forbidden by our laws and customs.

John wanted time to think about this. "If the roles were reversed you think women would marry men younger than

42

themselves. Also, under the double standard, they might have affairs with younger men."

"I don't doubt it, John. — We'll talk about this later, too. —Which of these patterns would you choose?"

"I don't like either of them! I want a home and children but I don't want to be a house-husband. And I wouldn't comply with my wife's restrictions, never to go with another woman — especially if she were having an affair," John said pounding the arm of his chair.

"I agree with John," Adam joined in indignation. "I wouldn't submit to either choice. The second one's as bad as the first. I want both a home and an occupation outside in which I can specialize and feel I have a part in the world's progress."

"But, my dears, you are in this society and most women would say, you can't eat your cake and have it too, you *must* choose!—This is just what I wanted you to feel— and feel strongly — that neither of these choices would you accept. They are too restrictive for most full-blooded persons. They deny basic human needs for *both* family and activity in the outside world.

"If men, however, did submit so they experienced these two patterns, some choosing marriage and housekeeping, other bachelorhood and business, they would, as you claim, soon revolt. The men house-husbands would sally forth with aprons and rolling pins, while the bachelors would come from their one-room apartments with wet clothes hanging to dry, and in the flashing eyes of both groups could be read the words: 'We won't stand for this.'"

Adam and John laughed. "I'm sure you're right," Adam said.

"You wonder why women submit to living within these two choices, I suppose. — But actually a woman in our culture is hardly allowed to live at all if she doesn't largely submit to one of these patterns. That is, if she refuses marriage restrictions but earns her own living and has a child or two, just what does society do to her? Have you known a case of this kind? I have. The mother is rejected socially and her children also to a degree. Her earning opportunities are limited, at the same time she carries the double job of housekeeper and bread-winner. She's far worse off than the women who fit into one of those choices. — Of course a woman may not flaunt the marriage laws but less radically refuse the restrictions offered her. A few, usually those with plenty of funds so they may engage servants, can manage to have a husband and children along with real interesting outside responsibility." Eve paused to light a new cigarette.

"And some mothers of moderate means hold earning jobs outside when their children are in school or college, but of course they carry on their housework too," Adam observed, "and, as you say their jobs are not the most interesting ones, they usually work as secretaries or clerks in stores, or as substitute teachers. I suppose that since they drop out of any former earning occupation or special field while their children are babies this breaks a line of progress to the better jobs."

"Yes, and when they take a job after some years at home, since they are still housekeepers they must choose something that eliminates long commuting trips." Eve added. "As to why women don't revolt, the way you men think you would, I can venture this. Older women, who have known through experience the various inadequacies of these two main choices, have insufficient power to change them. Sexual customs and marriage constitute the most delicate and explosive of all areas in which women can work for reform. Most young women don't know the full effects of this forced choice and since their lives are centered on keeping husbands happy they can't risk analyzing the marriage institution.

"And does not society use the blinding power of Cupid as it explains all these restrictions to the woman? She is largely assigned to housework, it is said, because this symbolizes her love for her husband. Likewise, her small opportunity for responsible outside positions is justified because her main job is at home to help her husband. A desire to have economic independence implies she does not properly trust him. Any freedom in her sexual life, even when her husband is away for years and has affairs of his own, is clear indication, society says, that she no longer loves him. All these limitations are explained by tying them to Cupid— if she is a proper loving woman she gladly accepts them, she is told. Few are those who will analyze or revolt at the risk of being considered cold, uninfluenced by Cupid. And where is the mother in this institution founded absolutely on mutual love when the husband's love flies out the window? It is humanly impossible for her then to carry on all these duties under a genuine feeling of love for him. In such an eventuality our society seems to assume that *she* has failed. It has made no proper provision for her and her children's future. — Young, single women often weigh these restrictions of marriage, but their natural desire for a companion, children and the fullness of life lead them to shut their eyes and move hopefully into the world of the family.

"Let us notice what our culture requires of the young woman as she enters marriage. She has been wooed for months or years while she has been denied any full sexual satisfaction. Then when she is in an ecstatic state of tension, hope and faith, having decided that she trusts this man sufficiently to give herself to him 'until death do us part,' the inherited law of the past descends upon her. After the wedding march has echoed through the church and the bride swathed in satin and old lace has whispered her vows, 'the law steps in and holds the parties to various obligations and liabilities,'—according to the words of the Supreme Court. [7] She is quite unconscious under Cupid's influence of the rigidity, demands and power of the laws which now surround her, as the two kiss each other under the palms."

"Very interesting and significant," Adam observed.

"Oh yes, almost unconsciously, society has developed a situation where the young woman has a mass of obligations dropped on her head — maybe that puts it too strongly. Those with funds can of course buy themselves out of future difficulties, but others cannot. The bride assumes the 'wifely duty' of submitting to her husband; the task of bearing as many children as chance may start, the job of caring for all their needs with no assurance that she will have sufficient funds for this. Likewise she has no assurance, as she bears babies, that her husband may not leave her with this task to shoulder largely by herself. No government or private agency has given her an understanding of the features of reproduction, nor helped her see into the future, for instance, that her family could be placed in a desperate position with eight or nine children. And various state governments have laws which interfere with her knowledge of effective contraception." [8]

"But, Eve," John asked, "can any other arrangements be made? It is hard to figure them out."

"If one looks at the present family setups in other countries and also variations in the past, he recognizes that innumerable changes could be made. To most of us it seems impossible that a woman could have all these things: freedom to choose her vocation, economic independence, children and life with a mate without being his sexual possession. Yet some society may well develop such a pattern. There are no contradictions here which could not be overcome if men were willing. Might a society which allowed women these basic things enjoy a new vitality? Might these liberated women — whose influence would bear weight in high places — who have great concern for the nurture of human beings, help us reorient our lives?"

They did not now attempt to answer all this but went out to lunch together. It was decided that Eve should write the next chapter since they couldn't talk further for some time. Adam was to read it over and make suggestions before their next discussion.

CHAPTER 3

1. James Boswell, *Boswell's London Journey, 1762-1763*, prepared from original manuscript by Frederick A. Pottle, McGraw-Hill Book Co., 1950, pp. 272, 273.
2. Ibid., p. 324.
3. Ibid., p. 237.
4. Clellan S. Ford and Frank A. Beach, *Patterns of Sexual Behavior*, Harper & Bros., 1951, pp. 101-105, 246, 247, 266.
   Alfred C. Kinsey et al, *Sexual Behavior in the Human Female*, W. B. Saunders Co., 1953, pp. 594-640.
5. Publisher, A. & E. Boni, 1930. The term hetaerae was rather broad since it probably included mistresses of the better classes. But it implied that they were sufficiently independent so they could choose or refuse their companions.
6. An excellent study of youth's sexual behavior and problems, by Dorothy Dunbar Bromley and Florence Hexton Britten, is *Youth and Sex*, Harper and Brothers, 1938, pp. 151, 152.
7. From a decision of the U. S. Supreme Court, Maynard V. Hill, 125, U. S. 190.
8. Harriet F. Pilpel and Theodora Zavin, *Your Marriage and the Law*, Rinehart & Co., 1952, chapter 11.
   Lee Rainwater, *And the Poor Get Children*, Quadrangle Books, Chicago, 1960.

CHAPTER 4

Thought Control

Control of women's thinking has been basic to fitting her into these patterns of sexual restrictions. No doubt men's greater physical strength in primitive and early societies played a crucial part. But other methods of control were soon discovered to be effective in supplementing their superior strength, always in the background. Various kinds of customs were developed to define women's sphere and duties. Religious conceptions proved a powerful means.

The study of primitive societies is fascinating, even amusing, for in these we find men's aims and desires very similar to theirs of today. The more primitive men, however, frankly express their thoughts — and their reasons why they do certain things. Present day men, however, simply accept the old customs and laws which they find helpful to themselves and allow them certain freedoms. They support them with strange explanations and confused thinking, such as we have noted regarding the double standard.

Methods of Control

To see the origin of these important customs which are later crystallized into our marriage and other laws controlling sex, we must look into the past. There is a ceremony found among various primitive peoples today in the Pacific Islands, Australia, South America and Africa. And it was probably common among most primitives in past ages. In New Guinea it is carried out through the cult of the Tamberan.

The Tamberan is presented to the women as a supernatural patron of the grown men, a being as tall as a coconut tree who makes weird sounds and will even swallow women. No woman must even look upon him at threat of death nor must she ask any questions about him.

The initiated men, however, know there is no Tamberan. They themselves play the flutes and gongs, which constitute his voice. The men also eat the meat supposedly laid out for the Tamberan.

On the big occasions when the Tamberan's voice is heard in the distance, all the women with their children flee from the village in terror and stay at a safe distance. After a few hours the men call to them that he has now gone away. When they return they are shown the Tamberan's large footprints, and are told that he has eaten the gifts of meat.

Such experiences keep girls and women from letting their minds wander in forbidden fields; their horizon is narrowed. They are trained in passive acceptance of men's demands as the only safe course in their lives. They are forbidden to take part in the important religious art productions of their tribes.

The little boys, however, who at first fled with their mothers from the village at the voice of the Tamberan, after their initiation at adolescence into the men's society, see the entire farce. Thereafter, the youths take delightful parts in pretending the Tamberan enters the village by playing gongs and making supposed footprints in the ground. They now feel superior to their mothers and all other women who flee in terror. They realize what can be done by scaring others and making them afraid to investigate.

"As the Tamberan cult dulls the imagination of the girls, it stimulates and quickens the imagination of the boys. And the quickening extends to other things, to greater interest in plants and animals of the bush, to greater curiosity about life in general." [1]

After these women are thus lead to maintain their own ignorance their subjugation is readily preserved. The spirit of inquiry is killed and they hold to their own bonds. Most significantly, among some peoples where such deceptive practices are performed, men have later gone to these women's graves and pounded on the ground muttering, "Forgive us. We have deceived you. Do not be angry with us."

Various other methods besides these cults described are used among primitive groups, such as telling women that they do not have guardian spirits to watch over them and protect them in danger so they must not venture into strange places. The men and boys may, for they are always watched over and protected by the spirits of dead ancestors, each one enjoying the power of a particular ancestor whose skull may be hung in his house. [2]

In India we find one of the best examples of conditioning women. Psychologists know how effectively this can be done by a combination of giving and withholding basic needs along with preaching certain attitudes. Indian wives were conditioned through the religious teaching that their husbands were their gods, so when they died wives' lives were not worth living. This teaching was supplemented by making any widow's existence one of destitution and servitude. This conditioning has led many millions of wives, eight years of age and older, to walk to fiery deaths upon their husband's funeral pyres. A rajah's many wives and hundreds of concubines have thus committed suicide upon his death. (Probably not voluntary for all.) Some cases of suttee have taken place as late as the 1950's.

In our society today certain conditioning leads to keeping women's minds in control through fear and ignorance. Some practices of the Roman Catholic Church through its hierarchy of men do this. [3] Through this Church's teaching that people may know ethical principles only through its agents, the officials and priests, the thinking of its members is walled in as desired. This influences women especially in an area of prime importance, reproduction. Almost every wife asks herself, shall I go through pregnancy and bear a child only when I feel well and able to carefully raise him, or whenever chance may dictate? How many children shall I raise, the number my husband and I have the strength and economic means to rear and educate, or the number who happen to be conceived? These questions are answered for her by the unmarried men of this Church. She must not question but obey, they say, and that this is the only safe course considering her life after death. She must use no really effective method to control the time and number of pregnancies. If she conceives when seriously ill, her life endangered by her continued pregnancy, no therapeutic abortion should be allowed, for she is told her life is of secondary value to that of the tiny joined reproductive cells.

In the impressive book, *People's Padre,* by Emmett McLaughlin, who knew this Church as a former priest, we read that it "preserves its hold . . . not only through fear but also through calculated ignorance — ignorance accomplished by the prohibition of certain reading and by mental isolation or separatism." [4] Confession to priests which keeps the Church informed of its members' actions greatly aids its control.

Even most of our Protestant churches have not yet freed themselves of the ancient teachings about the subjection of women found in the various books of the Bible all written by men. St. Paul said, "Let your women keep silence in the churches for it is not permitted them to speak; but they are commanded to be under obedience, as also saith the law." (I Corinthians XIV:34.) Also, "But I would have you know that the head of every man is Christ; and the head of the woman is the man. Neither was the man created for the woman; but the woman for the men." (I Corinthians 2:37.) And we read in Genesis that God made Adam, but Eve as a second thought was formed out of his rib to keep him company. The ministers carry on through the centuries these ancient attitudes.

But the Protestant churches are now allowing a few women ministers to speak in their churches. They do not prohibit women's reading widely or thinking independently. And they have stepped out of the past's darkness to the extent that they allow women to regulate the creation of babies according to their ability to bear them and raise them in health. They have not yet questioned, however, the ancient teaching that "the head of every woman is man" and that he should be the head of the family. To question this is a radical thought for today. However, in the light that the men's drives often lead them toward a change in mates and to admire the woman most for her sexually attractive qualities, rather than those qualities which cause her to give herself extensively to her children, one may ask whether making the man the legal head of the family leads to its well-being and unity. We are worrying about the extent of desertion and divorce, but we have not yet questioned whether a factor in the unhappy turmoil often within the family and its frequent break-up might be due partly to its very organization with the man at its head. What portion of family disruption is due to the husband's using his freedom in sexual relations by falling for a fresh, young woman, more attractive than his wife of ten or twenty years? No study has been made of this.

Included with these traditional legal and religious conceptions of the man-head are the current laws and customs regarding wives' economic position, which are powerful in their control. Outstanding among these is the custom, supported largely by our laws, that the family savings resulting from the efforts of both, the wife's work in the home and the husband's outside, belong to the husband. They are legally his to manage during marriage in all states, and his to take with him in case of separation or divorce in most states. Later we shall note what a small portion he usually pays for the care of his children after desertion or divorce. If in a partnership of two men the senior partner were allowed to keep practically all the partnership's earnings and savings it often would be a clear inducement for him to leave it and find a new partner.

In our further discussions Adam and I will note how these prevalent concepts of the man-head and the woman-follower, or the body of the head, are upheld for women's acceptance on all sides, in most books and periodicals, in much teaching of law, sociology, in our courts, as well as in considerable preaching from pulpits.

Women taught to be content under polygyny

We have already observed that mankind is just emerging

from a frankly polygynous pattern of living. After an extensive and careful study of the present customs of the simpler peoples, Hobhouse and others conclude that "The permission of polygamy is the rule throughout the uncivilized world." [5] Of the 434 tribes studied, 378 practiced polygamy generally or occasionally. Many Asiatic nations still largely practice polygyny or concubinage. The ancient Greeks and Romans ostensibly upheld monogamic marriage but resorted to concubinage. The Hebrews were polygynous into the middle ages. In such societies the leading men tend to secure several wives, the less wealthy fewer, and others only one. This pattern allows some husbands to obtain a series of new wives to carry on women's tasks as the others become worn or uninteresting to them. [6]

Recently we have had this Eastern pattern of marriage brought before us. As King Ibn Saud of Saudi Arabia has visited our country we have learned through the newspapers that he at present has four wives, which is permitted by the Koran, and he maintains, it is estimated, about one hundred concubines. Besides these, we are told, there are one hundred and twenty former wives who have been divorced. He has twenty-five sons. Since the daughters are regarded as less important their number has not been mentioned.

He made when here an address to the General Assembly of the United Nations in which he said "We must be guided by the fact that all peoples of the world are entitled to their freedom and independence in the name of the principle of self-determination. We believe in human and spiritual values. We stand on moral principles, on the freedom and dignity of human beings, on cooperation of freedom-loving peoples." [7] He was thinking of the less powerful nations of the Middle East and their desire for growth opportunities. The opportunities of his country's women compared to those of its more powerful men did not enter his mind. Whether one sits in the seat of the more powerful, or that of the weaker, determines usually the directions of one's thought. This is also true of most men in our own country, who currently uphold democratic principles but have not yet considered them in the relations between men and women.

In *The Good Earth* by Pearl Buck, the character Wang Lung, who is a typical Chinese peasant of today, took in his youth O-lan who bore him eight children and worked many years in the fields with her husband; then a second wife, Lotus, who was a beautiful young prostitute, in contrast to the strong but weather-worn wife of his youth; and last, when he was an old man he took Pear Blossom, a frail young girl, "half child and scarcely woman." [8]

It has been imagined, by men far more than women, that wives adjust themselves happily to a polygynous society and did so through the past ages. Many claim that since a woman expected to live under polygamy she was content accepting her husband's advances when he made them, going without him when he slept with a new wife, and when he later put her entirely aside. True, indoctrination helped women to accept this role of complete subjection in their sexual life. Yet extensive evidence shows that women did suffer, that they were compelled to suppress their sexuality and spontaneity to prevent excessive frustration when neglected. Such subjugation means a crushing of that and other sides of their personality the same as would be the case with men in a similar position.

Among some primitive peoples the wife's duties are so extensive, that she may be pleased when a new wife comes to share them. That is, physical weariness is so great that her sexual desire for husband's exclusive interest is secondary. However, if her work were not too heavy and if she enjoyed her marital sexual relations she would without doubt have much preferred to be the only wife.

If sex were something purely physical, it might not so often disturb a woman when she was one among several wives, nor would it disturb a man in a corresponding position. So long as either had satisfaction in accordance with the frequency of his desire everything would be all right. When the husband was ill or unusually tired he would not object to his wife's having relations with another man, as long as he could have her again when he felt well. Instead, sexual satisfaction is not purely physical but involves the whole personality. The sensitive man realizes that sex relations are far more satisfying when his wife is in tune with him due to her affectionate feelings. To even a greater extent the same is true of women. No matter what women have been taught about accepting polygyny or the double standard, they have not enjoyed being treated as though sex were mainly physical, or being desired or rejected as if they had no feeling of their own.

Pearl Buck describes well the bitter disappointment of the hard-working peasant mother, O-lan, when her husband puts her aside for the new wife, Lotus. As the new rooms built to her home for Lotus were being finished, Wang Lung ceased to sleep with O-lan. "During all this time he said nothing to anyone except to scold the children or to roar out at O-lan that she had not brushed her hair for three days and more, so that at last one morning O-lan burst into tears and wept aloud, *as he had never seen her weep before, even when they starved* or at any other time." [9]

"It was true that before the law he had no complaint against his wife, for she had borne him three good sons, and several daughters, and they were alive and there was no excuse for him except his desire."

In the film based upon this novel several significant changes were made, all of them being to present O-lan's life as less oppressed and to ignore her real situation. For instance, when O-lan's husband explains to her his plan to take the young Lotus as his new wife, O-lan in the film presses her husband's hand in friendly understanding. That gesture tells the whole story of the way men would *like* women to feel about polygyny.

I know no study of the devastation a mother feels when she learns that her husband with whom she has shared the deepest experiences — who has led her to place complete trust in him for her future; whose children she has carried within and passed through painful hours in bearing; the children who combine his life with hers — has turned his prime attention to another woman or has decided to leave her. All women who have experienced this know what such a study would reveal.

Kimball Young, a sociologist and a descendant of Brigham Young who has studied Mormon society, describes some wives' extreme suffering when their husbands took new ones. He tells of one mother who after many years of child bearing and raising broke down mentally when her husband brought a new wife into the family.[10]

Another sociologist writes, "The status of the Mormon father was greatly elevated. He was the High Priest of the family, holding the 'keys to salvation'; it was only through him that a woman could be 'saved' . . . " He ruled the members of his several families according to his own desires. Although the Mormon patriarchs thought a satisfactory family life could be obtained this way, they often suffered from "acute guilt feelings." One of the fathers said longingly that the happiest thing that could happen would be to see "his three wives all coming down stairs before breakfast saying 'Good morning' pleasantly to each other." [11] I believe no woman has ever dreamed of such behavior among a group of husbands to whom she distributed her attention. She knows human nature too well.

This situation whereby men, who have sexual relations with several women (wives and non-wives), punish and denounce as sinful the woman who has relations with anyone other than her husband, presents in essence the basic problem of all human relations. It is the problem whereby those in the position of advantage usually approve greater freedom and opportunities for themselves than for the others.

Is our country monogamous today?

Hardly a hair's breadth separates technical polygyny from a pattern in which a man may have several wives in succession and also extra-marital affairs of short or long duration. There is little doubt that if we recognized the full extent of affairs with "office-wives," friends and prostitutes by today's men, particularly those in big cities or who travel in business, we could hardly call our country monogamous, if we define monogamy as a pattern requiring a man to restrict all his sexual relations to those with his one wife.

We have noted mothers' reactions to polygyny because they are similar to those which occur today in our current pattern when wives must take second place or are completely pushed aside by husbands' new love affairs.

There are current suggestions that our laws and customs become more frankly polygynous with the slight surplus of men as an excuse. Among various articles Esquire Magazine published one supporting this view which said, "Biologically, at least, a woman is entitled to only half a man" and asked, "Are women ready . . . to accept legalized or socially approved polygamy?" [12] Some men are equipped to head two families, the author writes, telling of women he supposedly knows who are happy as one of two wives living in the same house with one man. A professor in England has likewise suggested changing laws to permit two or more wives. Actually the number of unmarried women in our country results mainly from the fact that about 15% of the men over thirty years of age are single. [13] The solution is clearly not polygyny, but a larger portion of men who would make good husbands.

As to how monogamous we are today, the Kinsey Institute studies constitute the best scientific findings to date. They indicate wide variance from the pattern set by modern precept and law, including pre-marital and extra-marital relationships, prostitution as well as homosexuality. At least some 200,000 illegitimate births, the large number of abortions by single women, by no means fully recorded, and the extensive sale of contraceptives to the unmarried are all indications of our non-monogamous ways, as is the following story:

> "When air lines were young and people were wary of flying, a promotion man suggested to one of the lines that they permit wives of businessmen to accompany their husbands free, just to prove that flying was safe. The idea was quickly adopted, and a record kept of the

names of those who accepted the proposition. In due time the air line sent a letter to those wives, asking how they enjoyed the trip. From 90 percent of them came back a baffled reply, *"What airplane trip?"* [14]

Women taught not to be jealous

In a book on marriage, a current attitude is presented as follows: "We don't need to whip ourselves into a lather of indignation about every deviation from pure monogamy just because we have been taught to believe that unfaithfulness is a sin. Too often nice people are . . . devastated by *emotions which they think they should feel . . .*" [15]

This statement and many similar ones imply that jealousy is not a basic reaction but is merely cultural. It may be aggravated or repressed by our customs but when we find sexual jealousy in animals, as we most certainly do, we are forced to recognize that it is a fundamental reaction to certain situations and not largely created by customs. [16]

Insecurity forms the fertile ground for jealousy. The mother is filled with panic when her husband shows her an averted shoulder, for is he not all in one the source of family support, companion, sexual partner and father of the children? When we tell her she should not be so selfish as to feel jealous we put on the pressure from two directions. We psychologically wound her by fault finding, at the same time we insist that she keep secret all signs of her frightening insecurity, hurt feelings and loneliness. If we tell her she is less attractive to her husband when she feels jealous, we simply cause still greater dejection, for although she can pretend to be free of it, she knows she cannot banish the feeling. Finding a new prospective husband is usually the only way this depression can actually be overcome. And when she has done this, both husband and wife are centered upon others, the present marriage is close to breaking.

Through history the wife has been expected to will away every feeling of jealousy toward her husband's "other women" or other wives, while the husband's intense jealousy of any "other men" in the life of his wife has been recognized as natural and justified. His great desire to be his wife's lone partner along with his jealousy has in fact largely created the double standard.

Husbands' jealousy has led them to keep wives secluded in inner rooms, their faces hidden behind dark veils, locked in their houses, bound in chastity belts and threatened with punishment. Jealousy has been considered so natural in men that "le crime passionnel" (murder of his rival) has been condoned in many countries.

The greatest need at present is to lift the security and opportunities of women to a higher level so they may be liberated for broader and deeper living. We cannot hold that equal opportunity is part of our democracy at the same time we place a sweeping group of restrictions around women alone. Democracy demands that a husband and wife should follow the same policy in their sexual lives and that society should hold the same standards for both men and women. There can be no widespread peace and happiness between the sexes, either within or outside the family, under a double standard. The road to better times is clearly a more democratic relationship.

In the story, *"Anna and the King of Siam,"* [17] we see the King in possession of every luxury including a harem of beautiful women. He thought, the greater his control of his women and the larger their number, the more extensive would be his sexual satisfactions. He accepted the thinking of his male ancestors and men today in his part of the world. He had not considered the possibilities of a deep companionship with one woman, freer, more educated, happier than the women of his harem, until he knew Anna from the West. It had not before occurred to him that there is a wide range of mental and physical pleasures a developed woman can bestow upon a man she loves. The King discovered too late that he was *lonely* among his many subject wives, for none of them were real companions.

In the same manner many men today are fundamentally

lonely, fundamentally unsatisfied with their sexual lives because they do not allow women to fully develop and to stand by their sides as equals and as friends. Instead of clinging to the old folklore about the great benefits of outgrown theories and attitudes, let us recognize that mankind today may be only the raw material, the half-finished product of something far finer, and able to create far better patterns of living.

CHAPTER 4

1. Margaret Mead, *Sex and Temperament*, William Morrow & Co., 1935 (Reprinted in *From the South Seas*, William Morrow & Co., 1939) pp. 63-73.
2. Margaret Mead, *Growing Up in New Guinea*, William Morrow & Co., 1930. (Reprinted in —*From the South Seas*, op. cit., 1939) pp. 99-101.
3. "The Roman system is essentially a man's world, as well as a priest's world . . . all the central agencies of power in the Vatican are without exception male." Paul Blanshard, *Communism, Democracy and Catholic Power*, The Beacon Press, Boston, 1951, p. 63.
4. Beacon Press, Boston, 1954, p. 239.
5. L. T. Hobhouse et al, *The Material Culture and Social Institutions of the Simpler Peoples*, Chapman and Hall, Ltd., London, 1930, p. 163.
6. This is the case among the Arapesh and Mundugumors. Margaret Mead, *Sex and Temperament*, op. cit., p. 190.
7. *New York Times*, January 30, 1957.
8. Pearl Buck, *The Good Earth*, Grosset & Dunlap, 1936, p. 200, 358. The characters in this story are referred to because they are known to many, and because the author observed carefully the interaction among individuals in such a family pattern. The fact that the family is Chinese is not significant. Polygynous families similar to this in many respects have existed among most peoples.
9. Ibid., p. 202, 203, 211. Italics are mine.
10. Kimball Young, "Mormon Polygynous Families," *Studies in Personality*, ed. by Quinn McNemar and Maud A. Merril, McGraw-Hill Book Co., 1942, pp. 299, 306.
11. J. E. Hulett, Jr. "The Social Role of the Mormon Polygamous Male," *American Sociological Review*, June 1943, pp. 279, 286, 282.
12. J. B. Rice, "The Unwilling Virgins," May 1949.
13. In 1955 about 15% of men between 30 and 64 years of age were single. There were only about 4% less men than women of these

same ages. *Statistical Bulletin*, Metropolitan Life Insurance Co., May 1956, p. 5, and Feb. 1953, p. 10.

14. Margaret Lyon, "And So to Bedlam", *Reader's Digest*, February 1945, p. 50.
15. John Levy and Ruth Munroe, *The Happy Family*, Alfred A. Knopf, 1938, p. 102. Italics are mine.
16. This will be considered in a later chapter.
17. Margaret Landon, *Anna and the King of Siam*, Garden City Publishing Co., 1945. This story has been presented as a play and also in film.

CHAPTER 5

Questioning Some Common Theories on Marriage

College was opening as students were surging around the campus in suppressed excitement, unloading their things from autos and greeting each other. Flower beds in their final brilliance added to the scene which Adam and Eve looked upon from their window. The severity of the office lined with book shelves and cabinets was relieved by ivy leaves and petunia blossoms spread over the sills from the window boxes Eve had arranged. They had just finished a game of tennis and had come to the office still in their tennis clothes.

Both had given considerable thought to their book since they last carried forward their recorded discussions.

"We must face the question, Eve, of whether our book is to be a college text book for courses on marriage and the family or not. As I think of our conversation on the double standard and your chapter on thought control, I am coming to believe that it is too incisive and outspoken for a text book."

"Perhaps so. Most features of present day marriage have been sanctified by church and state. They are upheld in magazines, radio and T.V. programs, in all the media which surround us — even in college courses. In most text books the material presents the current pattern of marriage, and persuades the young people to fit into its main features. They discuss the importance of marriage, problems of interpersonal relations and how the husband and wife can develop competence in these. They may touch on minor variations, such as the wife earning outside the home, but they are apt to steer away from major questions, such as that of the wife's sexual ownership by her husband, and his control and ownership of funds saved through the work of both," Eve replied.

"Yes, that's it. Our marriage institution is supported by laws which roughly define the husband's and wife's duties and the grounds upon which it can be broken. In the voluminous writings for students I have not come across much questioning of these basic laws."

How courageous shall we be?

"Of course the college's main job is to acquaint the young people with the present setup and show them how a successful family life can be obtained under these laws if each spouse is considerate toward the other, both understand children and do their best in raising them," Eve said thinking of her own teaching. "And this takes lots of time. We just don't get around to analyzing the pattern and weighing the pros and cons of some of its features."

"Yet, the students often do question some of these features, you know. They venture to think about the future centuries and changes which might be made. They ask some difficult questions. I agree we don't really dig into possible improvements of the basic legal setup."

"We might consider that our book will do just this which isn't usually done in college courses, that is, analyze the institution itself, which seems radical but is a most reasonable thing to do. The older, conservative persons may think it uncalled for, but most young people who are going to live in the more distant future and are in a mood of independent thinking, will find it stimulating, at least," Eve said smiling. "And we hope it will give some constructive suggestions for more successful marriages."

"That's right. We better abandon the idea we are preparing a text book, but do some objective scientific studying of the pattern itself in the light of new knowledge and attitudes. — Actually sociologists must look a little ridiculous to some bright, young people if they continue indefinitely to accept the present setup and laws which support it as ideal, and assume only the task of persuading the students to adjust to it. Someone must take the pioneer steps of treating the subject in laboratory fashion, seeking the truth wherever it may lead." Adam said with feeling.

"Fine, I'm with you. Pioneers often suffer for their efforts but I'll take the risk with you. Our procedure is well adapted to this plan, Adam. We'll talk freely — just you and I. We'll see where our frank investigations take us while our conversations are recorded."

Theories on the division of labor

Adam started the ball rolling by saying, "Let's break down the complex institution of marriage into its parts, then consider briefly the common attitude toward these and the purpose these features are supposed to serve."

"All right, we have already considered current theories on the two standards regarding sexual relations out of marriage and the supposed purpose for these. We put them under the microscope. — How about the theories regarding the division of labor between the sexes?"

"Yes, an important feature, Eve. I would say the common attitude is that the wife is expected to stay at home and do the housework, basing this on the false idea that she is born with an interest and ability in housekeeping. Likewise it is held that since she bears the babies she should assume practically all their physical care, tend to all the mechanics of their living, that is, prepare their meals, wash their clothes, clean their rooms, etc. during their childhood and youth."

Adam paused, so Eve carried on, "Then it is reasoned that since she does all this for the children, she of course should perform these tasks for the father, any relatives, such as the parents of either spouse, who may live with them and any visiting guests. The mother should also carry the main responsibility for the training and mental health of the children, it is held, since she is at home with them most the time. These are made primarily her tasks by our laws, though her husband may give some assistance if he has the impulse and time. She may be reprimanded, even imprisoned, by the courts for neglect of her children and may be divorced by her husband if she does not carry out these tasks."

"On the other hand, the prevalent thinking holds that the husband's primary job is to bring in the bacon," Adam observed, "by giving himself almost wholly to his outside job, resting in his free hours so he returns refreshed. This idea is expressed by managers of companies — 'the ideal wife realizes that her husband belongs to the corporation.' [1] All this means that many husbands do not, or cannot, give much assistance in home tasks and time to care for their children."

"One could ask, if he stands back and views the whole picture, whether corporations properly should consider that they *own* the husbands. And also, whether the fathers should not be regarded as persons who are deeply interested in their families, who want to assume responsibility for their wellbeing in other ways beside passing over some money. Don't children suffer from lack of their father's attention in such a pattern? Can wives alone raise and train the persons whom these corporations will use in the future?" Eve smiled.

"Today the father's income is regarded as of such prime importance to the family that he is made its legal head. Other considerations as to how he happens to be its legal head we should consider later."

"Actually, the mother's contribution to the family has tremendous economic value but this is customarily overlooked. If people were engaged at going rates of payment to do all the things she does this would be realized. And her energy-absorbing job of pre-natal nourishment and bearing of children should also be regarded as an extensive *economic* contribution. I'll mention here simply that the life insurance companies recognize the economic value of a person and of a child.

"Although," Eve continued, "the husband's income in cash is generally held as the most essential contribution to family life this can well be questioned. The mother's services are usually equally important. If a mother of several small children dies the family is as stranded as if the father dies— if not more so."

"Yes indeed! But to notice the husband's job as defined by the laws, he is required to support his family. And the mother rests in the feeling that this will be provided. Yet sometimes she finds that this legal requirement does not help much, for if she looks further into the laws she discovers it is only the husband 'having ability to do so,' who must provide support. And who determines whether he has the ability? No one, unless she brings her problem to court. If she does this, which in itself provokes him, the judge makes an effort to determine his ability, but it's not an easy job. Also in the laws we find he is considered as supporting according to his ability, if he is not 'failing due to idleness, profligacy or dissipation.' [2]

"In short this requirement is not very definite. The amount of support he gives, determined by the portion of his earnings which he uses for family members, is still less definite and poorly defined by the laws." Adam thought of the cases he had watched in court where mothers pleaded for support for their children and the judges were actually helpless to do much under the laws.

"Well put, Adam. The legal setup makes his part pretty vague but the mother's job of keeping her children alive is *very definite*. She must do it no matter what funds her husband provides.—And it's not only—keeping them alive—but out of delinquency, physically and mentally well, that she is expected to do, no matter what—," Eve opened her pack of cigarettes and went on.

"Along with these other common attitudes we should include the theory that since men are of greater mentality than women they are the ones who specialize for outside jobs. While housework and child care which do not require so much mentality—the theory goes—can be done by women. These tasks in fact are regarded by most who have not experienced them as busy-work, something which nicely occupies the mother's time while she is sheltered in the home watching the children."

"That does present many men's attitudes I grant you," Adam said as he lighted Eve's cigarette and took one himself.

"Along this line is the theory that women enjoy detail and repetitive routine, that they are timid and cautious, preferring the safety of home to outside adventure, so home is naturally their place," Eve said reaching for a book from the shelves and opening it at a place mark. "Here it is by some respected writers." She read, "Woman is (by nature) passive, patient, limited to her sphere of action. One sex revolts at monotony; the other takes naturally to routine'.[3] This thought is also expressed by business management, since women are assigned the more routine tasks.

"We should look into this, for it just can't be supported on the basis of studies which have been made of men's and women's mentalities. In colleges and universities where both sexes study under similar environment—that is, girl students are not doing the cooking and cleaning for the boy students—women's abilities to learn have been found equal to men's in all fields. In addition, mental tests have been applied with the aim of discovering innate abilities of each sex. Terman and Miles, who have done the most extensive studying on this, have written:

'Intelligence tests ... have demonstrated for all time the falsity of the once prevalent belief that women as a class are appreciably or at all inferior to men in the major aspects of intellect. The essential equality of the sexes has further been shown by psychometric methods to obtain also in various special fields, such as musical ability, artistic ability, mathematical ability and even mechanical ability.' "[4]

She added, "Scientific evidence fails to indicate such innate differences in the sexes as to justify casting men and women in radically different roles, as is done today.—Yet you know that some are so sure that women have this inferior kind of mentality, interested only in details and monotony, that they claim this was the chief reason for primitive men and women getting together as a family unit."

Adam interrupted with a laugh, "As if sexual attraction weren't all important. The basic family of male and female living together probably existed long before the species we call mankind had developed."

"Yes, it is found even among the sub-human primates, monkeys and baboons, as I have been reading.—That theory that females were doing detailed, routine activities *before* the family existed I agree is laughable, Adam. It implies that primitive men saw primitive women cooking and carrying water, and said to themselves, 'Let's live with them. They *like* these routine tasks. We don't.' Of course if these men and women had not been living together as a family unit, each man and each woman would have had to perform *all* the chores that sustained his life; the women hunting and fighting wild animals, as well as cooking and carrying water. The men likewise doing the same things for themselves.—But this inference that women chose detailed stay-at-home tasks before the family existed is still written in some college text books."

"The cart is put before the horse there, isn't it, Eve? It was the male heads of the earliest families who determined what their mates could do, who arranged the division of labor."

"Of course. They kept their females 'at home' under their surveillance mainly to prevent other males from conjugating with them or taking them away. Neither the female's mentality nor her supposed love of routine had anything to do with the division of labor. I must tell you more about the book, 'The Social Life of Monkeys and Apes', I've just read."

"I'd love to hear about it. That false theory is an attempt to find an explanation which ignores the early male's domination of his mate's activities and whereabouts, I'm afraid," Adam observed.

"Women's frequent pregnancies and extensive baby care in those past ages did lead many women to stay near home.

But these reproductive tasks cannot provide the reason for the usual assignment to her of carrying the family water from a spring or well and gathering the fuel, two of the heaviest, most time consuming and uninteresting chores. If one travels in eastern Europe, Asia or Africa today he can still see them working at these." Eve paused to whiff her cigarette, then went on, "Let us look at some business men on a holiday, returning to the simple life in the mountains to hunt or on the shores to fish. Those who arrange the trips and engage the guides arrange the division of labor. What tasks are assigned the guides?"

Adam smiled, "Well, I happen to know. The guides are usually asked to haul the water, gather the fire wood, do most of the cooking and wash the dishes. The business men may help a little, depending on their feelings, and whether they've been sitting or walking a lot. If the vacation lasts for a week or more those tasks become tiresome and fall more and more upon the guides. The business men spend hours sitting in groups making the important decisions on tomorrow's plan and enjoy the adventures of fishing or hunting."

"You've put it better than you realize. If one asked these vacationers how they happened to give the guides those jobs I'm sure they'd say frankly, 'Why not? We don't care for them!' They wouldn't say, 'The guides like the routine jobs such as washing dishes', or that, 'Because of their lower mentalities we assign them these tasks.'—And as for the serious discussions of tomorrow's plans by the vacationers, that is the ego-satisfying job cherished by most people— the talking and decision-making.

"Do you remember that study made by Hobhouse?" Eve asked as she opened another book on her desk. "Of 434 primitive groups which are living today he found that in all these groups except 19, it was strictly the men who sitting in special sacred places discussed and made the important decisions for the tribes.[5] Even in our country Pueblo Indians still use kivas, underground council chambers, which women enter upon threat of death. Hobhouse also found that the wives performed more tiring work than that done by their husbands in the majority of groups studied and usually worked longer hours." [6]

"Most significant." Adam rose from his chair and began striding back and forth across the room. "All you say, Eve, does make us think of our council chambers, state and national legislative bodies, boards of directors of business companies and institutions, made up almost entirely of men."

"Oh, yes!—I'd like to ask if the division of labor was based upon the women's reproductive role and care of babies, whether sitting in the Indian kivas, centered in their villages, making decisions through lengthy talk fests would not be an excellent job for the pregnant or nursing mother— restful physically, a good change from home confinement. I think far more appropriate for them than carrying heavy jugs of water on their heads.—The women might not know as much about fighting neighboring tribes but they'd probably know more about the richness of the soil and health conditions for their families."

"But here," Adam remarked, "we meet the idea that women are of lower intelligence, held by the Indians as well as many of us. People confuse women's innate abilities with those which they have opportunity to develop. That is, if a woman's movements are greatly restricted; of course her knowledge is less in certain areas than a man's who has freely ranged distances and met challenges in hunting. Like- wise today a man who has wide business experiences, travels about, meeting many kinds of people, naturally may know more in certain fields than his home-caring wife."

"Do you remember, how surprised people were in World War II when because of labor shortage women in great numbers performed jobs, called 'men's work'—complicated jobs in metal welding and riveting, operating giant cranes, woodworking, laying-out work, inspection and instruction— and were found able to do these as well as the men and sometimes better? Thousands of women were employed in

70

aircraft, firearms, automobile plants and shipyards.[7] Most people had never realized that these abilities were simply dormant until they were given a chance to develop. Actually it is wishful thinking by men that women are innately adapted to repetitive and confining household tasks."

"And as late as Shakespeare's time, you know, they thought women could not act on the stage, so men took women's parts. Also women were imagined not able to sing or play a musical instrument before an audience," Adam added, remembering accounts of Greek drama and those of of the middle ages.

"Anthropology shows us definitely that women can perform widely different jobs, according to what they are allowed to do. And likewise men develop very different natures and abilities according to what their culture expects from them. The Tchambuli men of New Guinea, for instance, decorate themselves elaborately, dance gracefully before their women, while the plainly garbed women admire them and efficiently perform the tasks which support the tribe." [8]

"Yes, a lot could be said on the subject of just what is woman's nature and what she would do if entirely free to choose her activities."

"Along this line, Adam, it should be recognized that among the relatively few women who have been freed from endless household tasks and child raising there have been many who showed great abilities. Just to mention a few who occur to me in recent times: there are the scientists Madame Curie, Lise Meitner; the first class writers, Jane Austen, George Sand (pen name for Amandine Dudevant) and George Eliot (pen name for Marian Evans), all of Europe. (I'll mention some of this country later.) Then the women who happened to be passed the crown of England proved some of its best rulers, Queen Elizabeth I and Queen Victoria."

Eve continued while Adam still paced the floor. "I grant that it's difficult for men who are exposed on all sides to advertising pictures of women wearing lacy underwear, pointed ruby fingernails and perfectly set hair to believe that women don't voluntarily choose to do all this.—Likewise most of us think that the doorman of a hotel in his impressive gold braided uniform and obsequious ways has voluntarily chosen this dress and manner. He probably lives in poor cramped quarters, is far worse off than the simply dressed business men he serves. He is doing only what is required to earn a living at his job. His employer and hotel patrons are well pleased over the air of affluence he presents.

"This is exactly the situation with many girl stenographers and clerks. They must be attractively dressed, look pleasant and feminine to obtain and hold their jobs, though this may require them to spend an unreasonable amount of time and money on their clothes, covering up the fact that they often struggle to keep well fed, obtain sufficient sun and rest, while they help support a parent, their children, or younger brothers.

"And it is not only such employed women who are forced to fit into our social requirements, but all of them, if they are to be attractive to men, have beaux and husbands. Some for a period in their lives genuinely delight in the energy and money spent on making themselves beautiful since it is combined with the thrilling game of finding a husband. But I wager that every woman at some time finds the task a wearisome burden, but she must keep on in order to be accepted.—There are women who would love to belittle all this and venture into hundreds of other fields, exploration and scientific research, astronomy and archeology. But they hesitate to assume the warped celibate and childless life in order to participate in these. Why shouldn't women be able to have both?"

Adam settled in his chair again. "I grant you, it is hard for men to see this as you do. They cannot help but believe

72

that women *are* free and show their natures all the time. They think of Egyptian women in 2000 B.C. using rouge and eye shade, and conclude this self-adornment is basic in their nature, never realizing that women then, as now, through social compulsion had to comply to win their beaux and husbands, as you say. Actually there is a desire for self-adornment in men shown through history. Take the primitive group, the Tchambuli you mentioned. The men deck themselves with headdresses of bird-of-paradise feathers over their carefully arranged curls, wear great chains of shells which extend below their waists, bustles of straw and carvings, with flying squirrel tails from their sides." [9]

"And we must remember, Adam, that not far back men of our country wore wigs with long curls, embroidered velvet vests and pants, with lace ruffles falling over their hands. Clearly the customs of a culture encourage self-adornment of women or discourage it—as well as of men.—Lately I have heard men condemn women for their pride, for giving too much attention to appearances, as if men had not demanded of each woman through the laws, an incomplete existence unless she pleased some man sufficiently to become his life-long mate."

"It looks as though right now we find a tendency for men to adorn themselves a little more, at least in gay colored sport shirts and bathing suits. Probably both men and women obtain similar enjoyment from self-decoration; that it is not an innate interest of women alone," Adam concluded.

Economic value of the mother's contributions

"But to turn to another common conception on marriage today we have the theory that the wife is being *protected* by staying at home, which is most questionable considering the high rate of home accidents with stoves and knives.— This is still combined with the idea of the mentally superior husband taking upon his shoulders the care of his dependent wife and children while she performs the simple, easy tasks in the sheltered home."

"Yes, Eve, I saw lately in a government pamphlet a picture of men supporting with their upraised arms a platform on which stood children, wives and elderly people. It was prepared by some men to show their economic burdens. They completely ignored the work of equal economic value by the mothers. Since her services to her husband and in raising the future citizens is not converted into dollars but is given directly as service its economic value is usually not acknowledged."

"How true, Adam. Her work not only helps her husband but is usually fully as valuable for the country as his efforts in business. That is, if we take men's work in business, industry and farming on the one hand and the mothers' of raising the next generation on the other, who can say which is more important? Surely all men's efforts would be for naught if there weren't a younger group to carry on, if the life of the country came to an end.

"Excuse me, if I return to her service in producing a baby. Here is the figure I wanted." She opened a book by Louis I. Dublin, of the Metropolitan Life Insurance Co. "He gives a value of $9,000. to the new born baby.[10] Of course it is a rough estimate but far better than considering the result of the mothers' months in prenatal nourishment, the strain and stress of childbirth as *no* economic contribution."

"Good, if a mother has five babies she contributes $45,000 roughly of population, or man and woman power to the country.—And if her hours of work for these five is calculated at going rates we'd really have an impressive figure. We'd hardly dare mention it," Adam said as he thought of what could be worked out.

"And to these hours the mother gives her children must be added what she gives her husband. Striking facts regarding this are published in the bulletin of the Metropolitan Life Insurance Co. It compares the health and death rates of men with wives and those without wives. The life-giving value of their service is impressive." Eve read from one of the Statistical Bulletins, " 'Among men aged 20 to 44 the death rate of the married is only about half that for the single, and an even smaller fraction of that for the widowed and divorced.' [11]

"Whew! You do present a thesis on the value of the mother's work."

"And with all this contribution she is made financially dependent upon her husband according to our marriage setup." Eve concluded in the low voice which she used when deeply concerned.

"It is an astonishing situation when you consider it. I can't think of another group contributing so much whose members are in a similar dependent economic position resting upon the ability, good-will and continued life of another particular person for his roof and bread and butter."

"There is no similar group. But this situation among mothers is an undeniable fact. People usually cannot conceive it possible to have another pattern. Most have never viewed our particular culture as something made by the people themselves, not by nature, nor by God. Nor have they come to regard our culture as only one among hundreds of others, in the past, at present and probably in the future."

Views of some pioneer sociologists

"Would you like me to read to you, Adam, some quotations on this matter of division of labor?—Here is one from Lester Ward, who is called our first great sociologist:

'That the subjection of women was due entirely to her physical inferiority to man seems beyond controversy. ... The man saw that he was the master creature, that woman was smaller and weaker ... and at the same time could be made to contribute to his pleasure and his wants, and he proceeded to appropriate her accordingly. The tendency to deny and escape (this fact) being inspired wholly by shame at admitting it.' [12]

"This one is by John Stuart Mill, true, written a while ago, but observations on primitive life were apt to be as accurate in his time as those of present writers:

'The legal subordination of women was not first adopted

because comparison and experience of other social arrangements proved it best for mankind. The mere physical fact of men's superior strength was converted into a legal right and sanctioned by society. The subjection of women does not rest today on considerations of social expediency . . .' [13]

"They hold in other words that many of the customs now embodied in the marriage institution which are viewed with reverence were originally based on man's ability to coerce those weaker than himself. The rule of the male was in accordance with the principles operating in animal and human life. Albert Einstein writes, 'Nowhere have we really overcome the predatory phase of human development.' The principle that might makes right still seems to be largely the law among nations, and among individuals and groups, with might often converted into economic power. The theory that the subordinate position of women within the home was established for her protection and has worked for her benefit cannot be demonstrated," Eve stated. "And I regard Einstein's objective observations on society as valuable as his in the physical sciences."

"I do too," Adam spoke up, "I also agree with the quotations you've read. But we should not criticize men too much for taking advantage of their greater physical strength. They have simply been those in the position to exhibit the general human lack of generosity and broad vision.—Women were forced to accept the role assigned them because it was usually the only way for them to live.—Even today a woman who does not accept her role as housewife and sexual possession of her husband suffers for it one way or another."

"Oh yes. The wife who ventures into business and shows real ability may well make her husband uneasy, causing him to find a more dependent housekeeping wife," Eve added, thinking of other ways wives have stepped outside their assigned role, then continued.

"When men obtained their wives through purchase, by payments of cattle and other forms of wealth or by cap-

76

turing them, they freely admitted that they were *obtaining something very valuable.*[14] They did not then claim that marriage was for wives' protection. Only a more modern society with all its rationalizing has held that the institution is mainly for the protection of the childbearer.[15]

"If marriage in the past had been designed mainly for woman's well-being we would expect the division of labor to have been somewhat different. Instead of many laborious tasks being assigned her, as we have noted, some of the more interesting and lighter work of making weapons, musical instruments, ceremonial objects, trapping small animals could have been allowed her but these were largely assumed by the men.[16] In many parts of the world one can still see a man riding a horse or donkey while his wife walks behind carrying a heavy load," she observed.

They were resting quietly when the telephone rang and Adam was called out of the office. Eve took the opportunity to slip on a skirt over her shorts and go into the quadrangle where a beautiful sunset spread a rosy glow over the scene. Station wagons and cars were being unpacked. Some fathers of the girl students, seldom seen on the campus, were helping them. Lamps, record-players, radios were among suitcases, boxes, and sofa pillows. She wondered if the dormitories would hold them all. How we humans depend upon our possessions, she thought. Many joyful "Hellos" for old college friends were mixed with "Goodbyes" to parents. Eve drank it all in, then studied the unusual colors among some of the zinnias and the shades of blue and lavender in the ageratum buds and blossoms, then returned to her office.

Adam soon joined her and remarked, "Talking about housework—what was really amusing during World War II was to hear the soldiers' attitudes toward kitchen and cleaning jobs, called 'Kitchen Police' or 'KP'. They recognized such duties as both mentally and physically wearing, so much so, that extra time at 'KP' was used as a form of punishment."

"Yet," Eve laughed, "even these very soldiers think women regard preparation of three meals a day for seven days a week during thirty or fifty years as the form of activity they love and freely choose.—One could ask why are house-maids scarce? Why do millions of employed women prefer the factory and other jobs? Today much of the work formerly performed by servants is now carried on by mothers. And if we compare the activities of each mother with that of her husband, I believe, we would find most mothers' working days longer, more monotonous and more of a strain than their husbands', especially while she cares for babies and young children, and if we include the energy-absorbing reproductive features of her life, menstruation, pregnancy and childbirth."

"You are right, Eve. Many wives in order to have a cleaning-woman and a washing machine find employment outside the home. It is one of the revolutionary changes taking place." After a pause Adam went on, "I'll again put in a word here for the men. They accept the customs on the division of labor, thinking them tested by time and beneficial to all. They often carry them forth feeling they are doing the right thing. Rarely does a person take the trouble to submit a custom to criticism and determine its origin and effects."

"Yes, that is true," Eve replied thoughtfully, "but all the time a certain interaction is taking place. Constantly men face some inherited mores which give them privileges and freedom along with others which impose burdens. They exert persistent pressure usually to preserve those which are pleasing and to change those irksome to themselves. For instance, women's preparation of meals is surely a great time-saver for men and has been a custom pretty well maintained, even on Sundays and vacation days when men could help. On the other hand the custom that men give women seats on trains and buses is often not so pleasing and is therefore not very well maintained. The men do not exactly figure it out—though there is a recent book advertised as suggesting tried-out dodges for fathers in the home. Some do little or no calculating but simply do what pleases them." Eve picked some faded blossoms in the window box as she thought. "Let me see how I can put this.—Long-legged men often manage to get seats in subway trains ahead of the short-legged men. The tall don't consciously plan to subject the short ones but they often actually do in certain respects."

"In case we are thought too hard on the men," Adam added, "shouldn't we stop to say there are roughly two kinds, those who are constantly humanizing the customs which give themselves undue advantages and those, on the other hand, who are intrenching those same customs? That is, those who help a tired wife with meal preparation and those who refuse to do so."

"Oh yes, that must be said. We could call one group of men the sportsmen, the fair-play men, those liberating women from past chains. The other group could be called the big-front—too big to stoop and help—the insensitive to women's needs, the enchaining men. Some of the latter group, it is true, are led to this through calculations, others from lack of any thought. Some keep their advantages noisily like a growling dog and others quietly like a fish sliding smoothly between one's fingers."

Customs develop through myriad small steps

"That's right, Eve, the building of customs favorable to those in the advantageous position is not a scheme planned by them but rather a development through myriad small steps."

"Yes, we find in history that women have sometimes resisted certain over-restrictive customs but usually they have possessed insufficient power to change them. The Greek women in ancient times tried to get the vote.—However, there is a limit on how far the dominant group can go in gaining its extensive desires for property and service from others. Sometimes a situation has been developed wherein the subjected have been reduced in numbers as a result of too heavy demands. In all probability groups of primitive people discovered through experience, for instance, that women cannot maintain their health while continuously bearing babies every year. And therefore they developed the custom of prohibiting sexual intercourse between a married couple until their last baby could walk or had finished nursing, which gave the mother some intervals between pregnancies.[17]

"This matter of custom development looks something like this to me," Eve continued. "There is a constant interplay between groups which results in the growth of certain accepted ways. Some groups exert far more influence than others. For instance, the conquering Greeks, then the conquering Romans were able to press their ways upon the peoples they governed; in our country the whites as against the Indians; also the whites as against the Negroes have likewise been able to encourage customs which pleased themselves. But in all these cases, the same as in the relationship between men and women, there were points beyond which the powerful groups could not go if the life of others was to be maintained.—In my mind's eye I see a sheet of water after a cloudburst running down a wooded hillside. Boulders and hillocks divert its course but the great force of gravity is the overwhelming factor which directs the flowing water. The boulders and hillocks which exert some influence here and there are the basic needs of the less powerful which must be heeded to prevent their sickness and death. The all-important force of gravity corresponds to the dominant influence in custom-building, which is the wishes of those on top to keep their privileges."

"That's a good simile. I can see it all—I can see the customs formed by the rulers and influential persons diverted only by essential needs of others." Adam lit a fresh cigarette and added, "You have a visual mind that pictures relationships through moving objects. I do, too, but not to the same degree.

80

"All this leads us, Eve, to the subject of why it is important for people to understand what is going on; why customs should be appraised as to whether they work for the benefit, or the turmoil and weakness of mankind. Of course the easiest course is to accept them and their many accompanying illusions. Harmful customs live on and on for centuries if no one stops to weigh them. The killing in cold blood of innocent men and women, such as, the kings' sons, as was done in the Bronze Age in Old Uppsala, Sweden, or certain chosen young people at the pyramids in Mexico, to appease their gods was common among many early cultures. Each succeeding generation was raised to accept these practices until some persons were independent enough to reconsider them—to question the myths and study the facts. And doubtless a difficult struggle ensued while these deep rooted customs surrounded with religious theory were in the process of change.—This seems to be the method of progress."

"It is surely so," Eve leaned forward, "which means someone must help people today see clearly some of the old myths and customs among which they have been raised, and view them with the same cool rationality with which we now view the myth that certain persons should be killed on altars to please the gods.—We have been mentioning some: the theory of women's inferior mentality; that she is best restricted largely to home tasks; that the double standard of morals should be continued; that the mother and children should be made financially dependent upon the good-will and ability of one man; and that no other pattern is possible. I shouldn't omit that theory that the man should be the legal head of the family. No doubt a struggle will take place while these are reconsidered."

"In other words, could we be as foolish in some of our ways as the tribes whose customs fairly knock us over? The painful, disfiguring initiation ceremonies boys and girls pass through, the worrisome taboos that fill the lives of all with fear, seem so horribly ill-conceived by us. For instance," Adam paused, "it is the custom among the

'Hairy Ainu' for twelve year old girls to cut the surface of the skin away from around the mouth and keep rubbing charcoal into the flesh, leaving a permanent wide black area. They who don't will not get husbands.—In a northern group young girls are sewed into leather vests for solid years, which prevents the growth of their lungs."

"To understand our culture which we accept like the trees and grass around us we must try to imagine ourselves outside of it viewing it as strangers. It's hard to do. If a person gets acquainted with other cultures than his own, that helps." Eve's eyes were fixed on a deep velvety purple petunia blossom as she was thinking.

"I must mention another custom in our society which needs to be appraised, Eve. It is that of men wearing long trousers, coats and neckties in their offices and while teaching in 90° weather while they fairly steam. I'd like to appear in a loin-cloth." Adam chuckled, then went on more seriously, "Most of us do not recognize to what extent our attitudes and actions are determined by these customs. Nor do we realize that when customs are carried on for a period they become sanctified and made into laws. *Laws are only customs crystalized* and enforced by punishments. When a judge makes a decision that certain action is legal because it is a custom he is making the conversion before our eyes. This is from a law book I am reading:

> 'The unwritten or common law ... has its origin in ancient customs, ... which have been transmuted into positive law by decisions of courts of justice.' [18]

And this English common law in the basis for most of our laws in this country today."

"That puts the matter clearly and it leads into our next conversation which will go into the customs of monkeys and apes. People will think us crazy to jump to the apes but it will be most enlightening.—You know the recent book by C. Wright Mills, 'The Sociological Imagination.' [19] It hits the nail on the head. He claims the most promising method today in dealing with many social problems is to bring together our knowledge from various sciences crossing academic boundaries. For instance, if one is considering a typical problem, such as the marriage institution, he should select materials from all areas—biology, anthropology, history, animal and human psychology and political science—which deal with his topic. Material from one discipline often throws light on the conceptions in another."

"I have read it and admire his thinking. So off we will go on another courageous line. Let the chips fall where they may."

CHAPTER 5

1. William H. Whyte, "The Wives of Management," *Fortune*, October 1951.
2. Chester G. Vernier, *American Family Laws*, Stanford University Press, California, 1931-1938, Vol. II, p. 55.
   Walter Gelhorn et al, *Children and Families in the Courts of New York City*, Dodd, Mead & Co., 1954. Report of Special Committee of the Bar of the City of New York.
3. William G. Sumner and Albert G. Keller, *Science and Society*, Yale University Press, 1927, Vol. I, p. 122.
4. Lewis M. Terman and Catherine Miles, *Sex and Personality*, McGraw-Hill Book Co., 1937, p. 1.
5. L. T. Hobhouse, et al, *The Material Culture and Social Institutions of the Simpler Peoples*, Chapman and Hall, London, 1930, pp. 170, 173.
6. Ibid., pp. 154, 157, This was so in 86 cases out of the 112 studied.
7. During the war papers and periodicals carried statements on their "remarkable" work. An article, "New Women Workers Speed Plane Production" mentioned assembly processes speeded 25% and 50% when done by women. *Readers Digest*, June 1942. "Women Workers Excel Men in Thousands of War Jobs," *New York Post*, January 13, 1942.
   Over the radio an officer of the Firestone Tire Co. said "women are found satisfactory in practically every job ordinarily held by men..." Voice of Firestone, November 17, 1941.
8. Margaret Mead, *Sex and Temperament*, William Morrow & Co. 1935 (Reprinted in — *From the South Seas* op. cit. 1939) pp. 240-258.
9. Ibid.
10. "The infant just born is an economic asset — because if he be allowed to reach maturity, he will produce more than he cost to

bring up, plus what it will cost to maintain him," Louis I. Dublin, *Health and Wealth*, Harper & Bros., 1928, p. 52.

11. The difference in these rates for the married and unmarried women is small in comparison. *Statistical Bulletin*, Metropolitan Life Insurance Co., February 1957, p. 4.

12. Lester Ward also quotes statements of other anthropologists who hold the same view. *Pure Sociology*, Macmillan & Co., 1903, pp. 345, 349.

13. *The Subjection of Women*, Longmans, Green, 1924, p. 9.

14. Wife capture is mentioned in Nordic, Greek and Roman tales. The story of the Sabines is still carried on among some Australian tribes. Women of different tribes have been exchanged or traded. They have been purchased by service of the bridegroom such as Jacob's working seven years for Rachel in the Bible story and by property such as horses, sheep, money and products of all kinds. As late as the 18th century in England women were sold in the market place as wives.
F. Muller-Lyers, *Evolution of Modern Marriage*, Alfred A. Knopf, 1930

15. "The Compulsive Basis of Social Thought; as Illustrated by the Varying Doctrines as to the Origins of Marriage and the Family," V. F. Calverton, *Journal of Sociology*, March 1931.

16. We find women among 224 tribes studied by Murdock doing over 90% of the water carrying, grain grinding and cooking; 70% of the "burden bearing" and 77% of the fuel gathering. Among these same tribes the men were doing the lighter and more interesting work; weapon making, trapping of small animals, and making of musical instruments and 85% of the fishing. George P. Murdock, "Comparative Data on Division of Labor by Sex", *Journal of Social Forces*, May 1937, p. 551.

17. Margaret Mead, *Sex and Temperament*, op. cit. pp. 36-38. George P. Murdock, *Social Structure*, Macmillan Co., 1949, pp. 266, 267.

18. Roger W. Cooley, *Brief Making and the Use of Law Books*, 5th ed., 1926, West Publishing Co., St. Paul, 1926, p. 5.

19. *The Sociological Imagination*, Oxford University Press, 1959, pp. 138-142.

CHAPTER 6

Dominant Factors
in the Beginnings of Marriage

A few days later Adam and Eve again found themselves centering upon the earliest beginnings of marriage.

Eve opened up with the question, "Have you ever stood in front of the monkey's cage in the park and wondered just who is observing whom; whether you as a curious *homo sapiens* were studying the monkeys, or whether their bright eyes were studying you and your strange clothes as you exhibited yourself before them?"

"Yes, often," Adam chuckled, "Do tell me of that book about their social life."

"You should read it for its most amusing, as well as most significant. It's by Zuckerman, entitled, 'Social Life of Monkeys and Apes.' [1] If all I say now is printed in our book I do hope our readers won't be shocked. But since we've decided to be scientific in our considerations we can't omit this material."

A glance into the animal world

"When we look into their ways we see the naked desires of these animals exposed to observers. The monkeys are not restricted by taboos. Zuckerman first shows us that a comparison of human beings and the sub-human primates can profitably be made. He and other authorities on animal life agree that all primate behavior is influenced to a large degree by the physiological sexual nature of the female.

"To clarify this he first discusses the lower mammals, not primates, such as the deer and the horse where the female is able to have sexual relations only at certain periods of the year, only during a few weeks, the rutting season.

85

As a result of this physiological fact the males live in herds separately from the females most of the year and join them only during the short rutting period."

"That is, the males' sexual desires play an all important part in the social structure of their lives.—This makes me think of a beautiful film by Cleveland Grant on the wildlife of Alaska and the Canadian Rockies, Eve. Such fine pictures of herds of male bisons separate from those of the females and young! Also, similarly constituted herds of elk, mountain goats, mountain sheep, and Dall sheep, deer, and moose. Such vivid views of them wandering over the mountains and valleys, with close-ups of the males' faces and enormous horns. Then of their joining the females during the weeks of rutting and the males' furious fighting with each other for their sexual possessions. I'll never forget those scenes— and the social pattern of their lives."

"I wish I had seen it.—Now the contrast of their pattern with that of the monkeys and apes stands out clearly. The males and females of these sub-human primates don't separate into herds. They live together most of the time.[2] And why?"

"Because the females do not have a rutting period, but instead the males can conjugate with them at any time," Adam replied, interested in this line of thought.

"Yes, that's it! But the two sexes don't pair off one male living with one female usually. Each male instead tries to bring under his control as many females as possible. I'll read you a description he gives of a chimpanzee harem:

"The dominant male 'kept himself aloof up at the top of the cage, seated on a board, observing and controlling the doings of the others. If a quarrel arose he sprang down from his seat and made an end to it by blows and bites. He never indulged in games or sports, but preserved his austerity which was respected by the others. The sexual appetite of this male was interesting to note. He was very exacting in this respect, and demanded repeated intercourse every day with his females. For this purpose he sprang down, and seized one of the females who, even if she struggled at first, had to yield

86

finally to his superior strength, and submit to copulation.... From my observation the old male exercised his power and strength in a despotic manner, and demanded sexually implicit submission. The harem was a captive troop....'[3] There was beside the male head a young male who could copulate only when the dominant male was asleep."

Eve continued, "I should bring out here that zoologists say there is a remarkable similarity in the reproductive processes of the human females and those of these sub-human primates. The pattern of social life of monkeys and apes therefore, though more crude, is embarrassingly simlar to that of primitive men and women, we must admit—"

"Admit—probably with a blush."

"Perhaps. Zuckerman gives lengthy accounts of a large baboon colony which was maintained in nearly a natural state in a Munich park. From these studies, as well as those by others of the primates in their native habitats, it has been shown that the baboons' physical strength clearly determines their social position in respect to each other. That is, the position between the males themselves, as well as between the males and females is established by one's muscles and size. Here is another important section:

> From observations of various groups of monkeys and apes it is clear that the males win their mates by fighting and capture. Fighting does not occur on every occasion, however, since the weaker males learn by painful experience not to challenge those who are stronger . . . and the stronger learn by experience to threaten and intimidate, which often obviates fighting. Yet there are occasional desperate struggles during which the helpless female is snatched, pulled about and sometimes killed by would-be owners.[4]

A family unit, consisting of one male, one or more females and their offspring, lasts only so long as the master is strong enough to withstand any attacks from competitors who may desire one of his mates.

"Since physical strength rules supreme, the strongest males capture and hold the greater number of females. At one time, for instance, there were in the Munich colony 25 males and 25 females, all adults. Soon the five strongest males possessed all the females, one baboon 'sheik' owning seven, while 20 males were left mateless." [5]

"I see. Rule by force, or threat of force, results in subjugation of weaker and younger males, as well as the females," Adam observed.

"Oh yes. Isn't that something? The largest baboon overlording seven females, the next largest six, until we see the weakest males as forlorn bachelors hanging around the outskirts of a harem, or going off in a small group by themselves.

"Here is another impressive scene. Can you see it in your mind? The head male of a family sitting jealously guarding his mates, for 'extra-marital' relations are strictly forbidden the females. He insists that harem favorites stay beside him, especially when they are in the period of heightened sexual attraction, called the oestrus period. Rarely indeed, does one of these closely watched females conjugate with anyone other than her lord and master and then only when he falls asleep at the post, or when she wanders beyond his range of vision. Fatal battles between the overlord and the seducer sometimes follow discovery of these rare 'adulteries.' " [6]

While Adam was mulling over this with a suppressed smile, he filled his pipe, pushed down the tobacco and lighted it, not being able to word his thoughts. Eve watched him, then said, "Excuse me, if I insert one of my own thoughts here. It is that the male baboon head does not imagine that the female is strictly monogamous and desires no one but himself, the way most human husbands do.—Nor does the baboon overlord imagine he keeps his wives at home for their protection. He knows it is to insure his sexual ownership of them. If you, Adam, like some others should hold that *protection* of these females and their offspring is the basis of this baboon family setup you'd stumble over an explanation of why the male so desperately contends for these responsibilities. We know that responsibilities for care of others involve burdens. The baboon lord would not fight to acquire burdens. He fights for personal satisfactions."

"Of course, and so did primitive man," Adam added. "Certainly the basis of the baboon family and that of early man is the male's sexual desires."

"Another feature which indicates the male baboon's harem is not kept together for the females' protection is brought out in Zuckerman's descriptions about the distributions of food between himself and his mates which we won't go into here.[7] He writes, 'Observations ... indicate that the female lower primate is completely dominated by her male overlord and her subjugation may well depend upon his physical superiority.'[8] Besides his larger bones which allow more muscle attachment, he is free from carrying the unborn young which also enables him to dominate her during her frequent periods of pregnancy."

Adam puffed his pipe, seemed to be looking into the clouds of smoke as he said, "I believe if one could see family life of earliest man, which was probably polygynous with wives kept near their home caves, it wouldn't look different from these descriptions of sub-human primate families. There isn't a direct line of development between the living examples of these sub-human primates and man, but scientists claim the common ancestors were so similar to monkeys or apes that they would be popularly called by the same name."

"Gradually, as man's mind developed this marriage pattern became strengthened and supported by supernatural beliefs about good and evil spirits and how the evil spirits threaten those who don't obey the overlords.—What is that saying—leading slaves to cling to the chains that bind them is the easiest method of control? We noted in a previous chapter how many primitive tribes keep their women cowed through fear of the evil Tamberan, only one of numerous similar ceremonies and devices. In these supernatural theories we see the beginnings of today's beliefs of men's greater innate intelligence and his headship determined by God.

And along with the growth of these theories through the ages we find the gradual covering up of the fact that the marriage institution is based on the sexual ownership of wives by their husbands, and in its place the development of the rationalized theory that marriage results from the male's desire to care for the childbearer and her children."

"That is, Eve, as I see it, marriage became culturally approved as if it were an institution of high moral order for the well-being of all, sanctioned by the supernatural spirits and their gods."

"Yes, it grew into what it is at present and what we are trying to analyze.—There is another group of studies we should notice here. They are the reports on experiments by Robert M. Yerkes and others with chimpanzees. In these, he notes who takes morsels of food given to a pair between their regular meals. For successive days an attendant comes to a large open-air cage and sends down a chute into the cage 10 small pieces of banana at 30 second intervals. He observes carefully which chimp gets the lion's share and how. The two have equal opportunity to snatch the proffered tid-bits so far as the construction of cage and chute is concerned. They could take turns, or a chivalrous male could let his mate take all, or he could take all for himself."

"What does happen?"

Eve leafed the packet of reports with marked sections and continued, "After repeating this experiment with several chimpanzee pairs during many months Yerkes found that the typical male took all the pieces of food, except during days when the female was particularly receptive sexually (in a state of oestrus) at which times he gallantly stood aside and let her have part of the choice morsels. He writes, 'Generally speaking this is in exchange for sexual accommodation.' [9] Of 25 consecutive days of these experiments described in his study the typical male took all the 10 pieces himself on 17 days. Then for the 5 days while the female was in oestrus he let her take all the pieces. And for the 3 days intervening before or after this period the male and female each took some.[10] Yerkes writes, 'when the female is not sexually receptive ... the naturally dominant member of the pair almost regularly obtains the food' with a spirit of 'assurance and assumption that the right of control is now his.'[11] 'Without threat of conflict' he places himself at the chute to receive the food and the female yields him the place. She knows that physical conflict with her mate is useless.

"These experiments seem to indicate that the male primate *assumes* his right of priority for the things he desires because he has the physical power to command them. Also, they show that the sexual drive in the male is extremely powerful in determining his behavior. They reveal also the importance to the female of her sex appeal. Clearly, this appeal is what gained the male's consideration, which allowed her a small portion of the choice pieces of food."

Similar mental traits of human and sub-human primates

"Extremely interesting, I must say. Do we dare include all this?—I wonder." Adam put his head back and stared at the ceiling.

"We'll decide that later, you know. But we agreed we'll not be afraid of mentioning now whatever seems true.— Just one more experiment by Yerkes I'll tell you about which brings in the matter of jealousy. A pair of chimpanzees, Jack and Wendy, were mates. Wendy had been 'eagerly aggressive . . . had striven hard for the male's attention,' and had won it. At a later time Jack was placed with the female, Pati, in an adjacent cage to Wendy during part of several days. Jack was sexually strongly drawn to Pati, the new female in his life. Later when he was transferred back to Wendy's cage she, having observed Jack's fixation on Pati and his corresponding sexual indifference to herself, exhibited what we call jealousy. She 'seemed subdued and repressed by his neglect of her.' As a result of her depressed feelings he allowed her fewer pieces of the food dropped down the chute than he had during the previous cycle before Pati had shaped the triangle." [12]

Adam sat upright in his chair remarking, "How typical of the series of reactions between the human male and female. Such actions indicate jealousy to be a fundamental emotion, not something found only in perverse individuals, or the result of cultural attitudes. Likewise, they show jealousy causes an unhappy state which leads the other to turn still further away and starts a vicious circle of responses."

"Of course, we cannot transfer in toto the motives and behavior of chimpanzees to human beings for the human situation is far more complex. But neither can we ignore indications from such experiments.—We musn't overlook, Adam, the male chimpanzees' seeming conviction that they were doing the *'right'* and natural thing in appropriating all the morsels except when mates were sexually attractive. With similar lack of analysis man seems to have convinced himself that his control of business, government and family today, gained through customs originating from his greater size, is right and natural. And he has felt it reasonable that his authoritative position thus obtained should allow him to gain greater economic power, for instance, to consider property won and saved through the work of both the man and his wife as being largely his own. We'll later look into this further. Most significant, also," Eve went on, "is the observation that the female chimpanzee's sexual attraction is somewhat compensating for her lesser size, so that her wants are sometimes respected. In human society this advantage of the female is greatly reduced from what it might be by restricting her freedom to grant men sexual favors as she chooses; through the widespread legal and social requirement that she give exclusive sexual rights to one man. If she gains any economic benefits through sexual favors outside marriage, she is stigmatized by one of our most derogatory words, prostitute. Thus we find in human society the prevalent attitude that it is *right* for man to gain through greater muscular strength extensive advantages; but *evil* for woman, except to a limited extent in marriage, to gain any kind of benefits through her basic compensating qualities, her sexual attraction and favors."

Adam recognized her point, "That is right, we have no bad word to call the man who uses his greater strength to arrange laws and gain extensive power, but there are many bad names used freely everywhere to denounce and ruin a woman who uses her sexual attraction to gain some wishes. It does give you pause for thought."

"Here again we must realize man has been the subject, expressing his attitudes and having them generally accepted, and woman, the object, he talks about extensively, and tries to control," Eve said. "The whole subject of prostitution we should later consider. Here is a final quotation from Zuckerman, 'Since few significant differences can be seen between the broader social mechanisms of different monkeys and apes, and since man is also an Old World primate, one may assume that the social level discussed in this book is one through which man passed in pre-human stages of his evolution.' " [13]

"That is true without doubt. But we must recognize the male has stepped forward from the social pattern of monkeys. We men restrain ourselves a lot, much more than you women think. We do, most of us take one wife and look after her and our children—perhaps along with a little sexual freedom. We are not allowed to kill our wives when we want a new and younger one as did Henry VIII," Adam said defending his brotherhood. "But of course there are many more of the primitive features in today's pattern than most people imagine. For instance, the man is still in a somewhat similar position to that of the baboon "husband," in that he owns sexually his "wife" or "wives"—the baboon and some men of the Orient owning several simultaneously, while some men of the West own two, three or more consecutively. The baboon and human male may readily take a new "wife" without suffering any great disadvantages.— If the human male leaves his wife and children she usually suffers in various ways, partly because she endeavors to care for the children. This is the result of our largely man-made pattern which in general allows a mother some return for her work in raising future citizens only if she pleases her husband. That is, under our basic pattern the man is paid for his work by society, but the woman is paid for her child-raising only through him. We shall later notice studies showing that only a small portion of a father's income usually goes to a divorced or deserted wife and often only for a short period."

"Yes, that is what people ignore. I must say again, Adam, that I can imagine a society in the future which considers the creation and careful rearing of its children so crucial for its continued life that mothers are assured proper economic independence and future well-being while they rear them. The wife and her children will not be forced to rely for their economic support upon the sexual urges of her husband and his possible passionate interest in another woman, often shifted due to no failing on her part but rather because he has become accustomed to her and irritated by their many years of close living together."

"I can imagine such a society, too—but way off in the future. Though men have moved forward toward a more democratic relationship with women, we still are living in a system where domination by the stronger physically or economically, is frequent. Only recently have the principles of democracy been conceived and they are just beginning to be put into operation," Adam continued. "The cartoonist —author of 'Mickey McGuire and his Gang' knows his sociology. Democracy is not natural, but artificial. It is a social invention which must be first taught, then arduously cultivated. At the same time it is assuredly a *better* way than the natural way. It is to man's glory that he can take Nature's given material and improve it; that he can achieve what we hope is the aim of Nature by more intelligent methods than Nature (before man) had devised. That aim is for man to live, and live more abundantly. Through man's intelligence he has invented not only the concept of democracy but scientific and medical discoveries which have lengthened and enriched human life, and can do still more to help us."

"Very good, the intelligent citizen *refuses* to avoid recognizing the blind and cruel forces which still operate in human society. But he supports every measure which tends to control these forces for the benefit of mankind. We are in a dramatic struggle between the powers which weaken our human race and the counteracting ones which strengthen and unite us, probably more crucial now than ever before. Will women be allowed a proper voice in how our new scientific knowledge is used whether in competition for property or to nurture our children? That is the question!" Eve glanced at Adam who came to sit beside her. It was dusk. They both were weary. He put his hand on hers as they listened to the carillon in the chapel tower play one of their favorite tunes, "Now the day is over, night is falling fast."

Then Adam got up smiling, "That music is all recorded on the tape. Well, it makes a good combination with our rather shocking discussion on the ways of baboons and chimpanzees," he said while he turned off the recorder. "It didn't record my holding your hand."

As they walked together toward their homes they discussed the next steps in their book. Since Adam was given some extra work with the freshman class he suggested that Eve write the next section. They then bid each other good night and went their separate ways.

During the next few weeks Eve wrote the following which was later read and slightly changed by Adam, so it largely presents the thoughts of both.

Marriage developed as a method of dividing the ownership of women among men

We don't know exactly the steps in the development of our present marriage pattern. It probably was somewhat different in some groups of sub-human primates and primitive men than in others. But from extensive studies certain fundamental features seem to have been present in its early phases.

As Lester Ward so clearly stated, early man was free to maneuver woman "to contribute to his pleasure and his wants" so proceeded to do so, logically considering sex her prime attraction. Every man not only wanted a mate but wanted to be sure he really had her. Life with no mate was unacceptable if it could possibly be avoided by the typical man. Furthermore he craved variety in mates as widespread polygamy and concubinage proves beyond question. [14] —How then could men's sexual desires be satisfied and community order preserved? Marriage was the answer. It divided ownership of women among men. Without such regulation life might have degenerated into a perpetual War of the Sabines. If each man were free to take any woman with no ceremony, regardless of whether she were a virgin or living with another man, there would have been "hell to pay."

> Ownership of human beings as well as of inanimate objects varies in degree. For instance, even when a man owns land there are restrictions upon his use of it. That a latter day husband lacks the right to kill or sell his wife, as he did in early Roman days, does not mean that she has not been his property in a measure for many centuries. Husbands have in general had the "exclusive right to possess and enjoy," their wives and this right has been "protected by law" (important elements of ownership as defined by Webster's Dictionary).

It is true that marriage in its rigid sexual restriction of the wife has protected her from other men's unwanted advances, as well as from relations she might desire. A certain degree of peace and order in the area of sex activity was thus ordained which freed mothers from being objects of constant rivalry between men and freed the fathers' attention for other things. It also has tended to hold parents together and aid in children's care.

96

To what extent are wives owned by their husbands today? We have already considered the man's present complete sexual ownership of his wife, also that he is entitled to her services in the home and her care for their children and himself. He can insist that she live in the home he chooses and in general be content with the money he gives her from his income at the risk of divorce. In some of our states today a wife is not permitted to earn outside without her husband's specific consent, while in all states his consent actually is necessary if family unity is to be preserved.

Yet most men do not now feel that they own their wives in any degree, and even wives do not feel this, because theories, customs and religious precepts have masked and supported various features of the pattern. Of course there is great variation in the extent a husband exercises these legal rights to control his wife. There are some husbands who generously grant their wives full autonomy to conduct their actions according to their own wishes, who give them as much freedom as they take themselves—who do not sit as judges assuming superior knowledge and passing judgment upon their wives' appearance and behavior. Such relationships are truly democratic. But our culture and laws largely lead husbands away from them.

Clearly the very earliest family, or the living together of two persons for an extended period, is the unit of mother and offspring. We see it with our pet dogs and cats where the father wanders off and hardly knows his young. And in the herds of male mammals living separately from the females and young most of the time which Adam described. It looks as though primitive men of the old stone age wanted sexual companions—and children incidentally came along with women. Men made the best of these little beings whom their mates nursed and tended. But they did not live close to the females to produce children.

Early men clung to their mates, the women clung to their children. The result was the three sided family unit of father, mother and children. In a sense man adopted the mother-child unit and became its owner.

Milleniums later, after men's thought processes further developed, they saw advantages in raising children who gave the clan continued life. But even when they realized this, their sexual appetites still dominated their lives during further milleniums far more than their concern for their young.

This is not said critically, for nature has constituted the male sexual glandular system to be a prime feature of his internal environment. Everyone's actions are influenced by his external environment consisting of food, warmth and shelter; and also his internal environment made by his physiological processes, his glands, his heart, his lungs. For instance, the fish's internal structure, his gills demand water to obtain oxygen while man's lungs demand air. And so even today it is nip and tuck with many men as to which is dominant in their lives, their urge for a high degree of sexual satisfaction with a variation in partners often including new wives, or, on the other hand, their desire to help their children by keeping their family well and united, foregoing some extra-marital experiences.

When, therefore, we study the present family institution, which men have largely developed, we should not be surprised to find features regulating sexual life more important than features regarding reproduction and the father's child care. We should pause here since this may be questioned. In our country today inability to propagate the species is not a legal ground for divorce, while inability or refusal to have sexual relations often is. "Copula not fruitfulness, is the test" of the requisite physical condition of the marriage relation. The statutes of the United States have not materially modified this common law principle.[15] Thus, a wife's refusal to have sexual intercourse with her husband for a certain period is a basis for divorce in several states. She may have born several children and be giving them excellent care—but that legally is not the crucial matter.

She may be ignorant of effective methods of contraception and raising all the children they can afford but that does not alter her "wifely duty."

Likewise cruelty by the father toward his children is not ground for divorce. And the support of children is legally a secondary aspect of marriage. The father's non-support of his children is not in many states ground for divorce. Where it is held as ground it must be established, not only that the husband has ability to support, but that the family is facing real deprivation, all of which greatly complicates the case. Also, as we previously mentioned, mere unfairness or wasteful use of income by the husband does not constitute non-support, nor is there any requirement that a certain proportion of a father's income shall go to his family.[16]

The right to bring into court a non-supporting husband sounds good, but the wife who most needs to do this often has little education and lacks funds. "Possession is nine points of the law," and the husband usually possesses the family income and savings.[17] Also bringing a husband to court breaks the basic factor of family unity, the spirit of trust between its members and is apt to send him away, the family thereafter receiving little or nothing from him.[17]

Actually the great number of deserting and divorced fathers is one of our major problems. We will consider later the some six million mothers and children in our country who are not supported by deserting fathers. It is also significant that under our present laws a father may choose to omit his children, whether minors or not, entirely from his will.[18]

If we turn to legislation on adultery we find further evidence that sexual considerations are the major feature of the marriage laws, rather than child care. The vast majority of human societies, from the most primitive to the present, have demonstrated the importance of the man's sexual ownership of his wife by deeming her adultery as a wrong against the husband. Whether she desired the extra-marital relation or had it forced upon her was unimportant. Since she was her husband's sexual property, through adultery she was considered "spoiled" or misused. He, as we noted, has been often accorded the right to abandon or kill his "errant" wife. On the other hand a *husband's* adultery was usually taken lightly unless it "injured" another husband's rights. Cato, the Censor, said: "If you were to catch your wife in adultery, you would kill her with impunity without trial; but if she were to catch you in adultery she would not dare to lay a finger upon you, and indeed she has no right." [19]

Dr. Samuel Johnson wrote, "Wise married women don't trouble themselves about infidelity in their husbands." [20]

> Under the old laws of Mexico a husband who killed his wife for infidelity was immune from punishment. In 1931 however the laws were changed to give him a punishment of three days imprisonment.[21]
>
> In the case of a husband's adultery with a maid in his house, later admitted by the servant, a New York Supreme Court Judge said: "Those relations were of a clandestine nature, quite concealed from (his wife) and unknown to the public. In my opinion such evidence does not measure up to the test of adultery as ground for separation." [22]

Adultery, the one ground for divorce common to all our states, applies to both sexes technically. But when we consider interpretations, such as the above and in addition the greater mobility of husbands, their office-homes with telephones at a distance from wives and the consequent difficulty to secure evidence against them; in comparison with the wife's risk of pregnancy, her circumscribed life and the more critical attitude toward her freedom, we can see that the whole system of sexual restrictions in marriage actually operates largely to restrict women.

Many states, as we have mentioned, deprive a "guilty" wife of property held by her at time of divorce and refuse alimony to her, even though she may have carefully raised a large family.[23] The harshness of our laws toward the disobedient wife may have led to the growing practice among more humane men not to bring divorce suits against their wives on this ground. Nevertheless the very existence of laws empowering a husband to ruin such a wife is a threat which enforces his sexual ownership.

Some sociologists even today hold a Pollyanna view regarding the development of marriage. For instance, one writer describes it as a nicely balanced arrangement between two equals. He says of the Trobriand Island family, that there the economic advantage of marriage goes to the man while the woman receives in return protection for herself and *her children*.[24] Let us examine with a critical eye this suggested sociological balance sheet. In marriage the mother wins protection for her children, he writes, and as a consequence foregoes economic independence. But we ask, why is the father's aid in caring for the children rated a service to her? Is he not interested in leaving progeny to carry on *his* life and that of *his* group? Since race continuity is as much to man's interest as the woman's, the energy the mother devotes to this purpose is a service to him as much as to herself. If he helps to keep the children alive he is not supporting *her children*, but only doing his part to continue his line.

This attitude, though, is still held by many, as shown by fathers who often vaguely regard the financial burden of the family as wife-imposed. We hear expressions such as referring to a wife as "my ball and chain" indicating the feeling that he is supporting his children to please his wife and upon her insistence. In cases of divorce when a father has married a second time and has children by his second wife, the first wife must often wheedle or compel paternal assistance. While almost always the *deserted* mother must legally attempt to force the father to aid in their children's support, if indeed any can be obtained from him.

It looks as though the dominant factors found in the beginnings of marriage, the men's centering upon their sexual lives and the control of their mates, rather than their offspring's care are present to a striking degree in our marriage institution today.

How is the father's care for his children won?

In the sub-human primate beginnings of marriage the father assumed practically no responsibility for the care of his young, rather unconsciously leaving that to the mother. Although primitive man gradually developed some interest in his children's care, he probably never consented to a mother's desire for his continuous assistance in child-care, for he assumed he was always free to give it or not, as he wished.

Since men at first completely owned their mates they did not need to give any assistance to their children in order to hold their mothers. But as women were given some protection by their own parents, men were led to assist their children in order to hold their wives—to keep them from going back to their paternal homes.

If the father at present were fully responsible in the area of reproduction, he would support his children in order to continue his line, the life of his group, or his country and because he loved them. He would do this whether he permanently owned his wife sexually or not. Just as the *responsible* citizen tries to understand government problems and vote intelligently to help his country, whether or not he is given further inducements. But history has shown us that the father *has* demanded further inducements before he would carry a share in child-raising—those of the mother's sexual ownership and services. The result of this arrangement, has constituted a step forward from leaving the child raising job entirely to the mother, but this present pattern still expects far too much from her.

In Russia during the depression and critical years of the 1920's when marriage laws were most lenient, innumerable fathers left their families so that masses of destitute women and children filled the country. This striking development and many others seems to indicate that the father is not so attached to his children as their mother, and that laws play an important part in keeping him with his family and helping them.

As to the present, we have noted that our laws in general impose child-care responsibilities on fathers but that many escape all, or most, of them through non-marriage, desertion, divorce or shiftlessness. Even today innumerable fathers think they should be free to give support, or not, to their children according to their wishes. Since mothers recognize that their children must be *continuously* cared for if they are to live—even if they themselves are ready to drop—they usually keep at the job through thick and thin, and often find themselves pleading with their husbands for assistance.

Thus, we find the efforts by men not to be burdened with the care and support of *all* their children and women's counteracting efforts through history to have them assume their half share of this essential task still continue. This is most clearly shown in the case of the unmarried mother and father. Here the father seldom supports his child, escaping on the grounds that he does not sexually own the mother.

Yet it is not mainly a father's knowing that a child is his which leads him to support his baby. Through the centuries men have had children definitely known as theirs by well-guarded slaves and concubines whom they have not raised as their own. And today many fathers know their illegitimate children but still assume no responsibility for raising them. It is for other sexual reasons we've mentioned that the man has demanded that the mother of the child he supports be his exclusive sexual possession during her marriage.

The big on-going task of civilization is to persuade fathers to care for their children with time and thought, as well as with material goods. This is so, not only within family life but in areas outside, such as the construction of family laws and the prevention of children-in-need.

A heartening new development is now under way in our and other countries. The more sensitive young men are discovering the personal satisfactions of fatherhood to a degree perhaps heretofore unknown in history. Many are becoming so attached to their children that they are willing to forego some sexual freedom, if not all, in order to keep their families happily together. But we still need men's interest in children's welfare in general, which undoubtedly can be improved through basic preventative work in reconstruction of the family.

How is the mother's care for her children won?

There is scarcely need for mentioning this to anyone who has watched his pet mother dog or horse tend and guard her young. Her concern for them is simply part of her nature. We used to say it was mother-instinct but now some call it tropism—the mother's involuntary turning toward the offspring, or the innate tendency to act in a protecting manner. It constitutes an important part of the most valuable drive in humanity, that to help and nurture the young, no matter what we call it.

All mothers know this tremendous urge to care for their babies. The strength of the impulse which the young woman discovers in herself upon the arrival of her first baby often is a surprise even to her. When she first leaves her baby for an evening she cannot keep her mind off of him. His well-being seems more important to her than her own.

This mother-love has made possible the continuation of human life. When her babies are older the mother has so identified herself with them and their helplessness that she continues working for their welfare. And the child's attachment to his mother becomes firmly imbedded, for he has found her the source of his sustenance and protection. She seldom has the heart to forsake her helpless child. She usually nurtures him without any further inducements, such as the sexual ownership and services of their father. Society counts on her care of her children even under the most difficult circumstances, during floods, earthquakes and famines.

She receives in general no economic compensation relative to the size and importance of her work. We recognize that thousands of mothers don't receive enough from the father to sustain their children's lives so they must earn outside the home while also performing lengthy and heavy home tasks. Other thousands whose husbands have died or left their families must carry this difficult double task. Both these groups of earning mothers perform child-rearing service, receiving for them absolutely no financial return for themselves but instead giving this labor as a free-will offering to society. True, some are now granted enough government assistance to allow them to live at a low level and continue this child-care, but they deserve a much higher standard of living, far more honor and greater independence while they rear our future citizens.

Does society take advantage of this mother-drive to protect her children? It looks that way. If certain men had a mania to build bridges over rivers and streams, so strong that they carried out projects of this kind with little thought of their economic return or their future well-being, how might society react? Indications are that people would think this *very nice* and allow them to continue their building generation after generation with little or no financial return, nothing commensurate with the value of their production.

Should fathers support all their children?

We have previously considered the false theory that man's desire to know *all* his offspring is the cause of his wife's sexual ownership. Put another way it is the theory that marriage is mainly to allow the man *to know* his own children so that he may care for them. According to this the husband says in short, "Since my wife has sexual relations with no one except me, I definitely know my own children."

This statement should be continually spiked by the question, "If husbands *do not* restrict themselves as rigidly as their wives, perhaps they do have children whom they do not know are theirs. Restricting wives is only part of what is necessary for husbands to know their own children."

Clearly wives' sexual restriction actually has *not* been to assure fathers knowing *all* their children. In fact, men often avoid learning of their illegitimate offspring. They have prevented any effective control of their own sex relations with prostitutes or other women not their wives. And they have made laws in every country hindering identification of the unmarried father. *"La recherche de la paternité est interdite"* (a search for the father is prohibited) was a legal principle in France until relatively recent times.

Man's extensive ability to reproduce has always been a problem to him. He has wanted abundant sex gratification but not the responsibility of numerous offspring. The South American Don Juan who is claimed to have had over one hundred children did not support them. Marriage might be considered an institution which, among other things, aids some men to know a selected few of their children, and so free themselves from supporting others. This would indicate that it is in some degree the reverse of an arrangement designed to allow fathers to know *all* their own children in order to shoulder their support. Man has never in history claimed he should support *all* his offspring.

The man has through marriage tried to assure himself that the children he supports are his own; and that he has not had to care for any children (even his own), if they were not borne by his wife. The motive therefore of avoiding support for any children except the issue of one particular woman, probably has contributed to our present marriage institution. The well-being of children again we find secondary in the family pattern to other matters, which here include the preservation and control of the father's property, so that he may spend it only for the children of his wife and pass it upon his death only to them or whomever he chooses.

We should recognize therefore that in many respects our family pattern and its supporting laws do not work toward the careful raising of children. Since all men are first children, they themselves often suffer from the failure of this institution to provide them a healthy, advantageous childhood which in turn influences their entire lives. This failure to give them what they need often arises from the fact that their mothers who faithfully try to nurture them are not themselves allowed the necessary resources for their task.

CHAPTER 6

1. S. Zuckerman, *The Social Life of Monkeys and Apes*, Harcourt, Brace & Co., 1932.
2. Ibid., Ch. 1.
   Howard Parshley, *Science of Human Reproduction*, W. W. Norton & Co., 1933, pp. 284-5.
3. S. Zuckerman, op. cit., quoted from description by Sokolowsky, p. 178.
4. Ibid., pp. 219-220. Thirty adult females were introduced to a group which was largely males on "Monkey Hill" in London. The resulting sexual fights brought death to 15 of the new females in the following month. Such struggles do not last indefinitely. A stabilized situation is established after a period.
   Similar accounts are in H. G. Wells, *The Science of Life*, The Literary Guild, 1934, p. 1445.
   This pattern of relationship between the sexes does not exist among all monkeys and apes. Ernest A. Hooton summarizes some other patterns in *Up From the Ape*, Macmillan Co., 1946, p. 260-263.
5. S. Zuckerman, op. cit., p. 211.
6. Ibid., p. 228, "The males of all primate series are larger than the females."
7. Ibid., pp. 234, 235, 244, 245.
8. Ibid., p. 212.
9. In arriving at the typical behavior, Yerkes included only experiments with experienced, normal and congenial adults. Robert M. Yerkes, "Social Behavior of Chimpanzees: Dominance between Mates, in Relation to Sexual Status". Reprint from *Journal of Comparative Psychology*, August 1940, p. 178. Yale Laboratory of Primitive Biology.
   S. Zuckerman, op. cit., pp. 234, 244, 245, 314.
10. Robert M. Yerkes, *Chimpanzees, A Laboratory Colony*, Yale University Press, 1943, p. 73.
11. Ibid., pp. 73, 76.

12. Robert M. Yerkes, "Social Behavior of Chimpanzees . . . ," op. cit., pp. 173, 174.

13. S. Zuckerman, op. cit., p. 315.

14. L. T. Hobhouse et al, *The Material Culture and Social Institutions of the Simpler Peoples*, Chapman & Hall, London, 1930, op. cit., pp. 159, 163.

15. Chester V. Vernier, *American Family Laws*, Stanford University Press, California, 1931-1938, Vol. I, pp. 196, 197.

16. Ibid., Vol. II, pp. 55-58.

17. See my chapter 9, pp. 163, 164.

18. This is so in almost every state.
    Legislation to insure the child a legacy upon his father's death has recently been enacted in England, Canada and New Zealand.

19. Willystine Goodsell, *A History of the Family as a Social and Educational Institution*, Macmillan Co., 1915, p. 122.

20. James Boswell, *Boswell's Life of Samuel Johnson*, Dodd, Mead & Co., 1923.

21. *Time* magazine, September 20, 1931.

22. New York Court of Appeals. Reported in *Poughkeepsie Eagle News*, July 6, 1935.

23. Chester G. Vernier, *American Family Laws*, op. cit., Vol. II, pp. 218-225.

24. Joseph K. Folsom, *The Family: Its Sociology and Social Psychiatry*, John Wiley & Sons, 1934, p. 14.

CHAPTER 7

Toward a Democratic Sexual Life

Men's preference for younger women creates social ill-balance

An important part of our culture is the age gradient under which men usually associate with and marry women younger than themselves.

During an ocean voyage to Europe on a *deluxe* liner, I studied the behavior of a segment of our citizens. The freedom of shipboard offered every opportunity for development of new friendships. There were approximately equal numbers of men and women, and their ages roughly corresponded. A balanced arrangement would have brought everyone into the games, the dancing and talk fests. There were, however, several middle-aged bachelors and married men not accompanied by their wives who by leaving women of their own age and joining younger women, threw the mixed gathering off balance. Some of the older women were charming, witty and beautifully dressed. Their masculine contemporaries could have found delightful companionship with them. Of course, the young men were also absorbed with the unmarried young women, resulting in a high concentration of men around them while many of the older single women were left without men companions. Few men paused to wonder whether they were unhappy. The younger women were sometimes spoiled by too much attention. The modern cut-in dance, which often made less attractive or older women embarrassed and kept others from the dance, formed an important feature of the unbalanced situation.

In every community, especially those of our country, on land as well as sea, one can observe this same age situation between men and women in companionship and mating. Far more men between 45 and 65 years of age are married than women, about one and a half million more.[1] Figures also show that men generally have wives younger than themselves. When they marry in their early years the wife is usually only slightly younger, while grooms in their 30's take brides who average about 5 years their junior. The average disparity increases to 8 years where the man marries in his middle 50's. And we all know of many cases where he takes a bride from 15 to 25 years his junior.[2]

The competition for the younger women is obvious among the unmarried men. Though less recognized such attraction for young women continues under the surface among married men and influences their attitudes toward their older wives and thoughts concerning possible affairs or divorce.

This age gradient affords men all the sexual security which women thereby lose. If a young man's marriage should be delayed, if a man should be divorced or widowed or if he should desire an extra-marital relationship, he has an amazing range of choice for a companion among those his own age to those much younger. This often makes him feel that there is a great surplus of women. The single women 35 and over, however, are in the opposite position. Most men slightly older turn to the women younger than 35. The result is clearly that men companions for these women near their age are very few.

Similar ill-balance of opportunity usually develops also where one group holds more initiative and freedom than others. The setting aside of older women is not done on purpose, it is only incidental to men's desired association with younger women. Nevertheless it involves a certain lack of sensitivity to the plight of some older women. Of course many men recognize all this and faithfully care for the wives of their youth and associate with women their own age.

The effects of men's general preference for women younger than themselves force upon a single woman of

30 or more an extreme sensitivity to her age. She cannot fail to recognize that she may be left in the neglected group, at last as far as attention from men is concerned. Even single women about 25 begin to worry for fear they will not quickly find mates. Therefore when marriage is delayed, when they are divorced or widowed, after some ten years or more of married life, only a small field of possible mates is open to them. This makes a tragic situation for millions of women. Although most of us are sufficiently mature to refrain from joking about persons suffering from discriminatory customs, the plight of the unmarried woman, 35 or over is still one of our most frequent sources of humor. James Thurber liked to sketch her crawling pussy-cat fashion along a sofa trying to snuggle up to some indifferent male companion. Here she is not playing her proper and assigned, passive role in mate-choosing. If one recognized that male initiative and the age gradient are largely matters of custom imposed on them, and that women have sexual desires similar to men's this would not be a joke. It would be as natural as a man's snuggling up to a woman. Since, however, men have imagined that women are passive creatures with no wish to take the initiative such a picture seems very amusing to them.

No doubt it makes an exciting game to grade women by appearance and age and then see which men can win the more attractive ones. Even high school senior boys often go with the freshman girls. But a game with different rules could be arranged, perhaps more fun for all. It would balance men and women of similar ages and would allow most women to feel secure in men's interest and affection. The reaction on men of such numbers of happy women might well bring men more pleasure than their keen competition which concentrates upon a smaller group. Just as the man is usually many times rewarded in his sexual pleasure if his manner toward his mate is a generous one, so it may be in the broader social relations between men and women. A pattern with equal opportunity for all players is always

111

worth trying, particularly in this matter of sex where women's pleasures so definitely are reflected in men.

There are many indications that the healthy woman living a full life keeps her sexual powers into the later years as well, or better than the man. It has been maintained, however, that the reverse is true and this false theory has been used as ground for the marriage of men with younger women. The age gradient doubtless also results in part from man's taste for a dependent wife who gives him confidence by looking up to him; also for a companion likely to maintain her health and able to care for him in his latter years. Helping to establish this gradient has been the fact that older men usually having more income can often win the younger women away from the younger men. But these advantages men should weigh against others they gain in marrying women about their own age.

At present in our country the results of this age gradient are striking. Since widowed and divorced men far more readily find new mates than do the corresponding women, these women who have not remarried are almost twice as numerous as men in this position within the age group 25 to 35 years. While in the older age group, 35 to 75 years, the women widowed and divorced, not remarried, are three times as numerous as the corresponding men in this position.[3] These figures reveal that many more women formerly married are left to live out their lives with no companion than are men who were once married.

The striking result is, we have at least ten and a half million unmarried women among us. (Over seven million of these were once married, and three and a half million, 25 years of age or older, are never married.)[4]

All these women must make the best of a society which welcomes the single men at gatherings more readily than themselves, and gives approval to older men's befriending younger women. The perennial bachelor or widower attends one party after another, while the single women are told by wives in various ways in effect to keep away from their

112

husbands. What do these current attitudes leave for the widowed or single women in approved male companionship? She may properly go to the theatre with her brother or her son. And only comparatively seldom does she join recreation of married couples while carefully watched. Our laws and customs demand her celibacy. At some future time one feature of today's social life may be written under the heading, "Ten Million Lonely Women" or "Ten Million Segregated Women." Of course if a single woman has a fortune she may in some degree buy her way out.

Two private bureaus which have aided in promoting acquaintance between men and women have made similar observations that the older unattached men were seeking women under 35 years of age. On the other hand the unattached woman over 35 seeking men their age or older were so numerous that they were usually discouraged from even registering.[5] *The Marriage Society* in England has found the same situation.

Little has been written on the ethics of discarding older wives for young ones. A shaggy haired primitive surrounded by wives of assorted ages differs but slightly from some modern man with his latest wife, 10 or 20 years his junior, while his other wife or wives (or mistresses) are omitted from the scene. If the primitive man were asked why he had several wives he would frankly say, "When a wife gets worn I take a new one. I also like a change." He might add, "I get more help this way than by simply keeping my first." If, however, the modern man were asked why he took a second or third wife he would invariably reply, "Well, my first was too extravagant"—or "too bossy," probably never admitting even to himself the basic truth, that he just wanted a new and younger one.

How much verity colors the common opinion that divorced and deserted wives have grave faults? All indications are that first wives' character is generally about on the same level as other men and women of their group and that other factors usually destroy the marriage. Instead of her failure at her job, the break-up is likely to be caused because the husband sees a greener pasture and lets the warm feelings within his first family cool off and then become frigid.[6] A most revealing order of events usually takes place which we will later look into further.

There are men today distinguished in journalism, government, education, drama and music who have left first wives and children. The stimulation of new marriages probably aided their progress. But these men often ostensibly working to bring further understanding between people in inter-racial, labor and other personal relations have themselves fallen into the easy path of over-riding the opportunities of others. While they preach progress through their chosen fields they have often denied their first wives a chance for the advantages they themselves enjoy.

The Mormons, often feeling guilty after taking several wives, sometimes left not only their first wives, but all of them. These husbands found an excellent escape from the confusing complexities of plural families by arranging to be "called" by their church "to new districts on religious missions or colonization expeditions." [7] At present, some men likewise leave their wives and children, as they convince themselves that duty or personal progress requires this.

Many husbands fall out of love—not with their wives but their *wives-bound-to-children*—that is, with preoccupied wives, tired wives, wives who discuss bothersome problems. In fact, *if the wife were in the position of one of these single women, the husband might now be falling in love with her.* The woman now his wife would be offering the glamor of fresh adventure. What the husband often resents and unconsciously escapes is the burden of child care, in time and money and energy which has been and continues to be required.

The depth of loneliness felt by thousands of women, never married, who, forbidden the revitalizing experience of sexual love, and companionship with mate and children is,

114

because of their nature and their restrictions, probably far greater than the loneliness of unmarried men. Besides her shackled emotional life she recognizes that the passing years probably destine her to permanent matelessness. We need effective and frank life stories by the single woman who sublimates into other interests her deep longings and who tries to take it all smiling. Through some thirty years of her prime, she silently contends with the discomforts of menstruation. Her rounded breasts develop and wither untouched by lover or nursed by a baby. The pleasures through bringing into use her extensive sexual and reproductive system are denied her. Though she gives vitality to these, society pretends they do not even exist. Most of these important denials of a woman's full life are also required of the widowed, divorced and deserted women who do not remarry.

While wives and prostitutes must often accept more sexual relations than they wish, the "respectable" single women often go through life with the whole world of sexual experience closed to them. The result is that perhaps a majority of women one way or another are denied the sexual pleasures they want combined with love.

Let not men think this is a minor matter. Let them not continue to imagine that women are essentially passive sexual objects who have no desire for a satisfying, rounded life, who are simply made to be recipients of men's sexuality, content to be neglected whenever it suits the men, for years or for a lifetime. The frustrated woman does not generally show her desires because she has been told with harsh and threatening voices through the centuries that she *must* be passive sexually except to the man who controls her, her husband. And even the wife has been generally expected to be a passive recipient of her husband's attention until recent times when some husbands create secure and happy situations for their wives which encourage them to be entirely natural with their husbands. It is a tragic error when men force women to conform to certain customs and then say it is their nature to do so.

Some philosophers hold that a principle of action which cannot be broken without automatic suffering by the breaker may be considered a natural law—a law more fundamental than those made by men. Thus one natural law may be that men cannot find real happiness in a pattern which denies women security and pleasures equal to those of their own. And this seems reasonable, for the deep relationship of love and understanding between a man and woman depends upon sharing their thoughts and feelings, and the union of man and woman is basic to life's fulfillment.

On the whole men and women of roughly the same age can give each other the greatest mutual understanding. If their relationship includes their whole personalities this is undoubtedly so. A new attitude toward older women would afford mothers more emotional security and undoubtedly, through raising their morale, would make them more attractive to husbands.

I like to imagine that those of about the same age are sailing on one vessel through the sea of life. They pass together through the same rough storms of personal and world events, have shared their lives and together created and reared their children. When a husband jumps off the ship and swims to another with a younger woman he fools himself into thinking he belongs there and has thereby dropped some of his years. He may later instead feel oddly old with his youthful wife and her young friends—older than if still aboard the ship with his first family. As the novelty of the new wife passes he may wish he were back in the circle with the wife and children of his youth. A certain husband has said he wished he had been denied the freedom to make such radical changes in the lives of his family members. And when he is still older, perspective on his life as a whole may cause him to dream of the deeper satisfactions he might have enjoyed if he still basked in the warm and vitalizing sunshine of his first and only wife's love and that of their children.

A husband who holds an understanding and generous attitude toward his wife may expect to reap in return deep understanding from her, especially in his latter years when his sexual power dwindles or disappears and he has lost most *joie de vie*. Then he needs a loving companion who can compassionately vision the flow of life with its strengths and weaknesses, her own and his. A man who has not won such close understanding and appreciation from a woman may be without such a needed companion. If he has left the boat with the wife of his youth to take a younger one, he may find later in his new wife only suppressed aggravation and little insight at this period.

Yet we must recognize there is a great desire for men to enjoy some change in mates. The question is, cannot this be arranged without leaving their families? Some day when we dare be frank about sex it may be said that if an older man has relations with a new and younger partner it revives his sexual life and renews his whole vitality—and that exactly the same thing is true for the woman. Men's recognition of this as regards themselves is part of the reason for the age gradient. In regard to women, however, this fact has been completely ignored. Yet only by facing the truth in all these matters can we place the situation clearly before us and consider what may be good for the future.

We have record of a New Guinea society whose sexual customs constitute in certain aspects a surprisingly democratic arrangement. They seem to lead to such contentment that men cannot be readily recruited to leave their homes and earn more money on the Germans' neighboring large plantations.[8] Their customs require that the young man be initiated into sex by a mature experienced woman, one of his mother's generation. Similarly the young woman is initiated by a man friend of her father. Later, marriage between a young man and woman of the same age takes place. Some years after marriage each is allowed extra-marital relations on ceremonial occasions when the man

117

and his ceremonial friend, all being about the same age, exchange wives. Still later when the couple's children are grown the father will initiate the bride-to-be of his ceremonial friend's son for about a year. The mother in the meantime will initiate the corresponding husband-to-be. During the life of each person, he or she usually has three temporary partners in addition to his married spouse; the age gradient is a balanced affair. And with all this change in partners, which we would expect to arouse jealousy on every side, there is almost none because women are not emotionally upset by the men's varied life. They are not denied the satisfactions of some variation themselves, nor the sexual companionship of at least one sexual partner all the time. This is only one pattern among the many which have been developed by other peoples. It is mentioned to indicate that the double standard and age gradient of our country is not the sole possible pattern.

In one of the decisions in Queen Eleanor's "Court of Love," previously mentioned, a different age relationship was approved between men and women from that in our society. The marked difference was that young men preferred mature women as companions—a relationship most of our young men today reject since the competitive game calls the winners those who gain the young ones. Also, in that circle of Queen Eleanor's where women had more power and initiative than in our society, they showed their interest in men younger than themselves.

> It was said "From the viewpoint of natural instinct, the younger men are wont to unite themselves more passionately to the love of a mature woman rather than a young girl who may be of the same age as themselves. While those men advanced in years strive to receive the embraces and kisses of young girls rather than of women of mature years. And, on the contrary, a woman, whether young or mature, seeks rather the embraces and the solace of younger men than of those of advanced years." [9]

There is extensive evidence that men and women in general chafe at the restrictions of taking one mate for a life-

118

time and denying themselves the slightest variation. An analysis by Murdock of many present day societies found that out of a group of 118 on which he had data 115 permitted or tolerated sexual relations outside of marriage, either pre-marital relations or extra-marital.[10] By few groups is sex confined entirely within marriage, he concludes. "Pre-marital license prevails in 70% of our cases," while extra-marital relations are allowed in 66% of the sample societies. But these sexual relations outside of marriage were restricted in various ways, such as with a brother-in-law or sister-in-law, or on certain occasions, such as festivals, funerals, weddings or religious ceremonies.[11]

Our problem today may be to recognize this desire for some variety and to make an arrangement which somewhat fulfills the need in a dignified and democratic manner, while it tends to keep parents with their children. Some pattern might be developed which would actually keep the family together and happier than today while it allowed some recognition of this need. Since a husband sometimes breaks up his family mainly because he wants a new sexual mate, if he were allowed this, while his wife did not feel desolately abandoned since she was equally free, they and their children might continue to live together long after their temporary and limited affairs were over and forgotten. But this is the question of questions. We don't know how it would work out; we will return to the problem.

Anthropological studies indicate we have far greater ability to shape combinations of customs and habits than was once believed. We can invent new codes of ethics and new modes of living as well as new machines.

Woman's sexual life ranges from paraíso to infierno

Numerous books have been written in recent years covering largely the physical aspects of sex. The emotional and psychological aspects fully as important have in comparison been little discussed. The world of material concerning degrees of satisfaction in different relationships, such as that of some married couples suffering from "cabin fever" after a few decades of a confining life together compared to that of some newly-weds, has hardly been touched. Publications concerning this side of sex seem to be still taboo.

To be realistic we must recognize that woman's reactions to union with a man vary without exaggeration from *paraíso* to *infierno*. To put it in Spanish does not seem so shocking, as to say, from heaven to hell. We are forced to abandon the conventional attitude that only those with her husband are pleasurable and beautiful. That theory is the product of wishful thinking by husbands with half-closed eyes. To bring the truth before us, again we must try to learn the facts.

Women's experience of these infinite degrees of sexual delight and anguish are roughly determined by the *extent to which her personality is favorably involved*. Men likewise know varying degrees of pleasure but not boredom nor pain nor resentment nor fear in sexual relations since they are physiologically unable to have sex congress if all desire is lacking.

A woman's experience may be pleasing mainly to her lower involuntary nervous centers, or it may involve the higher nervous centers and include even the conception of oneself and one's partner as unique and complex characters. She enters *paraíso* when sex relations pleasantly involve all phases of her personality. For instance, congress between two strangers is necessarily a different matter from that with her lover whose life supplements and enriches hers. The same may be true, but probably to a much smaller degree with the man.

The elements of the personality which can be drawn into the experience of a man or woman are roughly: that part of the nervous system centering around the sexual organs; that part which registers the tactual sensations from all parts of the body; the less tangible esthetic senses covering elements of sight, smell and sound of one's partner as well as the immediate surroundings; the mental associations and

120

memories of one's sexual experiences and particularly those relating to one's present partner. Then there are still further steps in the absorption of the personality. The experience may include satisfaction that one is giving his partner pleasure; that he is united with one whose character he admires and that his character is reciprocally loved and admired.

Beyond all these is a further section of the personality which may be drawn into the relationship. Most persons are interested in mankind's struggle for greater peace and happiness and are playing at least some small part in the great drama. When a couple falls in love, understands and approves each other's role in this human drama, their relationship especially for the woman, takes on an added richness. Their union becomes a conscious part of the whole web of humanity's struggle. Profound feelings seldom aroused by a less complete fusing of personalities are added to the many other delightful sensations, and the relationship reaches a zenith of satisfaction. Each feels a strengthening and deepening of his own personality through fusion with the beloved. Through their mutual aid and delight they may make contributions to social progress which could not have been made separately.

We all feel incomplete and want kindly companionship. With infinite variation in personalities among us we know there is a possibility of finding someone whose life will fit completely into ours. Yet the difficulties of two such persons finding each other are tremendous. They are multiplied by the necessity of finding each other in their youth before they are developed, if the pair are to marry and have children during the mother's most favorable years. Likewise, since we all have imperfections and peculiarities, the sexual relationship which pleasantly involves each partner's full personality is rare. The rareness of perfect matings however should not prevent recognition of the depth of satisfactions which are not perfect, and the range in satisfactions which are gained through the sexual life.

Besides the *extent* of the personality which is favorably involved, one experiences various degrees in *intensity* of other favorable feelings. The degree of the body's well-being and the nervous condition of each partner at times of congress play a part. Definite structural features of the sexual organs may add to or subtract from satisfaction. Then, in addition, each is influenced by events and feelings which have filled his hours previous to sexual relations; worry, insecurity and frustration may linger persistently in one's mind. In fact, all phases of the lives of each determine the degree of that elusive pleasure which he experiences.

That sex activity has been largely channeled into marriage has greatly influenced the love life of humanity both within and without marriage. Since marriage is usually a relationship between two who have unequal opportunities for growth and independence, it often does not encourage constant effort of each to please and satisfy the other. And since extra-marital relations in our society must be risky and clandestine, the full possibilities in sexual pleasure remain unknown. They have been too hedged and cramped by man-made regulations.

In these considerations I have not distinguished between pre-marital, extra-marital and marital relationships. A fundamental classification of types of experience can be made which uses the woman's actual feelings and not those supposed by convention to accompany "sacred" or "sinful" love. Marriage is a classification determined by the state and the state is sadly not always concerned with the satisfactions or dissatisfactions involved in the sexual relations of a married—or unmarried—couple.

Examples of different degrees of sexual satisfaction

An example of a relationship which favorably involves only a small part of the personality is one between a man and woman to whom he pays a few dollars or less for physical gratification. She may not even appeal to his aesthetic sense. The prostitute is usually to him, as he is to her, only a body. She may pretend to have pleasure, for that is part of her business, but she often regards her experiences as work. The patron likely is not concerned whether or not she is pleased. Nor is he concerned with her often virtual imprisonment to her manager or her pimp, nor with the poverty which may have driven her to risk disease and a rapid wearing down of her strength. Of course, some relationships with paid mistresses and more fortunate prostitutes may be on a higher level. The novelty or adventure of a particular experience may at times rouse in the man an intensity of emotion but only a fraction of his personality is involved. Since the woman as a person usually remains unknown to him she does not touch extensive areas of his full being.

There are corresponding relations within marriage which can be placed on the lowest rung of the ladder of satisfactions. In such cases also the wife is regarded only as a body used for her husband's physical relief, and the husband becomes therefore mainly a body to her, demanding obedience.

When doing social work among needy families Margaret Sanger discovered the worry and exhaustion of many mothers due to the burden of constant childbearing. She dedicated her life to help them. During the many years she has been active in birth control endeavors, thousands of letters from mothers have flowed to her. Some of them, such as the following, make one's blood run cold, especially when one realizes that they tell the story of innumerable mothers past and present.

Only a few excerpts from these letters are presented.

"I am a young woman in years, but an old woman in feelings. I have ten children ... and besides the babies I've had pneumonia five times ... My husband always told me it was a sin to do anything to keep from having children, but I know better. My little baby has been sick all its life ...

"We are poor people. ... We do not have what we need.... I get desperate sometimes and feel I'd like to

123

kill myself to get out of my troubles, then I am ashamed of my weakness and I am determined to stay and care for the little helpless things ... but many times I've got desperate and almost crazy. I never see a well day or a restful hour ..." [12]

Another mother of 31 years had endured eight pregnancies, had four living children and was recovering from an abortion followed by blood poisoning when she found herself again pregnant and wrote:

"It wouldn't be so hard if my husband was kind and sympathetic, but he thinks it all foolishness to be nervous and cross and will say the harshest things to me . . . No matter how bad I feel before confinement or how soon after that his passion is aroused, I have to submit to him."

A third letter represents one of the extreme cases.

"Pregnancy for me spells nine months of sickness and suffering untold . . . When I ask to be spared any more children he tells me if he can't be gratified at home he will go elsewhere . . . Even if my body stood another confinement I don't think my mind or reason would for I go nearly crazy with suffering at times."

Another letter said,

"My husband is always quarrelling at me for having so many children and every time I have a child I can hardly live with him.[13]

It is not in accordance with our Pollyanna tradition to pause to read these letters, much less to try to imagine the lives of the women who write them. If numberless women however are compelled to spend years in such fear, it is not asking too much of the more fortunate that they at least frankly recognize the facts.

At the other extreme in married love is a well-known partnership, where each loved both the other's mind and body. Each knew the way to gain mutual love was by aiding fulfillment of the other's many desires and needs. Each knew that no tricks, teasing or force won genuine love. Elizabeth Barrett Browning's aid to her husband in his mental life was reciprocated by similar aid to her. She was doubtless able to help him all the more effectively because he *did* reciprocate. Without such well-merged lives we might

124

never have read their gloriously impassioned poetry. Though they never wrote, I think, that their physical sex relations played part in their inspired lives the following sonnet and many others suggest this.

"The face of all the world is changed, I think,
Since first I heard the footsteps of thy soul
Move still, oh, still, beside me, as they stole
Betwixt me and the dreadful outer brink
Of obvious death, where I, who thought to sink,
Was caught up into love, and taught the whole
Of life in a new rhythm. The cup of dole
God gave for baptism, I am fain to drink,
And praise its sweetness, Sweet, with thee anear.
The names of country, heaven, are changed away
For there thou art or shalt be, there or here;
And this . . . this lute and song . . . loved yesterday,
(The singing angels know) are only dear,
Because thy name moves right in what they say." [14]

Similar to the married relationship between the Brownings were relationships between unmarried lovers such as George Sand and Frederic Chopin, and other couples where the highest degree of satisfaction was probably experienced by both, for although they were free to separate yet for considerable periods they clung to each other.

Many other beautiful relationships not known, through written records, and many simple lovers of generous spirits have doubtless held feelings toward each other well expressed in these lines:

"Because in this deep joy to see and hear thee
And breathe within thy shadow a new air,
I do not think of thee—I am too near thee." [15]

Space does not permit examples of relationships which fall for women between these two extremes, *paraiso* and *infierno*, on the scale of sexual satisfactions, those told of in letters to Margaret Sanger and those represented by the Brownings. Most matings should be placed at the infinite different levels between the purely physical and that which merges the lovers' entire personalities.

As for the men the distinction in degrees of their own satisfaction most widely recognized seems to be based upon the amount of a woman's aesthetic appeal. Their emphasis on woman's appearance permeates every corner of the world. Recently, however, more and more men are recognizing the importance of woman's personality. Still few have learned to find erotic appeal in the development of women's ability in extensive and varied fields. But as men come to regard women in a generous spirit as persons with many sides and abilities like their own, they will find these can add to her appeal and bring new depths to their relationships. Women are drawn to men by a great variety of abilities and accomplishments. The whole intellect and personality of the man concerns and rouses women.

Our sex-negating society

A society responsive to all its people would strive to build customs and laws which made sustained and genuine love widely possible. Our founding fathers wrote that all should have opportunity for "life, liberty and the pursuit of happiness." They did not say, "the pursuit of happiness except sex pleasure." A delightful play, "The Pursuit of Happiness," [16] with its bundling scene was based on the interpretation that happiness included a love relation.

A true democracy cannot denounce sex pleasure. Rather it must recognize and liberate the full vitalizing powers of sex, and at the same time insure against its misuse. As yet, this problem has not been faced. Instead our culture is rather sex-denying to men, and far more so to women. But youth in revolt is proclaiming through early marriages and greater freedom that it wants a more sex-affirming society.

Since early Christian times in western nations there has been continued effort to curb sexual expression on the basis that sex is evil. St. Paul wrote, "I say therefore to the unmarried and widows, it is good for them if they abide even as I unmarried. But if they cannot contain, let them marry; for it is better to marry than to burn." [17] To some early Christian fathers sex was still more detested. One wrote "It were better that the race did not continue than that it should be perpetuated by so foul a process." These views have influenced Christian attitudes through the centuries. A couple's marriage somewhat removes this cloud of condemnation from intercourse. After some liberal interludes, such as among the nobility during the middle ages when "courtly love" arose in Provénce and in the Elizabethan era in England when sex in general was freed from this attitude of evilness, Puritanism again placed sexual relations under this cloud. Why this attitude toward a natural and essential phase of life? The answer is complex, but a part of it is, I think, that in early Christian times when men thought of sex, they naturally thought of its excesses, of prostitution, concubinage and marriages often with many more children than parents desired or could raise. Sex to them was infused with exploitation of women and heavy family burdens which kept men from the life of contemplation and their religion. They recognized that men's unrestricted sexual freedom was combined often with an ethically low level of living. They could not then conceive that, if women held a better position among them so that they through simple refusal could control men's unreasonable demands, sex would be an entirely different matter.

Even today the inherited feeling that sex is evil is still among us reinforced perhaps by similar reasons, because we associate it with illicit affairs, prostitution and relations within marriage which are not conditioned by the mother's desire and satisfaction. Perhaps also, because it is an impulse which men must frequently restrain, they have associated evil with sex.

And even now, few people have glimpsed the fact that if women were in a position of equality, in opportunities to learn and earn in various fields and in relationship to their husbands, they would be free to refuse sexual relations without risking serious results. In contrast today, the mother often must consent to intercourse in order to preserve the family and win the father's care of his children.

127

If, however, relations took place only when desired by the woman as well as the man they would be free of any elements of the physically stronger making use of the weaker, or the economically more secure making demands upon the economically weak. That is, if all sexual relations were mutually desired and proper provisions were made for any possible resulting child, sex would be free from all elements of evil; it would then involve only beauty and the highest elements in men's and women's natures. A spirit of kindness and mutual respect would always provide its basis.

Of course raising women to such a position is a large and lengthy process. The important matter for us now is to recognize the relationship between the world of sexual life and women's secondary position, as revealed through our laws and in most situations found in our culture. A method through which a possible child, within or without marriage, could be insured care by its father as well as its mother is considered in a later chapter.

In short, the influence which could render sexual intercourse a matter of dignity and loveliness is the feelings of the woman, for whom sex is a most important matter, close to her very soul, a part of her innermost life, physically and mentally. When she is complete master of herself and freely consents or refuses relations, the union in all probability is good for her and for her partner. It is rendered a glorious feature of living, granted us by nature and by God.

Since the kernel of all genuine feeling is its spontaneity, a *command* to feel happy, or to feel sad, or to love another, usually falls on barren ground. Yet we embody in our laws and customs the thought that a desire for fusion of two personalities, the most delicate of all feelings, can be channelled by law and by iron-fisted compulsions. The maddening loveliness of love and even the moderate elations of sexual happiness are founded on mutual feelings that each is freely and constantly chosen anew by his mate.

A man has more opportunity to feel and express genuine love since he is privileged to take the initiative, clearly showing his interest or indifference to every woman, and is able to enjoy more freedom in his love life. Yet he will never know the exaltation of being chosen and re-chosen by a woman's free desire as long as the woman is unreasonably bound, is submerged and insecure. He will instead know only a woman more or less inhibited and apprehensive who is therefore often incapable of giving herself completely to anyone.[18] She frequently discovers that, due to her mate's greater freedom and temptations, bestowing her *full* erotic emotion on a husband or lover often leads to heartbreaking disappointment. Also, she is constantly asked to fit into a pattern which often ignores her desires and her needs for some continuity of the relationship and full backing in case of pregnancy. She often passionately wishes the complete embrace but the proposal of her husband, or her lover, often ignores her basic wishes. If it is a husband, he sometimes ignores the fact that she is only human and can raise only so many children; if, a lover, the whole one-sided double-standard bunch of laws and attitudes completely overlooks her needs and desires. It is time we recognize how many features of our culture tend to make a woman fearful of sex relations and later cool or frigid.

One of the most traumatic demands made of women is the command to avoid all sexual satisfactions before marriage and suddenly turn herself about completely and embrace enthusiastically *all* requests for intercourse upon the marriage ceremony. During her single state she is expected to maintain such a superhuman, non-sexual condition that she has strength to restrain a fervent lover, as well as herself. The heavy burden of preventing pre-marital relations has been largely placed upon girls and young women, as is indicated by studies of men's frequent approaches to them,[19] which are encouraged by the double standard. It seems to be imagined that the strong conditioning against sex of girls through their impressive youthful years has no influence during the following decades in their reactions toward their husbands' sexual desires. This is another case of wishful but unreasonable thinking.

A major theme of modern fiction writers who hold a mirror up to life is the tragedy hanging upon love's unrealized dreams. Secret desires of the unmarried and married alike are being powerfully presented and such presentation is preparing the way for a more humane society, a society which fulfills our needs more extensively while protecting all from exploitation. Perhaps our society has thus far achieved through its institutions no more harmony between men and women than between nations.

CHAPTER 7

1. About 84% of the men these ages were married and 72% of the women in 1955. U.S. Census, Current Population Reports, Population Characteristics, Oct. 31, 1955, Series P-20, No. 62, p. 8.
2. *Statistical Bulletin,* Metropolitan Life Insurance Co., May 1954, pp. 4-6.
3. *U.S. Census,* op. cit., Series P-20, No. 62, p. 8.
4. Ibid. In 1955 there were:

Widowed women, not remarried, over 14 yrs. of age to 75 yrs.	5,823,000
Divorced women, not remarried, over 14 yrs. of age to 75 yrs.	1,349,000
Single women, never married, 25 yrs. of age to 75 yrs.	3,506,000
Total	10,678,000

This figure probably does not include deserted wives, not legally divorced.
5. The two bureaus referred to, one was in Newark, N.J., and "American Service" was in New York City. They found that the less educated middle-aged men are sometimes willing to meet women their own age.
6. Williard Waller, *The Family, A Dynamic Interpretation,* chapter on "Marriage Conflict," The Cordon Co., 1939.
7. Kimball Young, "Mormon Polygynous Families" in *Studies in Personality,* ed. by Quinn McNemar, Maud A. Merrill and others, McGraw-Hill Book Co., 1942, pp. 302, 314.
8. The Banaro of the Sepik River region of New Guinea told of

130

by R. Thurnwald. A measure of the contentment of these men's lives is indicated by the small number who went to the large plantations where they earned more money but lived away from their families. Margaret Mead, "Jealousy: Primitive and Civilized," ed. Samuel D. Schmalhausen and V.F. Calverton, *Women's Coming of Age*, Horace Liveright, Inc., 1931, pp. 36, 37.

9. Melrich V. Rosenberg, *Eleanor of Aquitaine*, Houghton Mifflin Co., 1939, p. 224.

10. George P. Murdock, *Social Structure*, The Macmillan Co., 1949, pp. 263-265.

11. Ibid., pp. 265-270.

12. Margaret Sanger, *Motherhood in Bondage*, (contains a selection of typical letters received by the author), Coward-McCann, Inc., 1928, p. 44.

13. Ibid., pp. 280, 285, 274, respectively. That such situations exist today among the low income groups in our cities is indicated by a study made by Jerome Rabow, *News of Population and Birth Control*, International Planned Parenthood Federation, November 1957.

14. Elizabeth Barrett Browning, *Sonnets from the Portuguese VII. Poetical Works of Elizabeth Barrett Browning*, Thomas Y. Crowell & Co., 1883.

15. Ibid., (last lines of Sonnett XXIX).

16. L. and A. M. Langer, Samuel French, 1934.

17. Corinthians VII 2, 7-9.

18. Erich Fromm presents the importance of spontaneous action in the development of the self in *Escape from Freedom*, Farrar & Rinehart, Inc., 1941.

19. Eugene J. Kanin, "Male Aggression in Dating-Courtship Relations," *The American Journal of Sociology*, September 1957, pp. 197-204.

Some Most Delicate Matters

Since John de Dios, Adam's cousin, had wanted to join
another discussion, a time had been found which suited all
three. Again they gathered in the sociology office on a
cold rainy morning, when it was good to be inside together.
They chatted a while about personal matters, then got into
the subject of the day.

"I've mulled over our last conversation quite a bit, Eve,
listened to the recordings of your and Adam's discussions
and read the parts you've written. All very intriguing. We
men should stop to think about it! It's possible some customs could be developed to further liberate women, at the
same time men obtained what they want most. That is, not
what they often think they want in their reeling and excited youth, but what they come to realize they want in
their more mature years."

"I'm delighted, John, you think the subject is worth while.
— Today let us talk about men's and women's attitudes
toward sexual relations. It is a fundamental matter. We
have touched on it, but should consider it much further. If
men and women held similar attitudes, each group would
doubtless want the same restrictions and freedoms for itself and everything would be going much more smoothly
than it is."

"That's right. We men think your attitude often unreasonable and you women think ours equally so, I guess,"
John replied.

"When we talk about attitudes we are in the subject of
psychology which is a relatively new study. It's just beginning to be something of a science. Before the days of
psychology people held many erroneous theories about human behavior. They also felt that a person's attitudes could

be ordered from above, by the king or the chief, and that if the subject did not hold them he was disobedient."

"A good example are the heretics of the middle ages who were imprisoned or put to death for not believing as the church dictated," Adam observed.

The new subject of psychology is helping women

"All the sciences are helping women, for rational thought tends to correct the irrational ways in which they have been treated. The development of psychology is especially important for them. Through it a great deal is known about individual needs and natural results of emotional stress and conflict. Before scientific study of mental processes were made, many of the unsupportable theories were regarding women. The nervous housewife-mother was scolded and told to 'get hold of herself.' Today an intelligent husband tries to discover the cause of her nervousness which is not an innate weakness but the result of tasks demanded of her along with her working environment."

Eve continued, "Most cultures, including our own, have directed women's thought and then have in effect compelled them to pretend that they genuinely wanted to think this way. We may, for instance, consider the social pressures to make women want to do housework, one form of pressure being practically denying a love life without willingness to put on the apron. The constraining circle revolving around woman's life has these segments: the sexual restrictions with economic dependence of married life; the celibacy of single life; the social pressures that she act as though she wanted these restrictions and limitations; and then laws to enforce her obedience in case she fails to submit. Although some, if free, would have chosen the pattern assigned them, most have obeyed these dictates while inwardly rebelling at some feature. And many have broken under the strain of this strait jacket presented to them as shining raiment. Acceptance of these restrictions as inevitable and as nature's law, as same women do, has perhaps aided them as

133

individuals, yet such submission has entrenched their bounded lives.

"Some customs have interfered with the very life-demands of women, such as deforming the feet of upper class Chinese girls and others we have referred to. In spite of pathological conditions among many resulting from such customs they have been regarded as 'normal' and 'right.' But, sooner or later, the irrepressible *basic needs* of those subjected assert themselves and attempt to rebuild a more fitting culture, although the official calm of the society is shocked by their 'deplorable radicalism.' "

"Right, it's a matter of whether one's attitudes can be entirely ordered from above," Adam observed. "One can be led in certain directions through preaching and propaganda and by commands but there's a limit—"

"Oh yes. The mind like an eternal spring stimulated by the individual's physical and psychic needs will think, at least some of the time, just what it wants," Eve added thoughtfully.

"Well put. And such independent thinking must be encouraged. It is the basis of human progress."

"Psychology's study of attitudes is encouraging some people to look into their own independent views. Even some women are doing this. Many of them are now distinguishing their spontaneous attitudes from those which their culture demands. For instance, widowed women often distinguish between their real attitude toward their frustrating celibate lives and the attitudes society says they should hold."

This roused John. "Have you thought of this, Eve? Wouldn't it be interesting to use a lie-detector on a group of women and note what it registers as they answer these questions: To wives, 'Have you ever known a man, not your husband, with whom you wanted to experience some variation in your sexual life?' And to single and widowed women, 'Do you want to live without any sexual satisfactions for year upon year, for the rest of your lives?' "

They all laughed. "A fine experiment, John. If one carried

134

it out, could the results be published, I wonder," Adam mused. "Sometimes I think this subject of the relation between men and women so deeply pervades all our lives that it's filled with more fire than any other — even that of Communism. — In our country now we have published studies by the Kinsey Institute showing how some women refuse to obey men's unreasonably restrictive laws. But no one has dared to ask women what laws they would like. Nor, what restrictions *they* think most beneficial for themselves and others."

"How true," Eve replied. "Regarding this question of a person's thinking bravely of his own individual needs, I must read this statement by Karen Horney:

> 'The philosophy of life well represented in *The Late George Apley* . . . grants no place to the individual or his individual feelings and strivings. What counts is that he fit into the environment, be of service to the community, and fulfill his duties. Hence whatever individual fears or desires he has should be controlled. Self-discipline is the uppermost virtue. To give much thought to himself in any way is self-indulgence and selfishness.
>
> The best representatives of psychoanalysis, on the other hand, would emphasize not only the responsibility toward others but that toward oneself as well. Therefore they would not neglect to stress the inalienable right of the individual to the pursuit of happiness, including his right to take seriously his development toward inner freedom and autonomy.'[1]

"Statements such as these are revolutionary when applied to the mother. Yet it is being irrefutably discovered that women do have definite needs, bodily and mental, of various kinds and that adjustment to life implies some 'inner freedom and autonomy.' When we see where scientific thinking leads us, will we refuse to recognize the truth it tells? Or, will we say that maintaining women's traditional role is more important than democracy between the sexes or greater happiness for women — and men?" Eve asked.

"We seem to be feeling our way along to new ethical principles. And it is difficult, believe me!" John observed in an explosive way.

"Right you are. I think I'll read you also these remarks by Justice William O. Douglas on the attitudes of the Asian peoples and their recent turning toward recognition of their personal needs:

'For centuries Asia accepted that condition (control by conquerors and invaders) with the fatalism that has governed many of her attitudes. Asia became wedded to the view that she was born to the servant class. She accepted her servile condition and her poverty and fashioned out of them the *religion of the renunciation of life*. The influence of renunciation is strong in the East today. But Asia, awakened, is ridding herself of the notion that she was predestined to be exploited by the West.'[2]

"That is," Adam added, "as Karen Horney would put it, the Asians are now beginning to take responsibility toward themselves and their 'inner freedom and autonomy.' "

"Yes, this religion of renunciation has been preached to many groups, as well as mothers.—Even in the 1800's most women were taught to be content without learning to read and write. — You remember, we discussed the two main choices now offered most women, marriage with dependence or the single state with an earning job, neither of which you men said you would submit to. Things *could* be arranged so that she would have economic rewards somewhat commensurate with her work and also children and freedom to choose her vocation. Every time a person in sanctimonious terms advises a woman, 'you can't have your cake and eat it too,' he is preaching the religion of renunciation."

Adam asked Eve, "If women think more and more just what they want stimulated by their basic physical and psychic needs where will they be led?"

"We needn't be afraid. Our race is blessed by the fact that they embody vital drives toward the nurture of children — and other persons, their husbands, parents and grandchildren. Happiness for the mother consists largely in giving her children basic advantages. But let us leave this until later. Unless some reactionary forces gain control women will take steps toward their further autonomy."

136

"That is the course most restricted groups have found sooner or later," Adam agreed.

After a pause when all three were buried in thought, Eve said, "We could now carry our discussion of woman's probable greater freedom into the division of labor and her economic position, but we are centering upon the sexual side of life so we should turn to this again. — We could consider this urge for some change in mates."

John spoke up feelingly, "A fine idea. We shouldn't simply condemn this urge. It is too prevalent, perhaps impossible to eradicate."

The urge for some variety in mates

"All right, we'll try to be realistic about this," Adam answered as he drew himself up in his chair. "Shouldn't we first consider what often takes place within marriage?"

"A good starting point," John agreed.

"Well, have you ever heard of 'cabin fever'?" Adam asked. "It is recognized among men and refers to what happens when two men live in close quarters together as lumbermen, hunters or prospectors. They must cooperate in a thousand details to make their life endurable. They naturally talk over all their experiences and thoughts, going through the pleasant process of sharing each others's lives and learning each other's reactions to this idea and that. At the same time they prepare their meals and wash their dishes together, each tolerating certain ways of the other which are not his own. They decide together when to eat and sleep and when to turn out the light at night. This process continues a hundred days. Bill has a higher position in the forestry operation than Mike. Bill, however, quietly submits to Mike's snoring, while Mike tries to overlook the raucous way Bill clears his throat. When Bill shaves he badly musses up the table while he whistles the same tune *every* time. This all continues another hundred days. More and more Bill leaves the more disagreeable tasks such as disposing of the garbage to be performed by Mike. — Well, I won't continue further but 'cabin fever' develops. The peculiar ways of each grate more and more upon the other's nerves. If another friendly man appears upon the scene he is heartily greeted, perhaps hugged with delight. And if he offers to take one of them to another place, there's a real scramble as to who shall go. — I know something about all this from first hand experience," Adam laughed with suppressed feeling.

"You have said a lot!" John patted Adam on the shoulder. "If we apply this to a married couple we should add that the two live out of one pocketbook, what one spends the other must go without. Also, there are children with constant problems as to how they should be handled. Decisions are made together, or one person's wishes are often allowed to override the other's."

"Good, very good description of what often happens between a husband and wife. 'Cabin fever' is an excellent term for it." Eve said enthusiastically, "And we must recognize that where income is insufficient, everything is apt to be more trying. There's less space for each in the home, less outside social life, vacation changes, harder physical work for both. — And I might put in here that William Goode's study has determined definitely that divorce is more frequent among the lower income groups.[3] In addition, desertion (without divorce) by the father averages much higher among those same groups. This important fact has been overlooked until recently."

"I must say," John added, "for we are talking very frankly, that in the couple's sexual lives, also, a new feeling toward each other often develops after ten or twenty years together. How should we describe it?—Sex becomes prosaic — unexciting, shall we say?"

"Yes, we should admit this. After a couple has had relations two or three thousand times they of course thoroughly know each other, like a book re-read a hundred times so that there are no stimulating discoveries, no novelties," Adam observed. "Along with this frequently is 'cabin fever' from their years of too-close living."

"The wife still more than the husband is apt to find their

relations become prosaic, for the man obtains certain satisfying relief even if his experience is not highly exciting. But the wife when intercourse has become commonplace frequently feels little, if any, pleasure — and no relief. She is often left partially roused, longing for satisfaction, frustrated so she cannot join her husband in a deep sleep," Eve said speaking for women. "So very much could be said along this line, but we can only touch upon it here."

Adam continued, "So we must recognize, through these and other factors, that the thrilling, vibrating excitement of newly-weds often passes into a mutually warm and loving attitude for a lengthy period, perhaps twenty years, but then almost invariably, except for some unusually congenial, well-fixed couples, the mutual sexual pleasures become blunted. The husband may lose his self-confidence resulting from this situation or from other causes, such as small progress in his business, and even become impotent toward his wife."

"While she, as a result of similar situations combined with weariness from household tasks often becomes numb and indifferent toward his advances, try as she may to revive the feelings of their wedding trip," Eve added. "And when this state has descended upon them they are like the two men of the cabin—ready to hug any friendly newcomer."

"That is, two forces may then be present, that of a certain repulsion of the husband and wife toward each other, like two electrically negative charged objects; and beside this a great attraction by each toward a new, appealing friend of the opposite sex, similar to that of a positively charged object toward a negatively charged one," Adam nicely explained.

"You've said it! And I've never heard it put so well before. It's a terribly radical thing to say," John remarked. "And we could ask, why is that attraction toward a new person so great?"

"That's a big question. I'll make a stab at it—I think it is similar to the urge we have to read a new book, to see new places, the mountains, ocean shores, waterfalls we have never seen before — also other countries with their different languages and ways. It is a hunger for experience and knowledge." Eve said dreamily as she looked out the window and then continued, "But there is more than that. We all long for encouragement and emotional support from others as we wind our way between our problems, feel ourselves growing older and advancing toward the end of our earthly lives. Each is looking for another who will understand, who will share his basically lonely existence, with whom he may fuse his life and find new strength. I am not saying he, or she, succeeds in his search for the perfect companion, but that most of us do search. And most of us also have an appetite for the simple deep-sharing with others."

"That is all too true, and as John says, this is perhaps the most radical card we have laid on the table. But we can't overlook it if we are honest scientists. We should add that in this urge for a new mate is often the desire for companionship with someone older or younger than oneself, or of a different age than one's present spouse," Adam observed. "The most recognized situation is that of the older man who is drawn by the freshness and vitality of a young woman. And likewise her desire to gain a feeling of security and acceptance by a more mature man, one with greater knowledge and perhaps some achievement."

"And, though not generally recognized," Eve added, "there is the corresponding urge for age relationships opposite to those accepted in our society. As shown in the impressive play, 'Tea and Sympathy,' in which an insecure and floundering young man awed by criticism of his school mates and father gained tremendous help by sharing deeply for a time with an older motherly woman, richly experienced in many areas.[4] — A few older women show sometimes in their eyes their emotional interest in a young man, vaguely imagining the joy of feeling their youth again with him. But they are few and even this fleeting interest is frowned upon in our society. Most shut out such thoughts from their minds. Yet there are some, perhaps more in

Europe than here, who have made the amazing discovery that they can drink deeply and fully of the elations of sexual relations — even in their fifties and sixties when roused by a younger man. That is, they've discovered what many older men have known for centuries regarding themselves in their relationships with younger women. — But men are reassured by the fact that most all older women consider themselves rather sexless due to their age—not due to their walled-in lives."

Sex pleasure more mental than physical for women

A sudden downpour with wind attracted their attention. They went to the window to see if branches were being broken from the trees. As they returned to their chairs John began, "I wanted to interrupt and say at the point when you, Eve, were describing the husband with cabin fever, who was ready to hug any pleasant newcomer — that I imagined just at this time he happens one evening to notice his faithful, young secretary with tears in her eyes as she puts on her hat to go home. Both are lonely and forelorn. He kisses her in sympathy — a rush of warm feeling streaks through their bodies."

"Yes, John, that amazing power of touch."

"He then asked her out to dinner to cheer her up, to see if he could help. We can guess the steps — each discovered he *could* help the other.—The downcast, partly impotent husband even amazed himself at the new life he found growing out of this affair. New self-confidence helped his business and made everything seem happier and easier." John paused so Eve went on.

"He felt this would help his sexual relations with his wife and, from cases I have heard, it probably did for a while. He of course constantly compared his wife to his new companion for whom sex was a glorious glimpse into a previously unknown world. He became more and more involved, which meant more evenings away from home, more so called business trips. Gradually several little indications of what was going on appeared to her. Two stubs of theatre tickets, some long, curly hairs on the shoulders of his coat. At these discoveries her heart stopped beating, she lost her appetite, lost weight. When he was away on trips or evenings she couldn't control her imagination. Were all the fond kisses and embraces she had received, which were associated with the starting of their children, with the close family life she had dedicated herself to— were these all repeated with another woman? Impossible— yet probably so! Were they simply mechanical things applied to anyone to whom he took a fancy? She shivered at night alone between cold sheets as she tried to quiet her mind and sleep. She felt like a child whose devoted mother had died, and wept like one. Whom could she talk to, who could help her? She couldn't think of a soul. Things could well be made worse if she shared her problem with a friend or relative.

"And when her husband returned and slept with her — there were the nauseating problems—how should she act, what should she say? Her inclination was to sleep in another bed, but to maintain a surface calmness and friendliness. She couldn't pretend she was close to him and that she loved his caresses as before. She tried this but felt like a deceitful wretch.—No pleasure was gained, only agonizing doubt. She wanted to explode and tell him all her feelings. But that was hazardous, so she pulled all her resources together tied up her feelings and controls into a *self-imposed* strait jacket. It was a dangerous state—just what brings on nervous breakdowns—but what was she to do?"

John and Adam were impressed by this statement of Eve's. John passed cigarettes around and helped light them. They quietly whiffed at them a while.

"Well, I'll try to present the husband's thoughts in this situation," Adam remarked. "Of course this case is only roughly typical, there are innumerable variations. — He won't guess the inner turmoil of his wife. He is in a rosy cloud and can't see why she won't join him there. He is convinced he can love both her and his new friend, he has enough love for both. He may notice that his wife does not

142

react as warmly to his embraces as before, that her enjoyment of intercourse compared with that of his young secretary is now worlds apart. Then, he thinks this is probably because his wife is older, is bound up with care of the children and that she no longer desires much sexual attention."

"Oh yes. And he thinks probably that her slackening interest gives him new justification for his extra-marital affair. And so the downward spiral of their mutual affection and pleasure sweeps." Eve took a few more puffs on her cigarette, then said, "One such husband expressed the view that if a wife has as much sexual congress as she seems to want, she is taking a 'dog in the manger' attitude when she objects to his affair with another. He seemed to think that the extent of her desire would not be influenced by her uneasiness and hurt feelings.

"There we come to the fundamental difference between men's and women's values in sex," she continued. "That husband put well his attitude that sex is largely a *physical* matter. If he can carry on relations with two women why shouldn't they be satisfied, he thinks. — You remember, I tried to explain that the physical side of intercourse is only a part of a couple's relationship which makes satisfaction for a woman, when I presented her reactions as constituting a range of feelings from *paraiso* to *infierno*. The physical part of sex is nothing, or almost nothing, for women without the surrounding aura which raises it to an expression of regard or love. The woman is so constituted that she must be regarded, not as a sexual object, not as a body, but as a person with thoughtful attention in order to enjoy sexual relations. The feeling of her mate toward her is the prime factor which rouses her response. Actually, I could say most women fear and abhor intercourse which is purely a physical matter—it seems mechanical, animal-like, dog-like. She feels she is being *used* for the other's physical relief. Most men have not sensed this disgust at being *used* for it is impossible for a man to be used in a similar manner. He is protected from this by the fact that if he is not somewhat desirous he is simply unable to participate in intercourse."

"I had never thought of that, really, Eve," John said, "and that's an important feature."

"Most every woman while wondering about her mate's real attitude notices all the details in his treatment of her during sexual relations. And she usually successfully determines to what degree he regards her as a body, or as a being like himself with a complex psyche of her own, with interests ranging far outside of sex — a being who needs honor and help as she gives honor and help to him. She can tell whether his movements are the spontaneous result of a deep feeling toward her as a person, or are willed as a method of rousing her body for his own satisfaction. — It is like the difference between a violin player's performance resulting from his love of the composition he is playing, or his performance resulting from conscious fingering he has been taught will reproduce the notes he reads. In short, it is the difference between actions originating from deep pervading feelings or from calculated direction of movements, the great contrast between an artist and a technician. — The fact that he is physically able to have relations with another woman and herself is a small matter. Does he love her, she asks, as the violinist loves his favorite Beethoven piece or does he now give his love to another? — It is impossible for her to feel enveloped in his devotion, while he actually holds only a secondary or minor affection toward her.

"I must dwell on this further," Eve pleaded, "for above all things which are said to men about sex, this is the most important. In a few words it is that his actual feeling toward her as a person is the basic factor in their sexual relations and that she can't be fooled for long about his real attitude.

"Many books on sex instruct the man to say 'I love you,' to start with 'plenty of foreplay,' to do this and that; and yet they omit to say that he must in some way *feel* a great closeness to his mate and possess some admiration for her

144

person if he is to become the artist who shows some degree of genius in his sex behavior. The woman recognizes, far better than most men realize, the feelings in back of all he does, for they are revealed in many ways — by the depth of voice, the inflection, the muscles in his hands, around his eyes, his rhythm of breathing, the tightness of his hugging, the tenseness of the sexual desire of his organs. No learned technique can master or control all these matters. Only his *feeling* can make them authentic and convincing.

"And his deep feeling gives him the confidence which allows the relaxation necessary for his well-managed relations," Eve continued. "Though it may not seem from cursory observation that self-confidence is as important to the woman in intercourse—if a man could once take the woman's place he'd discover this, and it also allows her to relax and enter wholeheartedly into their relationship. Yet how often she lacks this needed self-confidence in her dependent position and especially when she finds herself only one in a triangle.

"Therefore, neither advice nor scoldings telling her she must overlook a husband's philandering will give her this confidence and security. Efforts persuading her to will a feeling of self-assurance and to be passionate are futile. The attitude of her husband toward her as shown in his actions remains the all-important factor in rousing and maintaining her love for him.

"So in short, when a husband falls in love with another woman, he leaves a great vacuum around his wife of mental and emotional elements. He tries with difficulty to cover it up but usually fails. And if we are scientific we must say that this vacuum can be filled only through these clearly sensed sustaining mental and emotional factors of love from another person."

"Really interesting, Eve!" John replied. "It is good for men and women to talk this over. They don't understand each other!" The beating rain which threw leaves against the window drew their attention. They noticed empty walks

145

and broken branches.

"What about the wife who doesn't bury her upset feelings?" John then asked. "Shouldn't we consider her? She does the natural thing, she tells her husband how hurt she is, how she cannot feel the same toward him or enjoy intercourse as before. She then tries to keep him from continuing his affair."

"I can tell you how some men react, for they have told me," Adam spoke up. "They think she's stubborn in not taking it all smiling; that there's no good reason for this affair to interfere with their successful relations. Yes, and some have said she's 'holding out on him in order to hurt him' and 'putting on a scene.' Most are irritated and feel their freedom is impaired—some just 'get mad.'"

"Yes, the husband probably freely expresses to her his antagonistic attitude," Eve said. "This piled upon her other feelings of being hurt, forsaken, desperately lonely and inadequate, completely devastates her."

"And the husband thinks his restrictions are *entirely* due to his wife's unreasonable reactions. Otherwise everything would be all right." John added.

"He doesn't see that her attitude results from her very nature, is beyond her control. He with man's usual attitude that sex is mainly physical denounces woman's attitude which holds that successful relations are basically mental. And what grounds has he, pray tell, for assuming that his attitude is *the* reasonable one!" Eve leaned forward to ask and went on. "He like the kings before the age of psychology thinks he can order certain attitudes in others and should punish them if they refuse to obey. He feels that his subjects' bodily and psychic needs do not direct their attitudes, or rather he doesn't think about this at all. — The woman's feeling that intercourse to be enjoyed must be combined with some security in her mate's affection may be laughed at and scorned, but her feeling is an undeniable and pervasive fact. Anyone who advises a mother in such a triangle to feel self-confident, relax and enjoy relations as before, is as foolish as if he advised a small

146

bird to feel calm with a hawk soaring over his head."

"Well, what advice can be given her, Eve? Suppose she asks a friend, a minister or marriage counselor," Adam questioned.

"The theory is today they should give her no clear advice but talk it over and let her work out her own solution from this slough of despondency. We've considered the course of pretending she doesn't know of her husband's affair, and we've recognized that this course, if carried out for a lengthy period, may well be the road to neuroticism or mental breakdown. Also, we've discussed the other course of telling her husband of her true feelings. Neither seem to be her way out."

"What can she do? Can't these advisers do anything to help her?" John asked as he knocked a fresh cigarette on the desk.

"They may do a little to relieve her strain *if* they have a real understanding of the mother's nature and her actual position. But, I claim, they can't do much under our present marriage institution and the double standard which together demand that she often do the humanly impossible. It's just that simple! — They can give her little or no assistance, no more than Sigmund Freud admitted he could give the women of his times, and for the same reasons. Our social structure places her often in traumatic positions with no happy solution possible. If she happens to personally hold sufficient funds to obtain economic security for her children and herself in spite of her husband's partial or complete desertion, she may be able to obtain other emotional needs and work out a somewhat satisfying mode of life. But we should have a social pattern which demands of the great majority of mothers only what is humanly possible."

"So what is the answer?" John ventured again.

"A change, many radical changes in her position. We have suggested some, and we'll bring up others as we go on. — Here the basic fact is that the husband gives her only part of his love and expects all hers in return. She should not be placed in such a position. It is the result of many features. Her usual economic dependence and that of her children upon this man of shifting emotions is a crucial factor," Eve added as if she couldn't put into words the thoughts streaming through her mind.

"If she were allowed a lover so she were not left so frustrated and alone what a mixed-up time we'd have," Adam muttered.

"Perhaps, and perhaps not. It might be actually far less tragic in its results than the mother's breakdown, going to a mental hospital, or dying from some accident or illness resulting from her depression. — Often people do not connect a mother's death with its main cause. I have known several such cases," Eve added. "Do you remember Mrs. Bentley who died after falling down the cellar stairs and Mary Brown who took too many sleeping pills, and what preceded that? Most people didn't know."

"Yes, I remember very well," Adam replied. "And each husband soon married the woman with whom he was having an affair."

"If the wife were not kept in that traumatic position she might be able to keep her poise and health until her husband found the other woman to be less novel, less fascinating undiscovered land and shift his main affection back to his wife."

"Yes, that could happen, Eve. But it could also complicate things still more and lead to the break-up."

"That's true, John. The way out from this problem is found only by analyzing further all the factors involved. And that's just what we plan to do."

Adam was called on the phone. Eve and John quietly set out cups and saucers and started to heat water for some coffee.

Then while they settled again Eve remarked, "I'm going to be bold and say we should also give some thought to this 'other woman' of the triangle. She is a person, too. If we are analyzing this in a complete fashion we can't omit her."

"That's right, she should be included. She might be a hetaera, the husband's secretary or a widow earning her own living. We musn't think only of a poor and ignorant young thing," John said. "The husband with his two mates does have difficulties with his emotions. They shift about in an unmanageable way and he may do some pretending with his wife."

"Oh yes. — And both women are constantly uneasy, weighed with fear, for each knows that her lover, can on the slightest provocation — perhaps only because sometime she is weary and doesn't react enthusiastically to him — switch his major affection to her rival. It is the easiest thing in the world for him to make this switch for he already has both women, wife and friend, in the close orbit of his sexual life. He can therefore turn the center of his passionate interest from one to the other for almost no cause. Thus, both women in tense uneasiness may be unable to throw themselves confidently and joyously into their relationship with him. The group of three, the man at the center, in fact, constitues a dictatorship or monarchy in microcosm and offers the man the same temptations toward misuse of others which kings and dictators have had. Therefore, the man at the head of the triangle can be selfish, and even degenerate and still have companions, even as did Henry VIII and many others. The factors dominating the lives of those men in these small triangular monarchies are not material objects, but matters equally important, the vitality and pleasures from life with a mate, intangible factors but none the less real and highly cherished."

"That's true, Eve. — With one breath men say, 'Sex is nothing, women should be happy without it; and with another, when they think of themselves they say, 'It is the very core of life and we'll keep our opportunities *willy-nilly*,'" Adam added, "and that puts it mildly."

"Right, and many women, too, hold that women can easily adjust to empty or emotionless, sexless lives. Dorothy Dix wrote: 'And every wife should be wise enough to recognize that men between forty and sixty years of age go through a period of indiscretion when they do foolish and irrational things and need to be treated with patience instead of divorce.' [5] She consigns the wife to a long period, twenty years, of uneasiness and fear. Moreover, this is a transition period when the wife herself goes through menopause and her children are leaving home. She herself craves heightened social and sexual security through her husband's loyalty at this time."

The whistling kettle called Eve to her feet. She poured the coffee. John passed the sugar and cream. The men discussed the college football team's latest victories. Then while sipping their coffee John remarked, "You know, men move about awfully impatiently."

"Yes, John, I agree. He is sometimes like an oil prospector who moves too rapidly, not studying carefully enough the area where he is. — Instead of recognizing that his own impatience is frustrating him he claims his women are obstinate," Adam replied, "when they are only sensitive human beings."

"And we might say that most men are feverishly trying to assure themselves at least one mate all the time," Eve added. "The husband of a triangle has as back log his wife to whom he can return at intervals or during an interim period between affairs with other women. When he is discouraged, old or ill he falls into his wife's arms. She often takes him, consoles and nurses him; the comforts of the honored marital relationship are reestablished. Yet this remarkable generosity is no easier for the wife than it would be for a husband in a similar position. — While the husband varies his life by enjoying two women for periods he demands that every woman center upon only *one* man at a time—or none. Then if her love relationship is broken, whether she be wife or hetaera, she necessarily is left alone, at least for a period, and often for the rest of her life. The hetaera, who has been in love with her companion for some years perhaps, is left almost as dejected as the deserted wife. — I know most people say, 'Well, she deserves

150

this — having an illicit affair like that!' But I would say 'Why does she deserve this any more than her man companion?' Both women suffer far more than the man of the triangle when there is a break. Each has probably given much more thought and feeling to him than he has to each of them. Whether he forsakes his wife to marry his sweetheart, or forsakes his sweetheart to return completely to his wife, or leaves one sweetheart for the novelty of another he smashes hearts. Many a man crashes like a bull through a flower garden knocking down magnificent lavender and blue sprays of larkspur and lovely canterbury bells in his search for something beautiful. — Take the college student who is quoted in a recent article as saying 'Although I never had any difficulty in finding and occasionally seducing interesting females, I discovered that I had no desire ever to see any of them a second time.' " [6]

"That bull trampling among the blossoms is a good picture." Adam chuckled to himself and asked, "You know since a surplus of women is developing in many countries, we hear the argument that men should be allowed more than one wife at the same time for long or short term periods. What should be done about this?"

John answered, showing he had accepted many of Eve's views. "If men were given this full permission while each woman was still restricted to one man, we'd have all the problems of the double standard — blown up — ready to burst! As I see it, there must be some balance in men's and women's freedoms if things are going to work."

CHAPTER 8

1. Karen Horney, *Self-Analysis*, W. W. Norton & Co. 1942, pp. 29, 30.
2. William A. Douglas, *North from Malaya*, Doubleday & Co., 1953, p. 322.
3. William J. Goode, *After Divorce*, The Free Press, Glencoe, Illinois, 1956, pp. 53-55 and Ch. 5.
4. Robert Anderson, *Tea and Sympathy*, Random House, 1953.
5. Dorothy Dix, "Should a Wife Forgive–" *Your Life*, Spring 1945, p. 42.
6. *Life* magazine, "The Unsilent Generation Breaks Silence," March, 1958.

CHAPTER 9

Greater Similarity of Men's and Women's Values in Sex Is Crucial

"That's just it, John," Eve replied as the three continued their conversation. "In men's rough conception of woman as a sexual object they have often considered her as somewhat inanimate, as something which can be shifted about to suit their passing feelings and purposes. She is often asked to turn her affectionate feelings on and off as if she lacked all the qualities of the living human being and were not subject to the delicate balancing of cause and effect on a nervous, mental and spiritual self."

Women are full persons with many sides

"A woman's erotic interest is roused by a complexity of forces which includes far more than a mate's request. We are not so foolish as to expect a person to feel sad, to cry or to be happy and laugh because another asks it. Yet men constantly make just such impossible requests in the realm of passion and sex love," Eve continued. "A husband may criticize his wife unduly and then expect her to grant his request to immediately forget and embrace him. Or after six months absence while she has been killing all her eroticism in order to remain faithful, he may return and expect her, without a period of love-making following his rather indifferent letters suddenly to transform herself into a highly erotic person. This just can't be done. The emotional and mental turmoil caused by such demands, most wives have experienced. In similar fashion, we've noted how the wife is thrown into sickening confusion by her husband's shifting attentions in a triangular relationship. And of course the woman who is required to live without sex during her husband's years of absence or after his death feels that she is treated like an inanimate object, compelled to fit into impossible requirements. As a result of being thwarted and pushed around many, or most, women are denied a satisfying sexual life. And to escape extreme tension they often cultivate a mild sex interest or become indifferent, almost non-sexual."

"It is interesting to hear you say this, Eve, for men complain a lot of women's lack of response to their attentions," Adam remarked, "You women don't hear it all. It is a major part of the general antagonism we feel in the air. — I must give you a good example. — On my trip to South America I was visiting with a handsome fellow who bemoaned women's lack of ardor. He seemed quite disgusted with women's unwillingness to satisfy men, even when treated with bouquets of flowers and trips to the theater. It developed that he was a real Don Juan and boasted of having had over a hundred different sexual partners. That is, while he spread himself thinly over many women he expected to receive deep affection in return. As you say, Eve, he had not guessed that women need much more than passing attention in order to relax confidently in a man's arms."

"A splendid illustration. — We must conclude," Eve added in her gentle but determined way, "that in the realm of passion a man cannot selfishly command what he wants as he often can with material things. He can call forth a mock love but that is all. He must give of himself deeply and with sincerity if he is to gain the glorious responses he wants from a woman-in-love. I believe this is a fundamental truth. Nature has made women full human persons, not passive objects, or beings. It is impossible for them to be maneuvered around while remaining poised, happy and able to enjoy their sexual lives.

"Balzac wrote, 'The destiny of woman and her *sole* glory are to make beat the hearts of men . . .' This thought is still pervading our times, as evidenced in the emphasis upon the woman's pretty face and her fine clothes in magazine pictures and articles. Yet her glory is far more. It extends

153

into her ability to lead mankind into a new society where all children are carefully raised."

John nodded his head while Adam poured second cups of coffee. Eve's attention however seemed to be far away. At length she said, "I have been trying to crystallize a cloud-like thought which has been floating about in my mind. To summarize some of our remarks, it seems to me that men's general conventional attitude that the woman is a very limited creature, mainly a sexual being and a passive one created by God only to respond to a legalized mate, is a result, I am afraid, of his pride which has also led him in all countries throughout the centuries to imagine that his highest God is masculine. This masculine God would make woman this way, he thinks."

Both Adam and John paused in their coffee drinking, then Adam said, "You've expressed a lot there."

"And we mustn't jump to the other extreme and think that since women are not entirely sexual beings that they don't love sex. Bernard Shaw presents man's love of sex for itself and his rebellion against the idea that if he enjoys intercourse with a woman he should want her companionship for the rest of his life. He didn't sense that women would probably have the same rebellion if it weren't for their concern regarding the child, and that women are feeling for something between a life-long joining of all couples who conjugate and complete irresponsibility toward one's offspring, who is considered an illegitimate."

They heard someone at the door. It was John's wife who had stopped on her way home from marketing. She was an old friend of Eve's and invited her and Adam to lunch. The four drove to John and Dorothy's little home just off the campus. Since Dorothy had the makings of a quick lunch she and Eve spread it out while the men built a fire in the grate.

When all were settled and eating Dorothy remarked, "John has told me about your discussions. You are giving him new insight into the relations between men and women. I have noticed a better understanding of myself since he's

154

taking part in them."

"Wonderful. We didn't aim at this. We are only trying to lay the cards on the table — some are radical ones," Eve replied.

"There's not a woman who hasn't given lots of thought to the double standard. Can't you put your ideas in a nutshell for me?" Dorothy asked.

"Good, Dorothy. Let's try," Adam looked at Eve and John who consented. "How shall we begin?"

"Let's use some simile. This often eliminates some of the prejudices and self-justifications people carry along with their attitudes. What could we use?" Eve asked.

"It should contain a feature which roughly compares with the pleasures of sexual relations. What could it be?" Adam glanced quizzically at John.

"I have heard them compared to drinking the right amount of highballs. We could have one group in an imagined society allowed all the drinks it wants, while liquor would be entirely forbidden to another," John replied.

"We're getting there," Eve said, "But I maintain that the denial of all sexual satisfactions, as is done to millions of women, and restrictions requiring relationships only with a husband who has lost interest in his wife, is more basic to a woman's pleasure and her health than the denial of all liquor would be. What about using some healthy food which is denied to one group?"

"Good, that's right," Dorothy spoke up. "I agree with you. Some luscious food which a person craves and which gives the body vitamins and minerals it needs to keep it thriving — fruit — ripe fruit — I love it. I'd howl if it were denied to me!"

They all laughed. "You've got it — luscious fruit — that's what we should use," Adam said. "And why not use tall and short men because that is roughly similar to men and women who average shorter. It also suggests that greater physical strength may have built up the two sets of restrictions.—Excuse an aside along this line.—I just heard a lecture on present life in Morocco in which the lecturer observed that whenever he saw bosses standing over labor gangs the bosses were big men, far bigger than the laborers doing the heavy work." [1]

Imagining short men are prohibited all fruit

"All right," John remarked. "We have it set up. The men over five feet eight inches tall are all allowed to eat any fruit they please and those under this height are forbidden it. The tall men correspond to the males in our society, the short ones to the women; and fruit-eating corresponds to the males' greater freedom which usually allows them some sexual satisfaction even when single and some variation in mates."

"The story would probably have developed that fruit was injurious to shorter men." Eve added, "It had never been scientifically established but the idea had been passed down for generations. An experiment to learn the truth would of course allow some shorter men to eat plenty of fruit for a year or so, and then compare their health with a control group which was forbidden it entirely. But that could not be tried! Since their laws on this had become sanctified, they feared the wrath of the gods if such a break should be made for only a period. The tall men, perhaps subconsciously thinking of their own pleasant control over the shorter, would impress all with the catastrophic results from such an experiment."

"That's right!" they answered.

"Let us imagine an incident," John said, rather proud that he was finding himself able to make contributions. "Here is young Peter of the shorter group wandering in an orchard with rosy peaches hanging around his head. He smelled them and felt their firm round form. Finally, he hid behind a tree, picked and tasted one while his heart beat fast with excitement and fear."

"Let me go on a spell," Adam volunteered. "On the porch near-by was a group of tall men with dishes of beautiful grapes, peaches, pears and melons before them — along with crackers, cheese and drinks. — One of them, let's call

156

him, Paul, spied Peter behind the tree, left his chair to get a good look and saw him taking a bite of the peach. Paul with righteous indignation shouted, then with others rushed at Peter, grabbed him by the neck, pulled him to the porch where the group lashed him with name-calling, accused him of nastiness, disgraceful behavior, no respect for the gods, gave him a whipping and sent him away. They then continued munching their juicy fruits in a holier-than-thou attitude."

"I'll go on a spell," Dorothy pleaded. "They continued to discuss Peter, predicting he would suffer still more. Paul sneered, 'Oh will he be sorry when his boss learns of this, who will have grounds to discharge him as an bad influence.' "

"From that day on this group of tall men who had discovered Peter's disgrace held their knowledge over his head. Some enjoyed rumoring it about. Others were kinder but let Paul know they held him under their thumbs," John added.

"Yes, John, the tall men's power over the short ones resulting from the fruit-eating ban extended over all areas of life," Eve said as she and Dorothy got up to clear the table and bring in the pie. While in the kitchen they mentioned certain women about whom rumors had been spread. Also, one case where they were positive that the wife was entirely faithful to her over-suspicious husband who nevertheless got a divorce from her. He led up to the separation by simply withholding some of his salary which was needed to keep the family going.

"You know," Eve said as she paused in handling the dishes, "It was back in 300 BC when Philip, king of the Macedonians, accused his beautiful queen, Olympias, of having an illegitimate child and on this unfounded suspicion put her aside for a new wife. And also, we should recall again, Henry VIII of England who had his queen, Anne Boleyn, beheaded on the ground of his suspicion, never proved to be true, that she had been unfaithful. It did not really matter if these women were unfaithful or not, for their husbands would have abandoned them anyway. The husbands simply found this accusation a convenient excuse to justify their high-handed cruelty and start a new marriage—as have other thousands of kings, nobles, propertied and common men."

When all were together again enjoying their dessert, John observed with a smile, "Every short man in our imagined society would have to watch his step so as not even to be seen alone in a room with a ripe melon for fear someone would assume that he had taken a bite."

"Good, John. Rumors were readily believed by the tall men," Eve replied. "Creating and passing them was a way to slap down a short one whenever he attempted to do or say anything inappropriate to his prescribed meek, submissive role. For instance, if he should ask a tall man executor embarrassing questions about his handling the funds of an estate of which the short man is a legatee, the executor need only show the world what a sinful, no-account fruiteater that short man is.—The important factor here is that the tall men are free of all these possibilities of being denounced and hurt for eating fruit—in addition to enjoying this health-giving food."

Dorothy went over to Eve and gave her a kiss, "You really see the significance of all this. I love you for it and hope so much your book will be widely read."

"Thank you, Dorothy, my dear. I appreciate your good wishes."

A while after Dorothy was back in her seat she observed, "We might wonder how the short men took all this. I suppose they were brought up under the teaching that they did not really want any fruit."

"Yes, and many tall ones kept wondering how well the shorties accepted their indoctrination—and enjoyed watching their inner struggle between their desires arising from their bodily needs and this teaching of abstinence. Jokes and stories the tall men told each other often centered around shorties' inner struggles. They never thought in-

cisively enougth to recognize that they themselves placed
the short men in this tantalizing position, for the superior
talls had themselves come to believe that it was the gods
who had forebidden shorties all fruit — not they through
building the customs and the laws," Adam concluded.

"Very significant and true. To switch to women, the
shorties in our society, this is what a man recently wrote:
—'Whenever a man sees a woman he feels he has before
him a being whose "inward humanity" is *essentially confused*," [2] implying this is an innate characteristic, never
guessing that men's traumatic restrictions have filled her
life with confusion," Eve added to illustrate Adam's remarks.

As Dorothy smiled her agreement she mused, "Going
back to tall men, I suppose some of them thought the
shorties showed their submissive nature by generally ab-
staining from fruit. But of course shorties were surrounded
by books and articles upholding this double standard, for
the talls controlled most of the publishing. A few independent shorties while reading of theories on democracy and
equal opportunities might apply these to themselves and
wonder about the justice and wisdom of it all. If any of
them then spoke or wrote their views, they'd be sticking
their necks out! They'd be accused of rank radicalism and
of eating forbidden fruit themselves."

"More than likely, Dorothy," Eve replied giving her a
knowing glance, thinking of how well it applied to herself
and what she should expect when her book was published.

John poked the fire and put on some new logs.

"Before we pull down the curtain in our drama," Eve
said, "we must give a thought to the effects of the double-
standard society upon the tall men. They felt they were
favored by their gods, evidenced by their very height, so
were entitled to special rights and privileges. And history
has shown us that it has been a demoralizing influence for
any group to imagine itself so favored."

Adam who had been taking in every word then slowly

said, "Looking at this tall man's culture from outside, we may observe that if they had considered fruit a dangerous food prohibiting it to all, such a messed-up society, demoralizing one group and suppressing another would not have resulted. Likewise, if they had thought fruit a beneficial food and allowed it to all this warped state of affairs would not have developed. But that double set of rules on fruit-eating was the most disruptive pattern they could have possibly devised. Actually it institutionalized, it approved wholesale domination of one group by another."

"Oh, Adam, I'm going to show you my approval too," Dorothy said as she placed a big kiss on his cheek. "Intelligent women perceive all this readily. But only unusual men like you and John can understand. You've put it well in a nutshell for me. Thank you, so much!"

They were all amused at her exuberance. Adam was encouraged by Dorothy's kiss to make another observation. "If the tall men were not raised as boys with myths and stories about their superiority they'd have been able to adjust to the changes that gradually took place as shorties won more opportunities. This may be the place to begin — with the tall men as boys — and the ancient myths, leading them when grown to expect to win every important game of every kind played with the short men."

"Along this line I must give you the sentiments in some recent articles on advice to women," Eve said. "This is the way they go: 'Be adroit and remember that a man's ego is a delicate thing and doesn't like being overshadowed by a woman's mental prowess.' Also, a man's ego cringes at the thought of playing second fiddle to his wife.' Another tells of some women's great endurance in swimming and mountain climbing, and ends with the man writer saying, 'Now, I climb mountains only in the company of other men. It is easier on the ego.'[3] Of course the men's sensitive feelings would not have to be so continually catered to if they had not developed this over-sensitive ego."

They broke out into a lively discussion of the subject,

160

then turned to lighter matters and a game of bridge.

Since Adam and Eve again could not find an early date to carry on their discussions Eve wrote the following section.

Men's sharing women's values in sex would heighten harmony

A woman usually feels that her new husband's passion insures his desire to provide for her well-being. His strong arms that so ardently embrace, his kiss that makes the blood of each tingle as though they were one, convince her that she is essentially the center of his existence and will remain so. It seems to her as impossible for him to separate himself, to become cold, or intentionally to hurt her as for the sun to change its course.

However, the man's sex feelings are apparently unlike what the woman imagines. No doubt he loves her as a person, certain individual features and ways have appealed to him leading to their marriage. But he is often fervent toward her, not exactly as a person, but rather as a sexual partner. Even within himself his intense emotion toward her as a person and as one who satisfies his sexual urge are so entangled that he himself cannot separate the threads. At least, we find his love for his wife frequently fades as the years pass. *Real love* of a wife implies caring and feeling responsible for her, for the growth and development of all her human powers, of knowing and respecting her. It implies such a unity that her feelings are so reflected in him that her happiness is a crucial part of his own life.

She in her conviction that he loves her as a person and will continue to do so, often gives up her earning job, cares for the home, bears babies and puts her future well-being into his hands, absolutely trusting that he will appreciate her contribution and resulting dependency upon him.

But as we view past and present human events we see indications that the main source of most men's fervent feelings is their sexual desire, since so many turn their passionate interest from one woman to another while the first wife's well-being becomes less and less important to them. This forms the basic problem concerning the marriage institution and our sexual customs. Wives depend upon lasting personal affection. The institution also requires that they do this, *trusting* in their husbands' love.

When men marry most intend to love and care for their wives throughout life, but various innumerable developments frequently change many a husband's feelings. He usually thinks then that this is because his wife has not lived up to his expectations. Since he is the subject who views it all and she the object of his reasoning, we should expect this to be so unless he has unusual insight and empathy. He does not intentionally calculate upon using for his own advantage his trusting-woman-in-love. But later circumstances often are so extremely tempting that he turns to another as the center of his interest, or as his new wife. We have mentioned the numerous factors which tempt him —in short, the younger, fresher woman; the novelty of a new love-life; his weariness of home and child-raising burdens; the sexual relationship which has become prosaic; the fact he can take with him the family savings and his earning power. Alimony payments which can be later avoided are usually a minor amount in comparison to his entire property and income. We should recognize that our laws giving him certain economic privileges constitute part of his temptation to leave his first family.

Aldous Huxley has presented the importance of reducing the number and extent of the dangerous temptations we face. We have reduced temptations to murder and steal through our laws but have done little in other important areas. Temptations of course cannot be entirely eliminated but we should strive to make our laws and institutions work toward the protection of mothers' and children's basic rights, as well as others'.

Husbands who leave wives and children in almost all cases have in fact taken advantage of their wives, have capitalized upon their *trust* in their husband's future love and care, whether the husbands intend to do this or not. There are cases where husbands have calculated from the beginning to take advantage of their trust, as presented in the powerful play and film entitled "Angel Street" or "Gas Light" but such cases are relatively few.[4]

I emphasize that the marriage institution places her in the position of trusting him to do his part because a husband often feels after some years that his wife holds a position similar to that of an employe. He comes to think of his work as providing the sole support of the family and his wife as paid by him for all of her endeavors, he becoming the owner and manager of the business and she, his employe, whom he may discharge any time he is not pleased. But her position is entirely different, for the husband is not the sole supporter since she usually contributes fully as much to the family's life, through childbearing, rearing and caring for himself and the home. Also he has not regularly paid her for on-going work as an employer does. Her room, board and clothes cannot be regarded as proper payment for her responsible, lengthy tasks. Usually she has been unable to save anything for her future from his payments. Instead the marriage institution expects her to trust that he will continue to care for her through life. But, in present times this feature is frequently disregarded by the deserting or divorcing husband — due to our inadequate laws and procedures on this matter. This feature, one of the weakest links in the marriage pattern today, has rendered the whole institution a faltering and fragile structure for the well-being of mothers and children.

Most of us are not aware of the amount of assistance most fathers give their divorced or deserted wives and their children. We read in the papers of large payments made by a few wealthy men to their former wives, but their number is very small compared to the thousands who give little or no financial aid. Where large amounts are paid we can be sure that the man can well afford these. The most recent

163

study on this by William J. Goode found the median payment by divorced fathers of a large random sample to be $8.50 per child per week and that almost one seventh of these children receive nothing from their fathers. Also that the fathers paid these sums for only two or three years then frequently stopped all assistance.[5] Similar facts were found in the extensive studies by Marshall and May. In almost all cases of divorce the children are assigned to the mother (about 95%). Almost all payments determined by the courts are made only to mothers with children. Usually funds for her own support while she cares for her children are not required. It was also found that the larger the number of children the mother alone attempts to care for, the smaller the amount of funds per child she receives from their father.[6] In short, the situation is the exact opposite from "an alimony racket" where the husband is imposed upon by his ex-wife and which has been publicized in our papers.[7] Let's hope that some day we will connect the superhuman task assigned these mothers with the extent of juvenile delinquency.

Therefore, when a father after accepting his wife's services during the prime of her life; then, as he thinks, discharges her from his employ, he has ignored a crucial feature of the marriage arrangement; namely, that she has worked trusting he will recognize her contributions and carry out his part of continued care for her. The husband's great error and that of our present laws which do not enforce this feature, is that of overlooking the full value of the mother's contributions—a great miscalculation. The situation is also confused by the fact that children are a product of years of expended energy, but do not usually bring a financial return to the mother (or father) that would come if she had produced saleable products, or given services of a kind paid for by society. Instead, the raising of children for future citizens (and soldiers) is regarded as a service freely given to the country by parents — especially the mothers. We will consider later how some countries are improving somewhat on this principle.

Thus, the marriage pattern has bound together the man's sexual interests with the mother's and children's welfare, especially in the matter of the continuation of his assistance. When we frankly note men's often shifting interests in women we are compelled to admit the weakness of this arrangement.

Therefore the man's attitude toward sex is fundamental. His physiological and psychological structure is largely responsible for his attitude, that is, his freedom from pregnancy and from the strong drive to care for all and any of his children. His interest often is centered upon the pleasures in sexual matters while secondary is his interest in possible resulting offspring and their care. His views on sexual relations and his responsibilities have been entrenched by their adoption in our culture due to his great influence upon it, and have been embodied in our laws regarding the double standard, the unmarried father, the prostitute, as well as features of the marriage pattern.

Turning to women's attitude toward sex, we find that she is interested in its pleasures but also greatly concerned over possible children and the personal relationship with her mate. Her physiological structure is inextricably fused with the complexities of her reproductive system. Ever since adolescence she has associated menstruation, pregnancy, childbirth and child care with sex. Each of these phases of her reproductive role colors her thoughts and feelings.

With her, sex implies not just an act in one moment of glory, soon to be forgotten as often happens with the man. There is always a chance that the consequences of the act, pregnancy, more than any other one event, may influence her entire life: that is, if single, the devastating experience of the unmarried mother; if married and in poor health, her very life may be endangered; on the other hand, her pregnancy may result in a desired child who is her great delight. Even if she understands contraception she realizes

165

that there is a possibility of its failure. And even though she trusts the method used, her mind has so closely associated the sexual act with reproduction that copulation seldom constitutes a fleeting experience. (Of course, there are the relatively few women, prostitutes and others, who have trained themselves to take sex lightly.)

Moreover the man's sexual organ is largely *without* his body. Her reproductive system is *within* and it extends into her two breasts, into her ovaries, and vagina, into the master gland, the pituitary, which influences her monthly cycle and controls many other glands. True, the man's system also spreads widely within his body but not in such an all-pervading manner.

Since the woman's sex is so closely tied to her entire being she yearns for a relationship with a man in which he takes her *whole self* into the range of his concern. She knows that if she has a child, she and the child will desperately need its father, that their very lives may depend upon his assistance.

The possible new being always so close to the woman is relatively at a distance from the man; a great distance when relations are casual and he plans to leave her; a greater distance if his partner is a prostitute. It is closer if he intends to care for mother and child, but never so close to him as to the mother.

Men's task is therefore difficult. If they want greater harmony they will through sensitivity bring their potential and existent children closer to themselves. They will transfer through the years their early, passionate, sexual love into close companionship and concern for their wives' and children's welfare. They will try to understand what sex means to women and try to share that meaning. If men conceived, carried and bore boy babies, and women the girl babies, we'd find far greater similarity in men's and women's attitudes toward intercourse.

We might also glance at the proposition that women's sharing men's values in sex would heighten harmony. Men's drone-bee tendencies, with temporary obliviousness to consequences, might be encouraged in women to create a more unified attitude, some might say. But unplanned pregnancies and deserted children everywhere would probably result. We already have encouraged women's ability to enjoy sex by the development of contraceptives. And this is working for the benefit of all.

In considering a pattern of sexual attitudes and customs which would bring better times, the first step should be a recognition of the biological facts. We must learn to honor and respect all natural functions and impulses which lead to bodily and mental health. Many hold instead a false philosophy which regards realism, biology and material facts as earthy, as the antithesis of the heavenly and idealistic. But our job is to use what is in our hands in such a way that our material lives conform with our ideals, that our biological lives become filled with beauty and are lived in an aura of heavenly light. This aim has seemed so difficult to achieve that we have in the past considered it impossible, with this resulting dualistic philosophy, that material, biological things are destined to be lowly, while the beautiful exists mostly in our imaginations and in the world after death.

Actual human relations are so often shot with selfish domination, cruelty, deceit and suffering we have naturally turned in our minds to the imagined kindness which is possible. Now that our knowledge has extended amazingly in all directions we should again ponder the questions of how we can bring into realization some of our dreams.

We have mentioned some of the biological facts which we must recognize and *honor* in considering future sexual customs and laws: that a man and woman together start the growth of a child (not a woman alone, if it is started outside of marriage) ; that a child is a full child with all potentialities of a complete person (whether conceived within or outside of marriage) ; that the mother is mentally and physically closer to the child during its prenatal life,

167

childbirth and babyhood than is the father.

Other biological facts we should recognize are that a man indulging in relations with many women could have a hundred or more children. We can honor his great fertility and along with this recognize the severe restraint which he must place upon himself if he assumes responsibility for his children's care. Without this and without his concern over a world crowded with starving people, human chaos would soon be upon us. Likewise we must recognize that a man can start the growth of some twenty children even when he confines his relations to one wife. And these are more than most men can properly raise and most women have the strength to bear and train. So even within marriage nature demands restraint from the man. Contraceptives have also come to his assistance here.

Perhaps the best example of refusing honor to biological facts is the widespread attitude toward childbirth among most primitive and Oriental people who regard it as "unclean" and as associated with evil spirits. Instead of regarding it as the most basic, most promising event of all human life, of celebrating it as nothing else is celebrated, primitive women during past millenniums have been required to go through childbirth outside the home, outside the village in the woods, deserts or on the snow fields and sometimes absolutely alone without even a woman assistant. Some peoples require this even today. Each man knew his own birth was the biggest event in his life yet he did not stretch his imagination to feel that his child's birth was equally important. Nor did he recognize that both the culminating event evidencing mankind's power to constantly renew life, and the mother's important and difficult role should be greatly honored. The attitude toward childbirth as "unclean" is strictly a masculine conception. We cannot here consider all the complicated reasons for his feelings, but anthropologists recognize that one of them is his uneasiness at not playing the central part in the birth process and instead having clearly demonstrated woman's unique, all-important power. In short, it hurts his ego. It is a power and service which should elevate her to a position of equality with him even if there were no other reasons. He may vaguely sense this and therefore want childbirth kept in the background and, as we shall later note, the facts confused by the customs of couvade.

Through the ages this attitude toward childbirth as lowly and unspiring has persisted. We find it in the book of Leviticus in the Bible where it is stated that if the mother has borne a man child she is "unclean" seven days; if a maid child she is "unclean" two weeks. She shall go to the priest after childbirth and "The priest shall make an atonement for her before the Lord for the issue of her uncleanness." [8] Some Christian denominations even today arrange a *'purifiication'* ceremony for the new mother (which now includes other factors such as thankfulness for her safety). Only in current years has the thought occurred that the father might give the mother moral and loving support during the hours of strain and stress of the first long stages of the process, rubbing her back, encouraging her so that he gains understanding, helps her and takes some part in his child's coming into the light of day.

Another example of refusing honor and respect to a biological function is the attitude toward sex held by most societies. We have noticed that in the early Christian period sex was regarded as sinful. This anti-sex attitude was turned against women, regarded as sexual objects, and women were thus denounced as evil. "You are the devil's gateway," is the statement of one early Christian writer which expressed a widespread attitude we will return to later. Luckily most people did not entirely accept this condemnation of women and sex, for relations continued, keeping the race alive! But there are many signs today that these attitudes have not yet passed. Clearly we must reorient our thinking, first accepting biological facts as beautiful and wonderful, then managing our lives in order to honor them and help them bring us our dreams.

169

In comparison to men, it is easy for women to hold attitudes toward sex and reproduction which are in harmony
with the needs of the human race. A quotation from José
Ortego y Gasset puts well the tendency for man to separate
body and soul but for women to more effectively unite them:

"The feminine ego's relation to her body is different
from the relation in which the masculine ego stands to
his body . . . Her body exists for her more than man's
does for him . . . Her body lives more closely with her
spirit; that is, her body is more permeated with soul . . .
In man, comparatively speaking, each normally takes
its own course; body and soul know little of each other
and are not allied, rather, they act like irreconcilable
enemies." [9]

When, for instance, a man's passion leads to rape; or
even to intercourse undesired by his wife, or to relations
with a woman not his wife without taking every precaution
against conception "his body and his soul are enemies" of
each other.

Men's rewards for sharing women's attitudes toward sex
and reproduction would be gloriously happy women, such
as no society has yet known.

At these times when tremendous attention and resources
are going into devices for destruction at the peril of all
humanity, women's deep concern for their children, which
extends into a drive for preservation of life, should be allowed full expression and influence. As evidence of her
interest in preserving and nurturing those far outside her
family we need only note the activities of her organizations,
which include sewing for hospitals and Red Cross, mending
and making clothes for needy families around the world,
raising money for scholarships and similar purposes, studying and bringing action for more humane laws and more
peaceful international relations.

As we look back in history what do we find?[10]Helena,
the mother of Constantine the Great, dedicated her entire
fortune to poor relief and was about the first to be concerned over the oppressed masses. Later Scotch Matilda,
Abbess Heloise, Catherine of Siena stand out as early lead-

ers in care of the sick. The medieval nuns gathered together the needy sick and from this action our hospitals of today evolved. During the same period organizations of nursing women who prepared to serve in epidemics and disasters were the forerunners of the Red Cross. Florence Nightingale, Clara Barton and Mme. Necker of France played leading roles in building the Red Cross and modern hospitals. Women in the 16th century developed the best methods of that time for aiding the mother in childbirth and gave their services without pay.

Dorothea Lynde Dix who saw that mental cases were confined in prisons and punished as criminals launched an international crusade which caused the founding of mental hospitals. In the anti-slavery movement Harriet Ward Beecher and Angelina Grinke Weld and her sister were some of the most active leaders. The pioneers in recent social work were Elizabeth Fry, Jane Adams, Lillian D. Wald, Mary E. Richmond, Florence Kelly, Grace Abbott and Julia C. Lathrop. Margaret Sanger has led the movement toward harmless limitation of too rapid population growth which may replace the former methods of infanticide, starvation, early death from disease and the slaughtering in war, which have in the past reduced our numbers. Of course these women are not the average ones, but they and thousands of others have exerted a tremendous humanizing influence.

Many men today have lost their bearings, have turned to superficial living, gambling, heavy drinking, graft and crime, have been led by the taste for power to dominate and use others for their own benefit. They are not the average ones. Yet Hitler and Stalin and alarmingly large numbers of men have recently taken part in the cruelest treatment of their fellowmen which our race has ever witnessed—in spite of centuries of efforts to become civilized. The marching of Jews into gas chambers, the forcing of confessions by leading citizens through exhaustion and then their execution, stand out as warning signals to all. We witness a tense struggle between forces disrupting

171

human life and those constructing a promising future.

Many men need a balance wheel, some wholesome, absorbing interests to orient their lives. This orientation could well be gained by entering the most dramatic and challenging endeavor of all times — that of preserving and improving human life. And this they can enter by further sharing women's interests, giving their sexual life significance and beauty by making it a generous union of two personalities mutually helping each other and those who are to carry on in the future.

In our present most extraordinary state of affairs, we see the witches' cauldron boiling away, all kinds of new and deadly weapons boiling up out of it one after the other — this, along with tense competition, bitter animosities between nations and world encircling wars. Does not man need to be drawn closer to the woman's side and feel with her a nurturing interest in all human life?

CHAPTER 9

1. Lecture by Robert Friars, "Morocco Today," at Bushnell Memorial, Hartford, Conn., November 1957.
2. Josè Ortego y Gasset, *Man and People*, W. W. Norton & Co., 1957, p. 130.
3. John E. Gibson, "Old Maids and Bachelors," *New York Herald Tribune*, Magazine Section, May 27, 1951.
   Richard L. Neuberger, "Are you tougher than your wife–" *New York Herald Tribune*, Magazine Section, March 19, 1950.
4. Patrick Hamilton, *Angel Street*, Constable & Co., 1939. This was presented also in film, entitled, "Gas Light".
   F. Vosper, *Love from a Stranger*, Samuel French, 1937, presents a similar theme.
5. William J. Goode, *After Divorce*, The Free Press, Glenco, Illinois, 1956, pp. 221-228. This is a study of 425 consecutive cases of divorced mothers living in metropolitan Detroit who were between 20 and 38 years of age when divorced.
6. Leon C. Marshall and Geoffrey May, *The Divorce Court, Maryland*, Johns Hopkins Press, 1932. *The Divorce Court, Ohio*, 1933, pp. 324, 337.

7. Ibid., Ohio, pp. 340, 369.
   Symposium, "Alimony", ed. John B. Bradway in *Laws and Contemporary Problems*, Duke University School of Law, Spring 1939.
8. Leviticus 12: 1, 2, 5, also 15: 19, and 16: 29, 30.
   David and Vera Mace, *Marriage: East and West*, Doubleday & Co., 1960, ch. 12.
9. *Man and People*, op. cit., p. 137.
10. Mary R. Beard, *On Understanding Women*, Longmans Green & Co., 1931, pp. 336, 449-453.

CHAPTER 10

Is The Mother a Human or Magical Being?

It was early October in the morning. Sunshine seemed to come from all sides as it shone through the trees of yellow maple leaves and was reflected from those on the ground wet from the night's rain. And here was a tree in deep maroon, another in shaded orange and brown. All the students seemed gay, some drinking in the rich, glowing colors, others oblivious to them but sensing the invigorating, cool air.

"It is too glorious to stay inside. But I guess it must be done if we are to make progress," Eve said as she came into the office from her walk.

"There's no way out of it if we are going to hold to our plans." After they had settled beside their desks, leaning back in their swivel chairs Adam remarked, "The part you wrote since we last talked together hits the nail on the head. I agree with it all. I made very few changes."

"Good. I'm so glad. Then we can look further into one of the ideas."

"Yes, the one we planned to take up looks like an interesting one. Wasn't it, the mother's abilities for work?"

"Well, the best way I can describe the subject is to put it into the question of whether mothers have magical powers or not. I've thought a lot about what is expected of mothers, expected by husbands and children, expected by our laws and customs. And I include in my question, not mainly the mothers we see in attractive suburbs but all mothers — those with less means, who are far more numerous, and those in city slums and on poor farms.

174

"It seems to me that," Eve continued, "most thinking about what mothers should be able to do belongs to the age of the witch doctor who shakes his gourd-rattles and chants to the spirits as he circles around the patient. Perhaps he holds a lock of hair from the sick person's enemy so he can cast an evil spell over the supposed source of trouble. You know how it goes."

"I've even seen it among some Indians along the Amazon."

"Of course any reasonable thinking about work demands of a person should include our knowledge of physiology, just what the body can go through each day and maintain its health; also our knowledge of neurology and psychology which is concerned with the amount of strain due to tense, prolonged vigilance, worry or monotony and the threshold of endurance beyond which the nervous system is apt to break. You know of the experiments with animals along this line — making them neurotic by submitting them to more anxious foreboding strain than they can take — of Dr. Howard Liddell's neurotic sheep and goats at Cornell University." [1]

"Yes, they're most significant. It looks as though we humans, as well as higher animals, have a threshold of endurance. If a situation requires us to submit to extreme tension which takes us beyond this threshold our system breaks down one way or another and we do unreasonable things," Adam replied as he adjusted the sound recorder.

"With this in the background of our minds let us see what is expected of mothers. To put it simply, our society roughly expects her to bear as many babies as are started by chance, for it seems to think her body is made of a magical substance so it can go through the task of pregnancy and childbirth in close succession again and again and even if she is exhausted or suffers from an organic weakness. All those who oppose the spread of effective contraceptive knowledge, or are indifferent to its spread and

175

its gneral use, hold this belief. In like manner society seems to think that her body and nervous system are of such super-human nature that she does not need a working day of limited time, eight hours or so. Nor does she necessarily need days of rest on Sundays and holidays when she can enjoy a change by leaving the baby, the children and the cooking, to enjoy some new sights or activities. Nor, does she need two or three weeks each summer to go fishing, while peacefully gazing at the sky and rippling water, eating picnic lunches on wooded islands with her pals, or something else equally restful."

Eve paused and smiled as she opened a package of cigarettes and Adam helped her light one. Then she continued, "All studies of the working hours of young mothers show amazingly long days of cooking, combined with child care, marketing, ironing, sewing, cleaning, etc., etc. — especially long when a baby is also tended. Horse breeders hold the principle that no nursing mare should be put to work. But mothers' working days often number almost 365 year after year.[2] It looks like 'fussing around' to some — not real work — but that is only to those who have never experienced such days. It's strange — you often hear it said that it's a valuable experience for a woman to be in business a few years before marriage so that she later will understand her husband's problems—but I've never heard of the valuable experience it would be for a man to carry out a mother's tasks for a few months, not for a few hours or days, but long enough so all branches of her work, cleaning and washing are included — so he will gain a first hand experience in it all."

"It would help his understanding. Of course there should be a baby to diaper, feed and train during his months of learning," Adam added.

"I believe that the father would be quite surprised to find how much physical energy is spent — and particularly how much nervous energy, especially when he does two or three jobs at once like keeping a toddler from putting pins

176

in his mouth, settling disputes between the other children, while he watches some three or four pots cooking on the stove and sets the table for dinner.—You know a ticket agent's booth with a window and a rail to make people get in line and take their turn in buying tickets? When they are quiet and orderly, and he cannot see the length of the waiting line, the agent is able to proceed calmly.— Well, what would a husband and children do if a mother insisted on such organization, so she could calmly listen to and serve one person at a time, ignoring others waiting? Instead the family members often think that she is so miraculous, that she is not strained if they all ask questions and demand her service at once. They usually feel sure a 'good' mother does not get fagged or cross even when this happens.

"And did you ever think of this, Adam? Our present pattern places the mother with the direct, first-hand responsibility of keeping her baby alive which of course involves extreme tension at times—preventing his falling down stairs, wandering into the road, or getting fingers caught in machinery, to mention only a few hazards. She must decide what to do about his refusal to eat, his ear ache or stomach ache. Most mothers can't consult doctors all the time. Of course she must make decisions on all these matters while she is carrying out her other tasks—perhaps when she is ready to flop with weariness.—I know I'm extolling the mother's job. It should be done much more."

Eve stopped to gaze out the window. Adam recalled that his grandfather had lost two wives and married three times. One died during childbirth and another in some home accident. He also remembered his mother had gone to a sanitarium for a period, she had developed some slight paralysis, while her fifth child was a baby. He thought there must be some truth in what Eve was presenting but he did not interrupt their discussion to mention his thoughts.

"Most people like to feel that they are being financially

compensated for long hours of responsible work," Eve continued. "They like to put something away for rainy days, for a vacation or a pet interest. But when it comes to a mother, society seems to think, she does not want this, she is entirely content to leave her rainy days largely to the chance that her husband will be alive, able and willing to provide what she in the future should have. She is imagined to be a super-being so inspired by her love of husband and children she ignores her personal future. As long as she receives her board and room — be it in a crowded tenement or leaky cottage — and clothes to wear, we generally assume she is content. This sounds extreme, I know, but the facts are that if she has not inherited funds she may well have little or nothing for her future. Our laws do not require that her husband pass her some of his income which she can hold for her own unpredictable years ahead. Of course some do this from the kindness of their hearts. But others cannot see why they should and nothing leads them to do so.—These extensive, selfless services expected from a mother can be regarded as somewhat reasonable only if we consider the very prosperous ones."

"Yes," Adam replied "when one is set up like Mrs. Spencer with a maid in the kitchen, a cleaning woman weekly, a well carpeted, radiant heated, sunny, sound absorbing house — with children called for by busses and autos for school and private lessons in music and art — or just some of these advantages a mother can often do all that is expected.—But any study of family income in our country show that only an extremely small portion of mothers enjoy most of these facilities."

"Another feature of this primitive thinking worthy of the days before psychology is the idea that all women are born with housekeeping natures, all with similar mentalities adopted to dishwashing and happy laboring at their chores until their 'knuckles are sore'—you've heard that expression. Along with this view is the assumption that there is no variation in their talents, such as among men, which lead some to be artists and others engineers. Also, that we lose no important contributions from gifted or genius women by pouring them all in the mould of house-keepers—that is, all the women who refuse to live the bar-ren, desert-like single life of a celibate.

"It is recognized that if a person is to make some mental contribution to society he needs time for concentrated thinking and periods of solitude," Eve continued. "To gain these he must enjoy a margin of security which frees his mind from constant concern over the essentials of living. We know the expression of being 'beside oneself' which means one's consciousness is not centered and organized in one's own body but is pulled out and scattered. How many mothers speak of being beside themselves as their minds dart about over their baby's and children's safety.

"Our civilization has allowed many a man, because he enjoys around him a margin of security, to temporarily free himself from his slavery to things so he may retire within himself, rest there and contemplate, but extremely rare is the mother in this fortunate position. If she has a margin of security for her own life, she probably is still under the slavery of the numerous things which serve the sustenance of her husband's and children's lives. The mar-gin of safety of her baby's life is seldom great as his older brother tips his high chair or passes him a marble which goes into his mouth. Perhaps when the mother is old she may have some short spells when she can retire within her-self and contemplate."

They heard some shouting and singing outside the win-dow, got up to look. There was a line of students singing and dancing conga fashion, each with his hands on the shoulders of the person in front, kicking out right feet, then left, in unison. Their team had won a football game. "I'd like to join them," Eve exclaimed. "I love that exuber-ance of youth."

Adam put his hand on her shoulder. "I'd like to get in there, too, but we're dignified teachers, you know."

After watching and singing with the others from their window they returned to their seats. "Adam, all I'm saying sounds crabby and complaining, but what we're doing is analyzing a basic institution which most all these students will enter. Only adults, like you and me, willing to study and concentrate can suggest improvements in its setup."

"Yes, yes, I agree, someone must do it."

A dream of pink ribbons and heavy straps

"The other night I had a dream which symbolized my thoughts on this. Would you like to hear about it?"

"Yes, dreams often synthesize thinking in a remarkable way," Adam replied, putting his feet on a near-by chair.

Eve, encouraged, began, "It involved glittering pink ribbons and thick leather straps. I saw the young mother deeply in love with her first baby, playing with him, feeding him, chuckling over his first words. She was clearly bound to him — at the expense of interest in all other things — she was bound by glistening pink ribbons. All was happiness. She, from her heart, wanted to forget herself and give this time and energy to her baby.

"Then she appeared again in my dream. She was older, looked tired and depressed as she was carrying on the complex pre-dinner task with three little children and another baby around her. The atmosphere in the kitchen was all tension. Clearly she was doing more than her body could adapt to healthily. A heavy strap seemed to bind her to the children and the stove.—As I now analyze it the strap represented *demands* that she carry out all these services whether she had the strength or not. They were the demands resulting from this unreasonable thinking that she is magical, that her powers are infinitely extendable.

"The family pattern compels her to carry on even if she cries with back ache, for her children must be fed. And she must carry on by herself. It is her only road, and it must be traveled without much complaint. If she complains or sighs too much her husband's love may turn away, even to the extent of losing him."

"We could stop to compare her environmental situation with that which Dr. Liddell created for his sheep and which led to their neuroticism," Adam interposed. "Her position, for instance, involved (1) being restrained in one place, the home, for long periods, as the sheep were restrained in the experimental rooms. Then (2) both she and those sheep were induced to carry out repetitive and monotonous tasks which also induced worry, and (3) they both worked basically alone without the sharing of other mature companions.—Again it is significant that as the women, who must support themselves through employment, have gained a wider choice, between factory jobs, clerical work in offices and stores as well as domestic work in homes, they have turned away from domestic work. It has become the least popular form of employment for most — and why? Ask them, and they will say that it is the isolation and loneliness, the long and indefinite hours and the monotony."

"A good point — and so the domestic job has fallen more and more upon the mothers themselves when they raise several children," Eve added and then went on with her philosophizing. "The family setup has made use of her strong mother-drives, the pink ribbons represent the bindings to her home and baby cares made through her own volition and in accordance with her health and happiness; the straps are the bindings to her extensive jobs which are impossible for her to continuously perform while she maintains her mental and physical well-being. In the process of imposing the straps around her is the unrealistic thought, the wishful thinking that she is a magical being, that her drives extend her energies indefinitely."

"She is thus given compliments about her self-sacrifice and abilities and then passed enormous tasks. It is easy for her to become confused," Adam observed.

"Yes, if she complains, then society, whose general attitudes today are still mainly determined by men, says, 'You are not a proper mother. You are weak and selfish. Look

at what other women do.' She feeling this prevalent condemnation hesitates to continue her complaint. She knows
she wants to care for her family, but she also knows she
gets worn out, nervous and cranky, that she often feels
isolated and depressed. And many a mother feels that her
mind is going fallow and dead, especially if she previously
has been stimulated by college or professional studies," Eve
explained. "One woman who was a brilliant physics student
in college told me after some years at housework that she
was like a wild animal in a cage pacing back and forth,
feeling the bars and figuring how to get out. She had great
sympathy for the lions in the zoo, she said. Another mother
who had shown fine musical ability told me she had thought
that after fifteen years of home chores she'd be able to
give some time to music again, but instead her skill along
with her vitality seemed to be going. She wondered
whether she could ever get into it again."

Adam emptied out the burned tobacco from his pipe,
cleaned it, refilled it, sucked and puffed at it till it was
burning smoothly. Then, as he settled back, for he was
having a restful time this morning, since Eve was doing
most of the talking, he asked "What do you think is the
solution? *Something* can be done."

"Of course, many people don't even recognize the problem and those who do seem to be stumped. We here in this
country largely regard our social patterns as fixed things
which can't be changed.—All one need do is to go to Sweden
to see that arrangements can be different, that mothers
can be assisted so their jobs are not so confining or such
a strain. When I was there I was impressed at the thought
which had been given to mother's jobs. It was like a fresh
breeze to learn that even the national legislature had considered at length how to help mothers — not relief for destitute and deserted mothers — but methods of aiding all
mothers, of preventing their crises and breakdowns.[3] I can't
begin to mention everything that is done there but briefly,
all mothers are given excellent, free medical care during

childbirth. The Swedish people reason that, since women give extensive vitality for the country's future citizens, the country should at least provide them high grade medical attention. Most nursery schools are cooperative and aided by the government. They are everywhere. Then an extensive organization of trained 'mothers' helpers' paid jointly by national and local governments aid in the homes if needed at times of mothers' or children's illness, or when a new baby is born. They also assist elderly people, perhaps with only two hours help a day or one day a week so the feeble person, or couple, may live in his own home rather than in an institution. The recipients pay these helpers according to their means but all fees are relatively small.⁴—And since they have become convinced that mothers should be free to choose whether they will confine themselves to their homes or not, laws have been passed which prohibit discrimination against their outside employment on the grounds of marriage or motherhood. When an employed woman has a baby, instead of being discharged she is given several weeks off with full pay. All these provisions and others assure the mother certain securities while she raises children, reduce extensive home confinement, allow earning experience which she may use if she wishes when her children are grown."

"That does stimulate one's imagination and desire to know more. You told me a lot when you returned from your trip.—Sometime let's go there together." Adam watched to see her response.

She smiled sweetly but made no answer.

"We can't go into the big subject of what Sweden does in this book. Perhaps we can in ours on the economic and other sides of marriage," Adam said.

The neurotic mothers

"Have you ever noticed, Adam, the number of plays, books and magazine stories which deal with the mother who is an unduly disturbed person, who upsets her family's life — or a neurotic one who is a great burden to her husband — or one who holds on to her children in an over-protective way, the "mom" picture. One could almost call this the age of the problem-mother.—Also, along with the so-called over-protective mothers we have those who are accused of not protecting enough and are held as a main cause of juvenile delinquency.— Here is another phase of the magical mother theory, that no matter what her situation and her education, she should and can give her children just the right amount of protection and attention, not too much nor too little."

"A simile occurs to me regarding this — not a fine dream like yours, Eve—but it may clarify the matter. It's like a driver swearing and yelling at the slow auto in front of him never looking to see that it is held up by a crawling car further ahead. The yelled-at driver is helpless in his position to do better. He is only human, he can't jump his car over that other."

"That's just right, Adam. All this barking and criticism of mothers is because these barkers haven't looked ahead to see what chances she is given to do better.—In these accounts and stories, some about real mothers, you know, she is often presented as very mercenary, over-emphasizing money and material things; she often can't understand her poetic, musical or writing husband who brings little or no funds into the family.—Those who present her this way clearly overlook why she values the dollars so highly — more highly than her husband seems to. Of course it is because these dollars represent to her milk and coats for her children. Money to these imaginative fathers or to these café-drinking fathers—and some have been important writers and artists — does not usually have such a meaning because the mothers and their efforts stand between the fathers and their children's need. Without thinking incisively, the father feels the mother has strength and time enough to make the small income he passes her supply all his children's wants. Thus, these accounts often present

184

an idealistic father whose life is not dominated by money, compared to a nervous, wrought-up mother who magnifies its importance.—I could name a long list of books, plays, even biographies, which present the mother as the big problem, the unimaginative, earthly, unadmirable person. I think of "The Rope Dancers," now on Broadway, which illustrates this current attitude.—Also of an article I just read which described Edward Gein of Wisconsin in whose house was found the decapitated body of a woman, ten human heads, and a chair upholstered with human skin. The writer of the article asks 'How did he come to be the man he was' and, then *briefly* answers, 'all evidence pointed to Gein's mother,' evidently thinking the reader would readily accept this without further evidence."[5]

Adam paused over this, then asked, "If she had had any of the bloodthirsty tendencies of her son I believe she would have committed some murders herself and not have carefully raised her son to his adulthood.—Then there are Philip Wylie's loud, assured criticisms about 'moms' with no consideration of what is expected from them in the way of work and adjustments." [6]

"Yes, he's about the best of them." Eve picked up a magazine article she had cut out, "and here's a good illustration. It shows Thomas Wolfe's attitude toward his mother — for children also frequently condemn their mothers without analysis. Tom's mother had eight children. He was the youngest. His father is described in this article as, 'dignified and rather dandified—fond of spouting poetry—a lover of beauty, lavish in every way, and a spree drinker of terrifying endurance and violence.'" Evidently Julia, the mother, found her job of raising these children and pleasing her husband a well-nigh impossible one, so she bought a large, old, frame house to run as a boarding house, then took Tom and her younger children there and cared for them while earning their living. Tom did not understand the size or difficulties of her task. Nor did Tom see that the dollar to her meant food for him in those days.

Instead Tom regarded her as shown in his letters and writings as tightfisted and mercenary with almost no love for him in his boyhood. She becomes in his *Look Homeward Angel* 'the evil power of acquisitiveness, losing every fine value through her insatiable love of property.'—And what makes his attitude toward his mother so striking is the fact that she was the one who appreciated his urge to study writing at Harvard College and financed his study there, while his father disapproved and did nothing to help.—Actually, of course, she loved him in his boyhood and felt that she expressed her love in her work to earn his support and look after him. But children are apt to take all this for granted. By the time each day was over and she had tended to her boarders' meals, rooms and endless demands in addition to her childrens' needs I do believe she was tired out, that she had little leisure to further show Tom her affection."

Adam thought of his own mother, whom his brother had criticized so roundly. "When children lack certain material advantages, attention, or encouragement they often hold their mother responsible, since they have regarded her as the source of their security since babyhood."

"Yes, it doesn't enter their heads that *her* opportunities are usually restricted on all sides, just like those of her children. She, too, is often in need of many material and psychological things, such as love and encouragement. But when her children feel frustrations, or when as adults they recall them, she is often made the end of the chain of circumstances they consider. Why do they stop there?" Eve asked.

"Well," Adam hesitated, "Perhaps it is laziness that they don't think further. Perhaps it is a revolt at her training in their early childhood. She is the one who teaches them the restraints which prepare them to live in civilized society. Perhaps they also find that placing blame on her is generally accepted as reasonable, that it is the fad."

"You have it. That's it. The children, young and grown,

feel it in the air. It could be regarded as a modern form of witchcraft. No scientific studies with comparative control situations have been made which establish that the mothers' bad management was the chief cause of her children's resulting poor adjustment or neuroses, as is widely held. Nor have any scientific studies been made of these cases where she is sweepingly regarded as responsible, which weigh the influence on her children, of their fathers and other family members, of their age group associates, of community factors, or of life in the army or under fire on the battlefield."

When Eve paused Adam went on, "And absolutely no studies have been made which determine what should reasonably be expected from mothers considering their usual restrictions—as to available funds for their work, their education for their jobs, the natural limitations of their time and energy, their dependent relation to the legal heads of their families and the confused and contradictory advice they have received from so-called 'authorities.' I agree, this 'momism' fever carries all the markings of witchcraft. We don't pass court sentences of death for them, but we often succeed in breaking their spirits, causing deep suffering or mental disorganization."

The story of Eve—and Adam

"The story of Eve in the Bible is full of significance.— Since I carry her name I have given the tale lots of thought.—It has many elements of the Babylonian myths which go back to 2,000 B.C. or earlier and are also found in stories of other ancient Asian peoples. In Sanskrit, the early language of India, we find a similar story. A common feature is that the first human being was a man and that woman was created later. In most, the woman introduced evil and represented evil in human life. Mohammed addressed women 'Verily ye are mostly of hell!'

"Then when we come to the later Greek mythology we find the first woman represented as Pandora, beautiful and seductive, given a box by Zeus containing evil spirits. When Pandora later lifts its lid all manner of misery and evil spirits fly out over the world.

"Since we have inherited much of our thinking through the Bible most people in our country even today feel that there could be no other order of events except that the first human created by God was a man.—Amazing that this myth carries on—even in this day of science—but there's a reason."

"Yes, I realize, there's a reason which we'll come to later," Adam said smiling.

"I should also give you here a tale of creation among the Iroquois Indians who have not inherited their myths through the Mesopotamian-European civilizations. This is the striking Iroquois story:

> The woman Aataentsic, fell through a hole in the heavenly realm above the earth to the back of a tortoise. She was already pregnant (she must have become so in heaven) and gave birth to a daughter. This daughter in time bore twin sons. One of these when grown in his violence killed his mother. The other made the beasts and men. Then he disappeared to the east and is said to dwell with his grandmother, the first human being, as his wife."

Adam sat forward somewhat stunned. "Amazing, the first woman came from heaven, evidently created by their gods. Then the second woman, her daughter, was fathered by some god. Two women were created before a man arrived on earth. This first man modestly grew in a woman's womb — shocking!—What a contrast to our story of the man's original creation by a special act of God who on second thought made a woman from his rib to keep him company."

They laughed as Adam added, "And in the Iroquois story the first woman is later married to her grandson — of all things!—Didn't the Iroquois know that older women should be shunned by young men — as they are in our society?"

"I didn't realize when I mentioned this story that it contained these striking features. You are good, Adam, to

188

spot them.—And did you notice that one of these two earliest men blamed a woman, his mother, for something and even killed her. That is, this story does not present the woman as bringing sin into the world, but does show man's tendency to dominate her, to use his greater muscular strength. Does it here symbolize the truth better than our allegory? I think so."

"And why such a different myth about human creation?" Adam asked and then answered himself. "The women must have had at least some influence among the agricultural Iroquois in determining their theories."

"How true! And how important an observation! Students of these Indians know this to be a fact.—Scarcely anyone today recognizes the connection between our Adam and Eve story with the fact that the men probably devised it, for men were dominant in all the cultures which originated and passed it on. It was natural men should have thought this way. They also conceived the main gods to be male.—The centering of their interest upon themselves and their role of the warrior is also revealed in the early art of these civilizations, that of Mesopotamia, Crete and Greece. Actually women's work of bearing and raising children, hauling water and cooking was fully as important as fighting. But the men who set the pattern of thought didn't recognize this, instead showed their first respect for the warriors and men priests in their pictures on the walls, vases and in their carved figures."

"I must introduce a thought here which, I think, *does* apply, Eve. Today the men of our weather bureau label the large storms every year with women's names. These storms are evil things destroying cities, by wind and water, killing people and ruining their homes. Why do they do this? Partly, because they have accepted the ancient prejudices and partly because they are men and it seems to be pleasing to them to consider evil as feminine. All our country's people each year hear of Alice and Bertha, Carol and Doris and many live in dread of their arrival at their home towns." Adam puffed at his pipe.

"An excellent illustration," Eve replied then explained in a sympathetic tone, "The weather bureau men, I guess, are not different from most others. They just happen to *demonstrate* their attitude in this dramatic way. The best advertising agent could not do better."

Adam chuckled as he glanced at the clock and jumped out of his chair. It was past time for the teachers' meeting. They rushed down the hall, across the green to the assembly room and fitted themselves quietly into some vacant seats. The talks won their interest only at intervals, since most of their attention continued on the intriguing subject of women; evil; men the physically stronger, free of carrying and bearing the young; men the ones who invent the stories of creation and name the destructive storms. These surged through their heads, circling around into various formations. They tried to place them in some order and gain some new perspective.

After the meeting they had lunch with friends and walked along the lake shore noticing the reflections of the brilliant colors in the water mirror.

Then back again to their office they came, to see where their explorations would lead them. They were filled with new thoughts and anxious to express them.

Eve started as she picked up some notes from her desk, "In considering attitudes toward women among different peoples we shouldn't omit here the writings we find by the early Christian church fathers about 200 A.D. They continue the more ancient attitude and make it still more denunciative. Here are some more of their remarks. The leading writer among them, Tertullian, declared:

'Woman! You are the gateway of the devil. You persuaded him whom the devil dared not attack directly. Because of you the Son of God had to die. You should always go dressed in mourning and in rags.' 'Natural grace must be obliterated by concealment and negligence, as being dangerous to the glance of the beholder's eyes.'

Another leader wrote: 'woman to whom it brings shame even to reflect of what nature she is.'

"They thus regarded woman as representing the flesh and man the spiritual life. Flesh was a hostile thing, tempting man from his religion.—Of course the only reason woman was regarded as flesh more than man, was because the men were doing this writing; they felt in themselves an intellectual and spiritual side which they refused to admit was also in woman. Their own flesh was regarded as a lowly matter and women's body still lower. And, as we have mentioned, since they denounced sex as evil and held women as the sexual beings, this was another reason why their bodies were 'shameful' things.—One could well ask, what is left that is not evil? And the answer can be only— the minds of men.—Could there be any connection between this belief and the fact that it was the minds of some men which were expressing their attitudes?"

Adam laughed, "I'll let some other man answer that. As to this view about the evilness of sex, we find it discussed again for hundreds of years in the middle ages. Some writers maintained it was sexual desire that should be denounced, not the simple sexual act without passion in marriage necessary for reproduction. Other writers held it was the pleasures in intercourse which were evil, not its indifferent consummation. While still others wrote that the evil element was the submergence of the rational faculty which often accompanies sexual relations, or the suspension of intellectual activity.[8]—I think the last, which of course is connected with the others, was the crux of the matter for them."

"I do, too. We have considered before other factors, such as undesired, heavy reproduction, profligacy and excesses in the general fear and denouncing of sex. — We mustn't fool ourselves into thinking the big argument is over. It still goes on with contraceptives complicating it all, and the degree of evilness in sex relations out of marriage being the present boiling debate."

"That section you wrote about recognizing biological facts and honoring them was put well. It must be done. It is the only course open to us. To denounce sex and consider child-birth unclean or not elevating, is to denounce human life and its survival." Adam interposed.

"I ask, how could the falseness of those long held views be better demonstrated than they have in the ages since Tertullian? We have seen that men are of the flesh and sexual; that as a result women have not been avoided; also that women embody love far more than evil, for they have raised generations of babies with infinite care.

"I should mention here another man of today," Eve continued, "who is one of the great exceptions in seeing light in the complex relationships between men and women. He is Ashley Montagu. I must read just a few of his sentences:

> "The love of a mother for her child is the basic patent and model for all human relationships. Indeed, to the degree to which men approximate in their relationships with their fellow men the love of the mother for her child, to that extent do they move more closely toward the attainment of perfect human relations.
> The genius of woman is the genius of humanity [kindness], and humanity is the supreme form of intelligence. Mankind must learn to understand that all other forms of intelligence must be secondary to the developed *humane* intelligence . . . It is that kind of intelligence with which women are so abundantly endowed."[9]

"Although one would think this might be recognized by now, we still find among us many remnants of the theory that women are sinful and as St. Thomas wrote that they are 'incomplete beings, kind of imperfect men.'"

"One could wonder why men have expressed such animosity toward women," Adam observed while again refilling his pipe, "Why haven't they held a calm and friendly attitude such as they have had generally toward children?"

"That is a tremendous question. Competition for power and control, the same as between other groups accounts for much of it. But, also, man's thoughts of women are filled with the fire of love and hate. His views are influenced by his sexual drives, his strong passion toward the receptive woman he loves; the blind, unreasonable passion toward the woman who turns him down; toward the desired woman who has relations with another man and the 'wilful' wife who is not at his bidding. Murder and suicide and neuroses have accompanied his intense feelings."

Eve continued, "Woman's urge to maintain her own life, and at times to be a full individual with autonomy over her own body and actions has sometimes collided with the man's desires. He has become as aggravated as a child who cannot obtain what he wants. — All those men through history who have written like Tertullian have evidenced their primitive and childish attitude. They have not been socialized in their relation to women and learned that co-operation, not domination, is the basis of happy, human relations. — And all the myths and stories about men's God-created superiority have continued to prevent this socialization."

"We must present here the recognition by psychologists that everyone's thinking is somewhat warped by his particular experiences and wishes," Adam said slowly. "Also the recognition that most every fortunate person has tendencies to feel superior to others, which is a form of wishful thinking that cheers him up. And every group and country especially if it is more powerful also tends to feel superior. This goes along with the human tendency to make scapegoats of someone, or some group, to blame others for undesired events. Those on top, anxious to shift any condemnation from themselves, claim others are responsible. Naturally those in the weaker position are made the scapegoats since they can't effectively defend themselves, their influence or economic resources being insufficient to spread their views or make an impression on those who don't want to understand the truth. Much of this scapegoat thinking is unconscious and follows the line of least resistance in relieving one's angry feelings, like the master kicking his dog when provoked over bad luck or a mistake he himself has made. He hardly knows just what he has done but his pet dog takes it in order to keep his home. One of the best examples is the Nazi persecution of the Jews for Germany's troubles. It should have opened the eyes of the world to this psychological tendency."

"A very important observation, Adam! Crucial in our analysis of this attitude toward woman, so vividly pictured in the Pandora and Eve stories and the other writings I have mentioned."

"And our book expresses the thoughts of a scapegoat group (the women) trying to persuade the more powerful of certain truths which their wishful thinking leads them to ignore." [10] Adam added as he looked at Eve, who was wondering if their effort would make a dent.

Other examples of warped thinking

"It's not only such tales of creation that reveal men's attitudes but their interpretation of all sorts of facts. For instance," Eve thought a while, "here is their interpretation of the facts of reproduction down through many centuries. They taught that women's part in growing the child before birth was simply that of giving it nourishment, the womb being like a nest for the new life placed in it by the all-important male, the woman's body adding no living cell which carried inheritance to the child. — Eventually scientists discovered that the woman provided an egg cell which joined the man's sperm, the two cells together of equal importance in starting new life, both carrying chromosomes which determined the child's inheritance. This discovery of 1854 men were forced to accept since it was in the field of demonstrable science, not of religious stories."

"The knowledge must have allowed women to hold their heads a little higher, Eve."

"Oh, yes, it's interesting how science keeps coming to their rescue from imaginative beliefs and attitudes which always belittled her abilities and contributions. We've mentioned how psychology is helping in the work demands placed on her and population studies in heavy reproductive requirements," Eve said. "Here is another illustration in physiology. The time-worn theory held by men was that if a pair is barren it is due to the wife's failure. And likewise, if only girl babies are born the wife has also failed. We read in the Bible of wives being put aside or divorced because *they* were barren, or bore only girls. Henry VIII of England used these reasons to get rid of some of his wives. In the recent year of 1948 the Queens of Egypt and Iran were both divorced by their royal husbands because they had borne no sons. Queen Farida of Egypt had born three daughters though she was only 27 years old but this was not enough.[11] — Of course biologists now know that the physiology of reproduction is such that on the whole men bear equal responsibility with women for infertility and for the sex of the child."

"All of those masculine theories offer an interesting relationship to the truth, an interesting bias. Could anyone claim no male advantages were gained by regarding women as solely responsible for these things? They gave him such self-confidence and provided such useful justifications for taking new wives."

Eve nodded. "Let's glance at some other theories such as those explaining why woman averages smaller stature and undergoes suffering in childbirth. As we have said, men have held she was smaller because she was less favored by the gods, but today it is thought that she is smaller because a girl's growth usually stops at time of menstruation when considerable calcium is absorbed in monthly relining of the womb and its discharge. Her puberty begins earlier than the boy's.

"Then as to suffering in childbirth, we find in the Bible that this is because she is cursed by God for her sins. I can't conceive of a more depressing and ego-destructive theory for women than that. Today scientists recognize that the birth process is more difficult for human females than for lower primates because we stand upright, which has meant a larger and more solid pelvic bone, and stronger attachment of the fetus within the woman's body. Also, the human head is proportionately very large, which likewise complicates birth. In short, the features which have allowed men's dominance through his physical powers in the primitive struggle are due to women's reproductive functions: menstruation with resulting smaller size, months of pregnancy, childbirth, nursing and menopause. All have incapacitated her in some degree during past ages for resisting the male's authority over her. These energy-absorbing tasks of course allow the life of all men to be renewed, as well as all women. Yet, she is not only refused proper compensation, economic and social, for these functions, but is still considered to be created an inferior being, less favored by God. And this view is embodied in many of our current laws, such as those making all men the legal heads of their families, irrespective of their character. — It's time we looked at it all in the bright light of day — and of science!"

They relaxed as they listened to the carillon again playing some familiar old tunes. Then roused themselves back to their discussion.

"We should add here that women's extensive abilities have been recognized for ages, her power to grow new human beings, to bear them, to work capably withstanding weariness," Eve said dreamily as if thinking out loud as she puffed her cigarette. "Clearly primitive man was overawed by her reproductive powers, as we said, and was uneasy that he did not share more in her ability to bring forth new life. An illustration of this is that ceremony of couvade in which the father pretends that he has born the baby, or helped through his own physical suffering, so he goes to bed and pretends being ill for some days. This ceremony has been found in all parts of the world—China, Africa, Europe and among the Indians of South America.—

196

I guess a young person in the family could not be sure whether father or mother had actually born the baby.— For similar reasons there is a ceremony among some primitive men of pretending that they menstruate."

"Yes, *couvade* nicely camouflaged one of women's main contributions."

"It must have been a trying job, to say the least, for women through milleniums to have lived under the control of those holding warped theories about their evilness and barrenness. But making things still more difficult were theories about their daily work. They could keep going most their waking hours, men thought, far better than men could themselves — and all their chores were regarded as a lowly nature, not like hunting wild animals or earning large sums in the business world."

"These theories about women did not need to be consistent," Adam smiled, "nor hold up under rational inquiry. Women could be held as lowly and evil beings while showing great patience, persistence and affection in caring for their families."

CHAPTER 10

1. These experiments have been described in many articles. *Scientific American*, January 1954. Also *Life Stress and Bodily Disease*, Association for Research in Nervous and Mental Disease, Vol. XXIX, 1949 proceedings.
2. In probably the most extensive study yet made the average time spent in homemaking by housewives was found to be 51 hours per week in rural households and 48 to 49 in urban households. This study did not include the poorest families. Study by Gertrude Schmidt Weiss, *Bureau of Home Economics, U.S. Dept. of Agriculture*, 1939.

   Also see, Jean Warren, "Use of Time in its Relation to Home Management," *Cornell University Agricultural Experimental Station*, 1939, p. 66.

   Margaret J. Hagood, *Mothers of the South*, University of North Carolina Press, Chapel Hill, 1939, pp. 42, 86, 110.

No such complete studies have been made in later years.

3. Alva Myrdal, *Nation & Family*, Harper & Brothers, 1941.
   Social Sweden, published by the Social Welfare Board of Sweden, 1952.
4. Reports in English by Margareta Nordström, Kungl. Socialstyrelsen, Stockholm, Avdehingen för Social Hempjalp, 1953-1956.
5. *Life* magazine, December 2, 1957.
6. Philip Wylie, *Generation of Vipers*, Rinehart, 1955.
7. Robert Coughlan, "Tom Wolfe's Surge to Greatness," *Life* magazine, September 17, 1956.
8. Clive S. Lewis, *The Allegory of Love*, Oxford University Press, London, 1953, p. 14-17.
9. *The Natural Superiority of Women*, The Macmillan Co., 1954, pp. 141, 142, 149 and ch. 10 entitled "The Genius of Woman as the Genius of Humanity."
10. Abraham Myerson, *Speaking of Man*, Alfred A. Knopf, 1950, ch. 5, entitled, "Woman, the Authorities' Scapegoat."
11. King Farouk of Egypt and Shah of Iran were the divorcing husbands, *New York Times*, November 20, 1948.
    The Shah of Iran divorced his second wife, Soraya, in 1958 for bearing no son.

CHAPTER 11

Is the Mother Often Divorced Just Because She Is Human?

"In considering whether the mother is a human or magical being we should look behind the curtain placed by marriage around the pair. How have these various theories influenced her sexual life?" Eve remarked as they continued their discussion. "We should not go back into the past here and we can only glance into the present."

Is the mother expected to be superhuman in her sexual life?

"A good way to determine present attitudes about what a husband may expect from his wife is to read the current magazine and newspaper articles about it," Adam observed. "They say she should strive zealously to keep him passionately interested by making herself perpetually young and vivacious—"

"Even if bearing and raising several children or if earning outside in addition to housekeeping—or if getting older and naturally more subdued—" Eve added.

"She must pretend happy effervescence, they advise."

"Yes, and she should rise above her husbands failings and weaknesses, quietly overlook and forgive them with great conciliation. In their sexual life particularly she must follow this policy. If he is too quick, clumsy or crude, if he does not inspire her response, she nevertheless must strive to satisfy him, for that is the way to hold his interest, to preserve the core of their marriage. — Even if she should fear another pregnancy just after a baby has been born, or is exhausted from her work and is thoroughly depressed over the task of trying to please him, she must feel affection and passion toward him, they write. — And even if she feels rejected she is advised by one writer to arouse him in sexual relations which involve 'her warmth, gaiety, charm, hunger and ecstasy.'[1] May I say that is humanly impossible." Eve thought a minute, then continued, "This adviser would reply to me, if she can't feel all this, she can *'pretend'* in order to stimulate her husband and help his ego. And again I say, that is also impossible. She is not magical. She might carry out this game a few times but it can't be done continuously.—Love is a two-way affair. It is more of a circular reaction—running from one to the other and back again—than any other feeling in existence. If a husband wants his wife's love there is only one course, that is, through his love for her, which includes kindness, helpfulness and effort to promote her well-being. Her affection for him lies in *his* hands. Her love for him is not the result of her willing its existence."

"Oh, yes, love and passion are the *natural consequence,* as you say, Eve, of many factors, just like crying and laughing are. The will to cry or laugh is relatively unimportant. — The husband's feelings and actions toward his wife are of prime importance in rousing or killing her love for him."

"So, for real love we need evidences of the husband's wholehearted involvement in the needs of his wife and her feeling of security in her relationship to him. She should not be in a position so that she needs to pretend that she is joyfully bubbling over if she is depressed, hurt, tired or simply cool. — And of course, Adam, all this can be put the other way around, the husband should not have to pretend. — Perhaps I should modify this by saying that some pretense may be tolerated to carry a couple over a difficult period but it cannot be continued for long without demoralizing the pretender and misleading the mate."

"And here comes in the economic setup of marriage whereby the wife and children are usually dependent upon the husband," Adam observed, "so that she often feels she *must* pretend in order to be the attractive, happy woman and the highly pleased woman in intercourse. We should recognize that many writers, whole groups of persons at periods through history have held that this very dependence

200

of the wife means that her complete freedom to be herself in the relationship is endangered, and that therefore the spontaneity basic to mutually-thrilling sexual experience is often lacking. A good example is the 'courtly love,' we mentioned of the twelfth century in France whose underlying theory was just this, that in marriage where a wife must obey her husband there could be little or no mutual passion. It was held that only relationships outside of marriage in the feudal courts, such as those between the lord's wife (the mistress of the manor) and her damsels with the knights and squires of the court could embody the highest degree of love. The basic elements in those relationships were humility on the man's part, courtesy and the 'Religion of Love'. They held it essential that the woman should be able always to withhold herself or reward her lover."

"I imagine," Eve added, "a similar view was held among the cultured and educated hetaerae of Greece and their men companions."

"Yes, we could talk at length about this. At present, I could say, all Christian countries are trying to turn their eyes away from some of these inconsistencies in our marriage institution." Adam glanced out of the window as the sun suddenly brightened, lighting the yellow leaves just outside while he tried to express his thoughts. "They are claiming that since a man and woman once freely chose each other for marriage, continuous free and spontaneous action in sexual and other matters is assured both the man and his dependent wife. They seem to think that if the man is preached to enough he will allow his wife to be entirely herself and to withhold her favors or grant them, even when he has the legal right to expect her 'wifely duty' and the opportunity to readily move to another lover."

"Well put."

"Adam picked up a book from his desk saying, "I'd like to read something which puts advice given wives today in more extreme form. It is from 'The Sacred Books of the East' and embodies attitudes found in the leading Oriental religions:

'Though destitute of virtue, or seeking pleasure (else-where) or devoid of good qualities, (yet) a husband must be constantly worshipped as a god by a faithful wife.[2]

'She who shows disrespect to (a husband even if he) is addicted to (some evil) passion, is a drunkard, or diseased shall be deserted for three months (and be) deprived of her ornaments and furniture.

'*She* who drinks spirituous liquor (however), is of bad conduct, rebellious, diseased, mischievous or *wasteful* may at any time be superseded (by another wife).'[3]

"Interesting—simply wastefulness, as determined by the husband, gives him ground to desert her. — But she must worship him as a god even if he is devoid of all good qualities," Eve observed. "Of course it is asking the impossible of her, asking that she rise above her husband with super-human understanding, forgiveness and self-control, though she is much younger than he, less experienced and educated, less secure and is taught that she is created inferior."

"Really not too different, is it, from advice given wives today in some popular periodicals?"

They sat up at a sudden rap on the door by one of their associates who wanted to talk to Adam. Eve excused herself, went out into the campus for a stroll. She met a neighbor, one of the student's wives who was doing clerical work in the library to help her husband get his Ph.D. degree and was also typing his thesis which was now half done. As Eve went on to pick up some ice cream she thought how awful it would be if her friend's husband later divorced her, taking all the advantages of his Ph.D with him. Eve knew that the wife, a bright person, could be studying for her own higher degree instead of pounding the typewriter for him.

Too rapid population growth and the mother

After Eve returned to the office Adam and she enjoyed their refreshments while they listened to news over the radio. Then Eve said, "Perhaps about the most important result of the required submissiveness of the wife in sex is a matter we have not touched on. It is the rapid growth of the world population, 5000 persons added every hour, or 120,000 more persons every day. Most wide-awake, intelligent people have recently become aware of overcrowding our earth. This rapid increase is due to lowering the death rate through spreading medical knowledge and care while the birth rate remains high especially in the extensive, less developed countries. The world's natural resources, mainly food, are not being increased at the rate of population growth, and resources cannot possibly be increased corresponding with the mouths to be fed, if they keep on growing in numbers as they are at present. Already in many of the backward countries we witness the tragic development of less food consumption per capita than in the 1930's. And gradually less vacant arable land becomes available for the peoples of crowded areas to move into.

"The connection between this and wives' 'marital duty' required around the world and the thought that their energies can be fantastically stretched may not seem clear. Many people have held that the mothers of these Asian and African large families have generally wanted them. However, recent studies have revealed that a majority of mothers in these teeming countries would like to limit the number of their children, to space their pregnancies and have smaller families.[4] These mothers know they could give each child more food and that their limited strength could do a better job in cleanliness and child-care if their families were not so big.—Yet, their culture is overlaid with assumptions that husbands should determine their sexual lives, that the more children they bear the better, the more sons they have the more sacred is the father's position. Their religions, laws and precepts, created largely by the men, under which these wives were raised, all tell them something contrary to what they learn from experience. — Even the men in our country — as we noted — are somewhat separated from the basic struggle of keeping children clean and fed. As a result they often do not appreciate the connection between the quality of children's care and their number — much less do they do so in China and Africa."

"Therefore," Adam interposed, "the crucial job of getting these mushrooming populations to decrease their birth rate will involve changing some of these ancient theories about wives and heavy reproduction. It will involve giving women more power than formerly."

"Yes, it's going to be a tremendous job to turn about — limit their births and incidentally lead women into greater independence. Yet the governments of India, Japan, Egypt, Pakistan and China have recognized this must be done and are starting such programs. Every country will soon become interested in its population growth and will develop plans to keep it within certain limits or at a level — and these plans will give mothers more autonomy and aid them in ways previously undreamed of. Sweden is the forerunner in working out such a program.

"We should drastically slow down the rapid world population growth at least until we learn how to manage ourselves. Without vigorous attacks we should expect a more and more crowded earth; with the struggle for resources becoming increasingly desperate; the irritations, maddening competition and clashes growing in number and seriousness — all along with the development of such weapons that a button pressed by an angry person can destroy mankind," Eve concluded, waiting for Adam's response.

"Yes, it looks like accelerated desperation in the struggle for the wherewithal of life. Perhaps before the remnant dies off its members will wander aimlessly around, raving maniacs." Adam added after a pause, "Paleontologists know so well the story of many animal species by their fossil remains in the rocks — how they evolved from simpler forms to the more complex, and sometimes how certain species grew elaborate organs that seemed to cause their destruction. For instance, there were molluscs which developed large, fancy shells with protuberances and then died out. Also deer which grew enormous branched antlers which caught in the trees, and then became extinct. These overdeveloped organs interfered with adjustment to their environment.—Homo sapiens perhaps has overdeveloped that organ called the brain, which has invented our array of life-killing devices — and this may cause its downfall."

"His urges or instincts toward peaceful living seem to be weak compared to those leading to the excitement of war and domination of each other," Eve went on. "Most important, this urge to fight is mainly in the male of the species psychologists are agreed — not only in the human males but the males of all mammals, probably caused by the male hormones.[5] It *could* be balanced by women's drive to preserve human life, to prevent injuries and suffering.[6] But men call them 'soft' and hold them unfit for the council chambers whose decisions often lead to war. — I believe that as we walk the razor's edge between our downfall or a bright new age the weight of women's voice should be heeded in all ways. It may well be sufficient to land us on the side of life filled with hope and progress. — They know what human behavior leads to strife, have seen it in their children and are sensitive to this whole area of personal relations. *They* know the dangers of bearing more children than can be raised in health, the tenseness of struggles when necessities are scarce and the wildness of angry men set against each other."

"That is a dramatic statement, Eve. I'm glad it is recorded just as you spoke it! — What a contrasting picture you present of women compared to that of the evil ones, the tempters and the troublemakers. — You know, I had a vague glimpse of what you say about women when I was in the midst of the purely male world in the Battle of the Bulge — wounded, crawling men around me, wagons carrying away the dead—all in the weird light of exploding bombs. Horror is a mild word for it."

Eve put her hand on his shoulder. After a few minutes she tried to summarize her thoughts. "The brute-force method of handling human life is fatal. It has led to the

205

present pattern, as we've agreed, whereby man's greater physical strength converted and combined with economic power has placed women in a weak position, excluded them from controlling groups and made them dependents in the family. It is leading to overcrowding our earth and placing confidence in nuclear weapons to bring peace. It is driving to excesses with no balance-wheel gained through vital love toward each other. New principles must be introduced to save us. They are those of cooperation, bending understandingly to the weak, caring for all children and planning ahead so these things can be done extensively."

Adam knocked out the tobacco from his pipe, cleaned it and put it away as he was forming a fresh conception of homo sapiens' lopsided pattern—and of the male hormones carrying too much influence. It was like viewing human life from the vantage point of a man from Mars who in his brief visit could notice only the major, all-pervading relationships such as those between women and men.

Eve saw his mind was not closed as so many would be at such thoughts. "Just one more area we should glance into which well demonstrates what we have been saying, the area of divorce. Here we see how slight the grounds may be leading the husband to leave his wife and children, and how he often controls her thoughts and actions through his power to divorce."

Noting some couples' steps to divorce

"Let us consider some of the divorced couples we know. It's interesting to gather together some of our first hand knowledge. Won't you, Adam, present the case of Henry?"

"All right. You remember he and Susan lived near me. They had four children who seemed to be well cared for. Susan worked hard, big washes were hung on the line twice a week. She did all the cleaning and made many of their clothes. Clearly it was a struggle to keep within a college instructor's small salary. She often looked real tired and of course her own clothes were very inexpensive. — Well, Henry told me at the time of their divorce that she was quite a bore, let her appearance sag, couldn't share his interest in physics, nor would she go with him to meetings and conferences. She seemed like an awful weight around his neck, he said. — We had seen him before the divorce playing with a pretty graduate student in his laboratory and some of us were wondering. The student was as fresh as a daisy, clearly had funds of her own and was studying physics. Later, we knew they were having an affair. Of course she was a more exciting companion. As Susan got wind of this she naturally became upset and said things which were not becoming a well-poised lady. — Anyway, next we learned *he* was getting a divorce on grounds of her mental cruelty and marrying his new love. He got a job at another college while she with the four children moved away. It would be interesting to know how she is making out. She moved to the town where her parents live."

"My guess is that most mothers who read your words will completely understand what happened, for they know Susan couldn't do the impossible," Eve observed.

"And many men who read it will picture tired, boresome stay-at-home Susan and think Henry was justified in leaving her."

They mentioned other cases. Then Adam said, "Excuse me if I make a general observation. Certainly the fact that great numbers of wives are weak and at fault is not the chief reason for the high divorce rate. Likewise, it is perhaps not mainly because great numbers of husbands are at fault. Instead it is likely that our ancient institution often demands unreasonable things of us and requires unnecessary restrictions."

"Ha, ha, you have it there, Adam. Perhaps we should have a variety of marriage patterns, some with fewer binding factors than others, some for short terms. Perhaps in the future we will live largely as individual units, give up the difficult job of living in twosomes. — I am later going to present an idea which would allow sex relations between these one-person units and still connect *both* partners with a possible or actual resulting child, and lift

207

relations above the irresponsible and fleeting."

"Well, Eve, that *is* something! But now we are discussing divorces today, the relationship between them and the marriage structure. I would say the features of marriage which lead to its breakup are: too close and continuous living together with some degree of cabin fever often developing and the strict pattern of sexual relations compared with the desire for some variation in mates."

"We must include the division of labor in marriage whereby the wife usually performs each day considerable work of a much lower nature than she is capable. Also her economic dependence upon her husband in spite of her work and child care activities."

"Yes, these and other features often cause a couple's problems to expand to an exploding point. Life together becomes impossible. The results are desertion, divorce, mental breakdowns and murder of spouses. Let us recognize it, Eve. — Can you think of another case you've seen inside and out?"

"Yes, there is George, my cousin, whom I know quite well. His income was rather small, so after their three children were at school Florence earned at a job near home, which at first allowed them some valued vacation trips and comforts. But George became a heavy drinker and made big bets at the horse races, where he lost quite a sum each year — about as much as she earned. Of course this was disheartening for Florence, who was getting worn down with the double job of clerking and housekeeping. When her health gave way George felt she was simply an oversensitive, complaining woman and after she gave up her job for a few months he urged her to return to it. He told me that he was sure it was good for her, it kept her mind off herself, and that he promised to give her 'the big boost' of washing the dinner dishes every Sunday. — Well, she went back to her job, he continued to lose in gambling and things within the family became more and more strained. She developed the strange uncontrollable habit of shutting her eyes even when driving the auto, and had frequent severe headaches. Her patience became short. George thought her shrewish and began staying away from home on business trips. I don't know if he fell in love with another woman or had an affair, but no doubt sexual life with his wife degenerated. — After the divorce he confidently gave me his explanation, assuming I would consider it entirely satisfactory. He said, 'she was impossible, too bossy, clearly a neurotic, and I just couldn't take it any longer. We fell completely out of love with each other.'"

Adam got out of his chair and played with a paperweight on the filing cabinet as he said, "The *order* of events is so important in analyzing a relationship! If George had come to a marriage counselor toward the end of his marriage, described Florence's actions and attitudes demonstrating that she was then neurotic, just what insight into the situation would the counselor have had? Would the counselor have held this as justified grounds for George's leaving her and the children, as he listened to the father's plans with passive assent?"

"You wonder. — Let's stop to compare these reasons the husbands gave for their divorces. Certain complaints about their abandoned wives occur over and over again."

"Yes, that's true, Eve, as I think of other cases. Let's see they are briefly that: — they have fallen out of love; she says things that are not pleasing to him; seems bossy; her mind has not grown as his so she's not a mental companion; she is no longer well groomed; refuses to fall in with his hobbies, be it gardening, mountain climbing or dogs — or does not adjust to his affair with another woman."

"That's about it. And *that list is all important!* It does *not* include her willful refusal to perform the basic tasks she assumes under the laws upon her marriage: that of caring for her husband and the children, cooking, cleaning, etc.; that of her sexual 'marital duty' and of being faithful to him; that of living in the domicile he chooses and endeavoring to run the home with the funds he provides. — I would say practically all divorced and deserted mothers have carefully raised their children and to the best of their abilities they have performed these tasks under the conditions provided them year after year, but all this is taken for granted by these husbands, whose complaints are that they did not perform them with the competence he, as the judge, thinks they should have used. Nor, with the joyful, loving spirit he thinks they should have maintained. Nor, did they expand their energies to join him in his hobby interests and adjust to his 'other woman.' — In other words it is these refinements and feelings, often unreasonably expected, which caused his complaints and rejection," Eve concluded speaking softly and slowly as she did when she was intense.

"It is always the person in the powerful position, such as that of the husband with economic control of the family, who may reject for minor reasons," Eve continued. "Remember that quotation from the religious books of the East which says a mother may be divorced simply for doing what her husband regards as wasteful — no more than that. Actually in most Oriental countries he need only be displeased and write a 'note of divorcement' in order to be free of her."

"In our country it is only slightly different considering the technicalities available to the husband in getting a divorce, such as withholding necessary funds from his wife and going to some easy-divorce place," Adam observed as he lit a cigarette.

"The wife's position is actually often one of submission to *arbitrary rule*. That is, no laws clearly define the work she is expected to carry out, nor do they define the husband's authority. His legal position as head of the family, plus his usual superior economic power, in addition to the absence of any restraining laws as to what he may demand from his wife, give him what is called arbitrary power over her — the power kings have held over subjects and which people have fought against since written history began. — Do you know the husband who admires and marries the practical woman who spends little money on her clothes and gives almost no time to make-up, then falls for an expensively dressed, carefully made-up woman and forsakes his practical wife? — Many husbands change their ideas and some don't really know just what they want in a woman."

"Quite true, Eve."

"Oh, I should add another case, one that goes into big business. I can speak about it with some assurance because I know some of the husband's business associates as well as the wife and the children who are now grown and married. — It was the marriage of a bright, intellectual woman who worked for a period in the field of investments, the same field as her husband's. During their first years her earnings were important to family support and in building up some capital. Then the husband, Fred, felt uneasy over her unusual abilities and insisted that she retire from business and devote herself to her home. She didn't want to do this, it seemed too confining, but she had no choice. The usual elements entered here, the close living together, weariness of each other, common problems with their four children, his taking her contribution in child raising and home care as of small value, their diminishing sexual pleasures and a younger woman on the scene who thought him a little god. As the years passed their relationship became more and more strained. When their children had finished college Fred finally got a divorce—instead of agreeing to a yearly alimony he passed her as a full settlement about a thirtieth part of the million dollars he then had in his name. He felt that the money he had earned while she raised his children was rightfully his own and overlooked the fact she might have earned and saved as much as he if she had stayed in business. His actions were encouraged by our laws which do not require a husband to tell his wife the amount of his income nor his total property, also allow him, in most states, to consider the family savings as his personally. — A few years after the divorce Fred married the woman who had been his secretary over twenty years and with whom he had been in love during the period the marriage was breaking."

"Very interesting, Eve. I can't help but think of that file of newspaper clippings you showed me of well-known men in various fields who have taken new and younger wives after they became wealthy or successful." Adam softly chuckled. "It would be fun to mention the impressive list."

"Some would say women should not be intellectual. It's true most men don't care for brainy wives. — Yet we find men leaving women whom they consider a bore. The truth is that our marriage setup allows a husband to ask of his wife whatever is pleasing to him and to reject her if she doesn't satisfy his particular wishes."

Adam nodded. "There is an old saying, 'Take a wife so she may carry you in her hands.' And it has more truth than a man thinks—unless he has had the experience of suddenly losing his wife so he alone must run the home and care for his children. It seems that some men need two wives, one to carry them in their younger years while they get established in business, and another fresh and stronger to give them a further lift, look up to them and aid in their sexual lives during their later years."

"And some men need three or more."

Adam then said, "We should recognize that in our country public opinion, which women probably now have a larger share in making than our laws, is having some influence. It is critical of the divorcing fathers who have abandoned two or three of their families. I've certain instances in mind."

"Yes, sometimes such fathers are not accepted in certain groups which include some thinking women. — Adam, to return to the matter of husbands' reasons for breaking up a marriage, we should recognize this: That after a wife realizes that her marriage is on the rocks, that her husband's love has gone forever, and that they may muddle along a while for the sake of the children, she may strike regarding some jobs required of wives, such as refusing intercourse, or performance of some minor household task. Sometimes a father will claim that because she has done this when completely discouraged, that this is the reason for his divorce. Of course that is unfair. Her behavior the last months of their marriage was a result of its actual breakdown and not the cause."

"Oh, I have heard many a husband's tale of a wife throwing dishes, calling names, or saying hateful things to him — these as reasons for his decision to leave the family. He implies that no one could live with such a person, never recognizing that she is a human being, after all, and is simply reacting as people do to what has gone before."

"The husband often expects here the fantastic impossible, that she remain sweet and poised while she comes to the full realization of her weak position in marriage and his taking advantage of it. — Of course, along with her years of chores she has gone through monthly menstruation, which is depressing to many, pregnancy, childbirth and perhaps years of menopause which are by no means easy. All this should be regarded as work—internal work—which is part of reproduction, and which alone should win some future security from her husband and society."

"When you think it over it *does* look as though many mothers are deserted and divorced because they are only human, because they haven't the magical powers their husbands would like," Adam said as he took a long pull on his cigarette.

"More truth in that than people guess! If that idea were realized, how it would help the millions of mothers who are made to feel they have miserably failed. They know they have given to the limit of their strength in working for their families—but usually do not see the whole situation in perspective and that this business of divorce might be called the modern form of polygamy or multiple wives."

"That puts it simply, Eve."

"One wonders if girls should be prepared for this — that

213

is, to be either a first wife of a young man who later leaves her; or a second wife of an older, divorced one, with the radically different situation in each. What are the pros and cons of the first wife's and the second wife's position? — It looks as though the man often learns during his first marriage what can't be done along with keeping his wife's love. He becomes somewhat socialized in his relation to women, and his second wife benefits from his experience and knowledge. Also the relation with the first wife has often suffered from the strain during the father's younger years while getting established."

"Yes, in many cases," Adam replied. "It's surely hard on first wives to be used for the process of their husband's education, then left with their children for no fault of their own. — Do you know that popular song which indicates that some men recognize this?

'Looking back over my life I can see where I caused you strife.
But I know, yes, I know I'll never make that same mistake again.
Once my cup was overflowing but I gave nothing in return
Now I can't begin to tell you what a lesson I have learned!'

"Good, Adam. That's to the point. — The usual extremely different positions of the divorced father from that of the mother make it a horrible solution to an unhappy marriage. Of course there are exceptions where the mother is wealthy or is young and attractive so she may find a satisfactory new husband. But the position in which most mothers are left does not square with their past years of service to their families. *If* they were as well off financially as their husbands upon divorce, had experience and opportunity for earning in as interesting a manner as their husbands, opportunities to marry attractive, capable men their own age or younger, as their husbands have to marry younger women, and children were well provided for, we might regard divorce as a good solution. But the marriage setup has built a situation wherein the divorced mother often has no

214

earning experience except in housework and almost no savings of her own. We should consider the advantages of placing her in a position so that a couple could separate and both satisfactorily adjust to a new life without guilty feelings and bitterness. This will be necessary if we are to move away from the rigid and unreasonable features of the present pattern.

"I see no other way except that the mother should be in a position similar to other working people. She should continually receive the wherewithal to assure her present and future health and growth. One step could be taken now, that is, that while she gives full time to care of children and home, one half of any family savings should be put regularly into her name.—At present, husbands may consider half their savings belong to their wives on their federal income tax returns. This reduces their taxes. Instead of just *saying* this on their returns, this property should actually be the wives' for her present or future use."

"And there are mothers whose husband's earnings are regularly all spent for the family who should also receive some future security for their work," Adam observed. "That and the whole problem of the economic position of the mother is a big subject and will have to wait until our next book, won't it?"

"This would be twice as long if we got into it, for the question comes in, to what extent should the government be concerned in the proper feeding and raising of its future citizens and much more?"

"I think Eve, we ought to add that there are some marriages where the woman has a fortune or is a big earner, such as a moving picture star, so she is not economically dependent upon her husband. There is one of these among perhaps every hundred thousand wives. She is in the position where she can leave her husband without her children suffering financially. But she takes the steps to break her marriage far less frequently than the economically independent hubsand, for if the father loves the children she usually feels the importance of keeping the family together."

Adam put a new tape in the recording machine while Eve studied the bright maple leaves swaying just outside. As they took their seats she remarked, "One may think I over-emphasize the influence of our divorce laws upon marriage. Let's see how I can put my idea—guess it will be a simile again. — When I was in South America I saw a herd of wild horses, not broken to the saddle, rearing and racing around in a manner most can't even imagine who have seen only our well-broken, harnessed ones. In our country the process of breaking colts includes driving them into a corral. Then one by one each is taught to walk and obey, later to become used to a bit in his mouth. Finally, to a saddle on his back.

"Well, all of us human beings are really saddled in the process of bringing us from a wild animal state, in which we would remain if raised by a wolf in the forests according to the stories of a wolf-child, to that of a civilized person. In particular, young folks when they become parents are broken-in to restrictions and responsibilities, for they constantly deny themselves many personal desires in order to care for their children."

"True, we could say that both wild horses and parents are taught to wear a saddle," Adam chuckled.

"This is my main point," Eve continued. "Besides the techniques of training the colts, they must be kept in the corral. Keeping them there for periods is as important as all the other steps in their training."

Adam broke in, "Oh yes, I see. Besides the process of training the father to trot in the saddle, which we could say was done by the requirements that he support his family — he must be kept in the corral. Keeping him there is as important as all the rest, if he is to care for his children."

"And the divorce laws correspond to the fence of the corral. If these laws have large loopholes so he can readily run away from his family, all the requirements for his care

216

and support become as naught. So I say our divorce laws are a crucial part of our marriage institution. They can actually determine the manner of life within marriage more than any other laws. They increase the temptations to escape which surround the father — the same as a large hole in the corral fence tempts the horse in training especially when he sees greener open fields outside."

"Good, very good, Eve! We have mentioned his main temptations: those of starting a new, exciting love-life and carrying most of the family savings and his income to his new home—this is allowed by our biased court proceedings as well as the laws. The person who can afford to engage the more clever lawyer has great advantages. — And I must mention the temptation to the husband who is a blunderer in business or of an irascible nature to gain self-confidence by taking a new partner and starting again."

"And we must include the ease with which he can obtain a divorce if he has the know-how and some funds." Eve then pulled out a volume from the shelf, saying "Chester Vernier who has made the most complete study of these laws writes, 'Divorce statutes are not a product of logic alone. They are a resultant of mixed elements. Religion, sentiment and historical accident all have combined to form an inharmonious and incongruous legislative product.' [7] And these are the laws which frame our marriage institution — different in the various states and such that most divorce cases are filled with perjury."

"I believe you have analyzed it correctly! No doubt there is a drone-bee tendency for men to want a variety in mates and for some to escape child support — and along with this we have a system of laws and customs which encourages these tendencies. I hope my brothers will excuse my frankness."

" 'Have no children,' some would say. That would eliminate the main problem in relations between man and woman. Women could then support themselves as men do, both sharing light housework. Husbands and wives could change partners perhaps without great tragedies."

They both smiled as Adam replied, "True, raising children is the crux of most man-woman problems. — Men may not like your picture of the saddle and the corral. We could ask them, if they don't do their full part in raising their children, who should carry it for them?"

"Recognizing and weighing all this, I'd say if we want successful marriages we should reconsider the weaknesses of the marriage pattern, the laws which surround it—all in the light of our new knowledge of psychology and physiology and our professed belief in democratic principles. We should ask ourselves: What pattern will best preserve mutual love between a mother and father— What pattern will best create the health and happiness of each? What setup is likely to accomplish these while children are provided careful care? And," Eve continued, "of course the main purpose of the pattern should not be to keep the father in the corral but rather to make him *want* to do his full share in the enterprise of raising his children."

"Oh, yes, we should not expect superhuman performance from the mother or the father. He must be allowed means of earning a living along with maintaining the reserves in vitality necessary to feel affection and show it to his wife and children. This involves his salary, his education, the requirements of his earning job and the number of his children," Adam concluded. "How all these influences dovetail into each other and determine the opportunities of each new generation!"

CHAPTER 11

1. Marion Hilliard, "Love, Life and Women," *New York Journal-American*, newspaper, September 8, 1957.
   Marion Hilliard, "The Art of Love," *The Reader's Digest*, June 1957.

218

2. G. Buhler, *The Sacred Books of the East*, translated by various Oriental scholars, Ed. by F. Max Muller, Vol. XXV, Clarendon Press, Oxford, England, 1886, p. 326.
3. Ibid., pp. 78, 80.
4. *Population Research Foundation of Jamaica*, Report of 1957. Hon. A. G. Curphey, chairman.

   C. Chandrasekaran, Director of United Nations Office of Population Studies in India, "Cultural Patterns in Relation to Family Planning in India," presented to the Third International Conference of Planned Parenthood in Bombay, November 1952. *Report of Proceedings*, published by The Family Planning Association of India.

   In Japan the birth rate has been *drastically* reduced from 34 per thousand in 1949 to 18 in 1959, as a result of a change in their men's ideology regarding large families and their laws. Since women had wanted these changes they accepted them with alacrity.
5. Carl Murchison (Psychology Laboratories of Clark University), "The Experimental Measurement of a Social Hierarchy in Gallus Domesticus," *Journal of Social Psychology*, February and May, 1935.

   Georgene H. Seward, *Sex and the Social Order*, McGraw-Hill Book Co., 1946, pp. 14-18, 30, 36, 37.
6. Helene Deutsch, *The Psychology of Women, Motherhood*, Vol. II, Grune and Stratton, 1945, pp. 14, 20.
7. Chester G. Vernier, *American Family Laws*, Stanford University Press, California, 1931-1938, Vol. II, p. 65.

   For an excellent presentation of the procedures in our courts as well as the laws, see, Maxine B. Virtue, *Family Cases in Court*, Durham, N. C., The Duke University Press, 1956.

219

CHAPTER 12

Our Laws Regarding Sex Lumber Along Like Dinosaurs

Several weeks had passed since Adam and Eve last discussed these matters. Since it was now Christmas vacation and the students had rushed off the campus a few days before, they enjoyed a real breathing space in the strangely quiet halls and met again in the sociology office among their books and papers.

"Many people think laws are not important," Eve began "— even some sociologists. They hold that most of us live within them and hardly know what they are. But actually they set the very framework within which we must act, supporting certain customs and discouraging or prohibiting variations. They to a degree even tell us how we should think."

Legal dinosaurs have clumsy bodies and little heads

"Yes, indeed. This is especially so in regard to laws on sexual relations and marriage. They have tremendous power."

"That power compares to their huge dinosaur-like bodies and the laws' incongruity and lopsidedness corresponds to their tiny brains. We've both stood beside that dinosaur skeleton in the museum and tried to imagine his slow moving body lumbering along, oblivious to its changing environment," Eve added.

"And his lumbering along is like the laws' embodiment of long outgrown attitudes and reasoning. We have mentioned many examples — in those concerning the double standard and the mother's position in divorce, for instance. Since laws become entrenched and regarded as containing divine wisdom, anyone who questions them is considered presumptuous — unless perchance he is a retired judge."

"But, Adam, in a democracy these laws are supposed to be made by us, the people, so of course we should weigh them and criticize them when we wish." Eve slowly formulated her thoughts. "In this area of sex and marriage we have noted the problems arising from nature's handiwork which gives sex a somewhat different meaning to men than to women, and that to bring greater harmony between the sexes we need laws which reduce the difference in these attitudes toward intercourse, pregnancy and child care. But our mass of legislation instead of doing this, often does just the opposite. It often encourages a still greater difference between men's and women's values."

"That is, some laws make matters worse than they might be without them, I agree. For instance, those regarding the unmarried father and his ability in court to escape responsibility for his child while denouncing his mate's character. Also, we noticed how the father may leave his family stranded. All social workers see this." Adam filled his pipe with his favorite tobacco, lit it and leaned back in his chair. "The early settlers brought to our country what is called the English common law, which is the accumulation of decisions by judges in the courts of England. Besides this, our state and national legislative bodies have been passing statutes and laws. Then the courts in our country have interpreted these, giving them one meaning or another. A lawyer must search in several great volumes at a law library for the precise meaning of a law."

A glance into men's legislative bodies

"The best way to understand how a law is made is to follow the process in relation to one particular piece of legislation noticing the forces at work — to study it as a laboratory worker studies a chemical reaction," Eve said. "I did this when the national House of Representatives and Senate were considering a change in the laws on birth control. These old legal restrictions on contraception had been prompted by an impressive man, Anthony Comstock, who holding some of the ancient indignation against sex had come to Congress back in 1873 with a large supply of pornographic pictures and other material, and succeeded in getting those laws rushed through which make it criminal to import, mail or send by common carrier, such as express, obscene material, which in their sweeping generalization included information concerning planned parenthood. His attitude and that of the congressmen, which regarded restrictions on distribution of obscene pictures as similar to the spread of some of mankind's most valuable knowledge, is an example *par excellence* of men's lack of understanding of women's reproductive task and of nature's way of producing far more children than parents can raise.

"These laws prevented doctors from giving information on birth control even in their private practice to their patients, to mothers with organic weaknesses who already had eight or ten children. It caused an inestimable amount of preventable maternal invalidism and deaths, and loss of babies shown clearly in the statistics covering those years. Most mothers were in effect powerless in controlling their own body functioning, they often could not prevent conception when ill or just after a previous birth, or limit the number of their children. — In the later period, after this law was reinterpreted to allow women knowledge of contraception, many have managed to conceive only when well and willing to have a child, and this has been an important factor in the big reduction of maternal and infant deaths."

"To return to the time of Anthony Comstock, most legislative bodies of the states passed restrictive laws which still stand on the books. Practically no women were in these state bodies either, to enlighten the men lawmakers. Most striking are the states of Massachusetts and Connecticut, whose people led the fight for human rights in our war of independence, and now are the most backward in granting women this basic right. Their laws still prohibit doctors to instruct weak or ill mothers whose pregnancy is likely to endanger their very lives. — Connecticut actually prohibits the *use* of contraceptives," Adam added scornfully. "It is a commentary on our civilization. Most people know that the Catholic Church is the chief influence in keeping these amazing state laws."

"Well, I must tell you of my dramatic experience in taking part in the effort to change the federal laws restricting birth control. I listened to speeches in Congress, was shown the mail received by a congressman friend on the House Committee involved, learned of the groups lobbying for and against, and attended the hearings. The proposed change was to allow *doctors* to give knowledge and materials *to their patients who needed them for health reasons.* — It was introduced into Congress year after year for some ten years. Active opposition as shown in the congressmen's mail and the lobbying, led by the Catholic Church, succeeded in having this proposition buried in committees again and again so that it *never* was passed by Congress. — We'll discuss later how it was finally reinterpreted."

"It is a significant story. Go on, Eve."

"Well, this of course was a matter which particularly interested women. They have the wombs of the race and know first hand about how they can be kept in a healthy condition. Women were backing the legal change and had formed two organizations for the task, The Committee to Change the Federal Laws on Birth Control and The Birth Control Federation of America. You remember it was Margaret Sanger, when a nurse, who in her social work became convinced of the tremendous importance of women's ability to space and limit their babies, and who started the movement. Gradually other women came to her aid who during twenty years spent millions of dollars in time and money for the cause.

"They brought before Congressional committees scholarly material showing the numbers of mothers dying because they became pregnant while suffering with heart trouble or other organic weaknesses — and thousands of neonatal

223

deaths of babies yearly because their mothers were not strong enough to give them a good start. Also how many families became destitute since they had far more children than they could support. Yet nothing was done by Congress. Do you remember what finally happened to break the deadlock?"

"Margaret Sanger and Hannah Stone arranged a case to be brought in a particular U.S. Circuit Court of Appeals where there was an intelligent judge interested in social conditions," Adam answered. "He made a re-interpretation of the old laws, 63 years after they were passed, deciding that they did not mean to prevent the sale or mailing of information or materials which might be used by doctors to save the life or promote the well-being of their patients." [1]

"Yes, one of the rare men, like you, Adam, was found who took the time to study the problem, had enough imagination to understand and then courage to act," Eve said as she looked at Adam, who was pleased at the compliment but made no reply, then continued.

"If half of Congress had been women members, I feel sure that either these restrictive laws would never have been passed or they would have been changed soon after. The women members would have known the tragedy of a mother's death leaving a family of small children. If you could have seen some of those men of the Judiciary Committee half asleep when the most impressive statements were presented to them by doctors and other authorities at the hearings around 1935, you would realize what I mean," Eve declared, imitating how they slumped, half asleep over the hearing table. "Of course some people claim that although men largely make up our state and national legislative bodies and are the judges in our courts, they are always carefully considering women's interests and are forwarding these as much as their own."

"If we honestly recognize human weaknesses, however," Adam replied, "I agree, we can't escape the fact that these legislators must think first of their own advantages while making laws. They are placed under great temptation to do so, we must admit. At least they embody certain masculine points of view due to their psysiology, experience and wishes."

"Whether they do or not can be determined by noticing how well our laws have protected women's interests. — If women had been regarded by law-makers as *full* human beings they would have been granted the knowledge of how to keep their health and preserve their lives through controlling their pregnancies—as readily as the knowledge on the prevention of diphtheria. Likewise they would be granted this in all our states now," Eve added as she got up to fix some tea and sandwiches.

Adam strode around the room as he told of some amusing college events. The falling snow was making little piles on the window sills. Everything induced them to stay right there and continue their discussion. It was fun for them to follow along certain lines of thought together, far more than working them out alone—a man and a woman, it also helped a lot for they enjoyed each other.

After they were settled with their tea Adam remarked, "If we study past legislation, we find one of the clearest examples of prejudice against women were the laws which prohibited them the right to vote for their own representatives until 1920. To obtain this took another vast struggle, this one lasting about a hundred years."

"A good example, for most people know about this." Eve pulled out a book from the shelves, opened it at a place mark, saying, "Here is a choice bit, a legislator's words about the women trying to get the vote, and his claim that since a man and wife are one, only the man should vote." Then she read:

> "It is well known that the object of these unsexed women is to overthrow the most sacred of our institutions, to set at defiance the Divine Law which declares man and wife to be one, and establish on its ruins what

225

will be in fact and in principle but a species of legalized adultery . . . Are we to put the stamp of truth upon the libel here set forth, that men and women in the matrimonial relation are to be equal?[2]

"He was sure that marriages would be ruined if wives could vote."

"Yes, and I should add that he based his views on the Bible for he went on to say:

'We know that God created man as the representative of the race; that after his creation, his Creator took from his side the material for woman's creation; and that, by the institution of matrimony, woman . . . became again one flesh and one being with him, he being the head. But this law of God and creation is spurned by these women.'"

"It's a wonder the women ever won with divine law against them," Adam laughed.

"I must read this quotation too, which fits in here. It is from our recent great Justice Oliver Wendell Holmes:

'An ideal system of law should draw its postulates from science. As it is now, we rely upon tradition and vague sentiment, on the fact that we never thought of any other way of doing things, as our only warrant for rules which we enforce with as much confidence as if they embodied revealed wisdom. Who can give reasons of any definite kind for believing that half of the criminal law does not do more harm than good?'"[3]

"That's a strong statement, Eve. But it's made by one who knew the laws as well, or better, than anyone else. Clearly we human beings are just beginning to build a rational society. We waver between tradition given a rosy aura by those who want to prevent change, and reason based on present knowledge and ideals. Those in power usually stand for the traditional ways which keep them in their advantageous positions." Adam continued between bites of his sandwich, "One would think that when laws are found to be clearly unreasonable they could be readily changed."

"You would think so. But I can't help but picture it this way. Here is some human being who is to be unreasonably punished because of some law's shocking backwardness. He holds up his hands in horror at the onslaught of these stupid but powerful legal dinosaurs and cries to the servant of the law, the judge, for reason and understanding. The judge merely murmurs in return, 'My job is to interpret the law as it is and apply it to you.'

"If this mere human being should then appeal to the opposing lawyer out of court and ask him why he fights for one who is taking advantage of an unreasonable law to oppress another, the lawyer would probably reply: 'Why, someone has to defend the scoundrel. We lawyers can't let our hearts rule us. It is not our place to consider the justice of laws. Legislators make the laws. Not us.'

"Should this baffled person later go to Washington and talk to his congressman he would hear the reply, 'Why, I can't do anything about that outgrown law. There is not sufficient interest. You know, we only represent our constituents. You'll have to go and see them.' And so, especially if a progressive change for women is concerned, the great legal dinosaurs and pterodactyls, unmoved by anything but a tremendous and costly organized effort, go lumbering along."

Adam chuckled, "Quite right. It is like an ugly nightmare."

They silently enjoyed their tea. Then Eve said, as if considering just how to express herself, "As to the matter of sexual relations, it seems to me that the laws have not in the past and still do not protect women from inhuman male demands either inside or outside of marriage. It is true that some have worked to protect women from certain unwelcome sexual demands of men, the most outstanding being those against rape. The great hue and cry about rape is however inconsistent with the other cruelties which the law allows. It suggests that the severity of punishment for rape may have been developed since it enforces men's sexual possession of wives.—Strikingly, one type of protection from unreasonable demands of men has been entirely omitted from our laws, that is, restrictions upon a hus-

227

band's sexual intercourse with his wife when she does not desire it, whether because she is pregnant, menstruating or nursing a newborn baby or for other reasons. One of our outspoken sociologists, Myerson, frankly states that some callous husbands force sexual relations upon their wives and often 'sneer' at a more considerate treatment as 'female domination.' [4] Sexual ownership of wives has been considered so complete that the idea of prohibiting rape in marriage has not entered our legal system. Instead, as we noted before, several states regard a wife's refusal of sexual congress as desertion or abandonment and as ground for divorce.[5]

"In short, the laws do not assure wives that they fully own their own bodies. The risk of complete or partial desertion by their husbands, if they refuse his requests, constantly hangs over their heads. Many primitive groups have taboos against congress at least during these periods when a wife needs to conserve her energies. The letters to Margaret Sanger we noticed, are evidence of this serious gap in protecting the basic human rights of women in our society. Of course, sensitive husbands carefully respect their wives' wishes but the many insensitive men should be guided by some laws, as they are in other areas."

"Your mind, Eve, seems to have wandered into so many considerations which most men's have never touched."

"Thanks. I think I've centered on this subject since I was in my teens. — We have already talked of male demands upon unmarried women. This includes prostitution. Don't you think this can stand further attention?"

Who is a prostitute?

"Yes, we should pull it out of the darkness and look at it with a steady glance. And weigh the laws and their enforcement which surround it. Who is a prostitute anyway?" Adam asked.

"*That* is the question! The laws made by men's legislative bodies in effect say a prostitute is a women, she is a criminal and punishments dealt out are almost entirely for women. Prostitution is regarded as a matter of women. The laws almost ignore the existence of the men customers and lay down no punishment for them. There is not even a word in our language for the man who pays for a prostitute, above all no word which corresponds to that of *prostitute* carrying censure and often disgust."

"And of course men are as essential a part in prostitution as women."

"Actually men play a far more important part than women. Roughly there are from four hundred to three thousand or more men customers in a year to every prostitute depending upon whether she is a call girl, house girl or street walker, how much her customers pay and other features. — I'll let you figure how many customers are involved compared to one woman during twenty years of her life. — Besides all these men who support and form the basis of prostitution, there are many other men who procure them, lead them on, manage their lives and take all or most of what is paid for these women. These are the pimps, the procurers, the owners of houses, the big vice lords and others. The women are only *tools* sandwiched between customers and these many men who control the racket. Why is prostitution considered an affair of women?"

"It's all in the point of view. It seems so, looking at it through the eyes of men buried in the double standard theories, which hold that the men customers are acting only as men are expected to act while the women are filled with sin when they act the same way," Adam answered with insight.

"How similar to the thinking that woman represents sex, the evilness of sex, as if it were not essentially a man-woman affair?"

"All that thinking is, I'm afraid, Eve, grey matter operating on the lowest level. Let's see. It first cuts out facts it doesn't want to recognize, such as that one. Then it adopts a conclusion which is gained this way and by means of contradictory ideas which aid one's self-esteem and denounce the other person. And finally it strengthens its conclusion by adding righteous emotions. Like this fellow I heard explain, 'Take every slut who walks the streets and throw her in jail for life.' He had previously said he goes out to find a girl regularly every week for sex — not love. He went on, 'A decent man loves his wife and ought never to get lustful with her, to wallow with her. But he wants to wallow at times so he has got to find women who are filthy enough to meet him on an animal level.' These were his words. Several contradictions here — wallowing in sex is all right for him but makes his partner 'filthy' — he needs to wallow at times but wants to lock up all the women who satisfy him." [6]

"Yes, there's the rub, Adam, he asks the impossible, his thinking is wacky but he feels very superior and righteous. He separates love and sex, the mental factor from the bodily, as we have noted is a common attitude of men.— I've just read that impressive book, 'Cast the First Stone' by John M. Murtagh, Chief Magistrate of the City of New York, and Sarah Harris,[7] which gives an authentic picture of what is taking place in prostitution in New York right now. It is scarcely believable."

"I understand the book tells of pimps who can afford to buy a new Cadillac every year from the earnings of the women working for them — and that they call these women their 'cows' or 'horses' and the group their 'stable'?" Adam asked.

"Oh yes, you should read it. We find students today looking for something dramatic to write about, playwrights seeking exciting material for stage or film, fiction writers imagining often impossible stories. Here is actual present day drama — nothing like it to present tragedy, the preying upon women, surrounded by public indifference and efforts to keep it quiet. Legislation and court procedures denying these women their constitutional rights of equality before the law. — And why? Because they are usually in a weak,

230

almost helpless position; lack education, funds, family or friends who can help them; and because they are caught in a web. Also, just because they are women with attitudes and laws which regard them as second-rate citizens —"

"— those created by God as a second thought, as persons *only* to keep men company and serve them," Adam smiled sardonically.

"Actually what is done by legislators is to create a caste system, placing women who take any sexual freedom in a lower caste; and in the bottom caste, women who allow relations for money payments. Then these latter women are denied almost all rights other citizens are assured. Without this caste system—that is, with the man customer and the woman treated alike under the laws and in court—the evil features of prostitution could be stopped."

Eve went on, leaning forward in her chair. "I have watched the proceedings of the Women's Court in New York. A similar process takes place to that in the courts of Stalin's Russia and Hitler's Germany which we so-called democrats have vehemently denounced. Under Hitler the Jews were put into a lower caste, then denied the rights of others. The feature which put them in that caste was not their doing—they were born with some Jewish blood.—And in our country putting these women in this lowest caste is not mainly their doing either, but because they are born women in a country which discriminates against them, makes laws which say if they do the same as men they are criminals.—Strange, one suppressed group can't understand and help another."

"It all goes on—as Hitler's work did—partly because the people are kept ignorant of it. The subject is avoided in periodicals in order to keep wives and young folks in the dark. Clearly all the men who use prostitutes want the institution continued. Other men are entirely indifferent to its exploitation or too busy with other things to even notice it. — And, Eve, 'respectable' women shouldn't look into it!"

231

Eve laughed. "And you aren't respectable either, to use your head in these matters and try to understand these low caste women."

The Women's Court

"I'll try to picture the Women's Court as I saw it. Here is the black-robed judge sitting behind his mahogany desk on the dais in a mahogany-panelled room with other officials around. Here is a group of young men in good civilian clothes confidently chatting together before the session begins. They are plain-clothes policemen who have trapped and arrested the young women to be tried. They have prowled around the city acting as though they were some typical civilians looking for prostitutes. The huskies with little sensitivity in their faces are in fact stool pigeons. They daily act out the part of a decoy which attracts friendly pigeons or wild ducks to come near them so they may be shot down. They also could be regarded as a secret police. Each member plays his tricks well, often snuggling up to a woman in a bar or smiling at her as he passes on the street in order to lead her on before he arrests her. He sometimes cruises in an unmarked police car along the curb at a slow speed, sits in his parked car, or loiters on a street corner, constituting an invitation to speak in exactly the same manner as does the loitering of a woman. The woman can be imprisoned for loitering but this man is performing his honored job of ensnaring her.

"The women are tried under the vagrancy statute of the New York State Code of Criminal Procedure. It doesn't define a clear cut act such as stealing or murdering. Instead it is vague and involves minute details, such as who speaks first to the other, the man or the woman. Of course a smile or a touch may be the first step in the conversation of a couple but the law overlooks that. The statute involves the question of whether the woman may have said 'Hello' with the purpose of asking directions or whether she spoke for the purpose of inducing a man 'to commit . . . unlawful

232

sex intercourse or any other indecent act.' That is, what is in her mind when she first speaks is all important, and who can tell that? And it defines a vagrant as a person 'who loiters . . . for the purpose of . . . enticing or procuring another to commit unlawful sex intercourse or any other indecent act.' [8] Again what is in her mind when she loiters is basic.—You can see, Adam, what a pesky law it is, with loads of opportunity for various interpretations in order to trap and imprison a woman."

"If the law were logical and clear defining the crime as intercourse outside of marriage accompanied by the passing of property it would make the men customers criminals as well as the women — and the legislators wanted to avoid that. They found their way out by passing that illusive vagrancy statute." Adam said.

"And added to this feature of the trap we have these plain-clothes sleuths who interpret what the women are thinking and their purpose in speaking or loitering. Each sleuth alone has the full power to decide this, to arrest her and tell his story to the judge which no one need corroborate."

"Of course each man of the vice squad gets credit for bringing women to court and convicting them. He must do it to keep his job. He is surely tempted to make the first pass. And more — tempted to make his court report contain the necessary features to win her conviction. — Real similarities to a Gestapo police," Adam remarked as he shoved his tea cup aside.

"You should hear their stories! One after the other, yes, containing the exact details the judge needs to find her guilty. They are actually monotonous they are so similar, usually including a statement that she speaks to him first, later that they talk of sex relations, agree on a price, then go to a room and she disrobes. At this exact moment he always says he shows her his badge and arrests her. It all goes like clockwork. It seems impossible that all this could happen with all the features going smoothly in the order he claims time and time again. But there is no one to dispute him.

"It's most significant that sometimes a new, inexperienced vice-squadman tells the judge the whole, true story including what he himself said as well as the girl. For instance, a newcomer told the judge he and the girl mentioned having a 'good time' and revealed that no offer of intercourse or a price was made, that he lied to her several times and arrested her in the elevator while going to what he had falsely said was his room in a hotel. She was not found guilty. This policeman later learned just what he should report and what to omit at the trials, to have his girls convicted. If he later in his career during the trapping process said to a girl, 'You are gorgeous and I'd give anything to go to bed with you,' (as some of these stool pigeons do) he carefully omits this in his court account. Legally he is allowed to say such things if she spoke first but it looks pretty crude when the policeman admits it.

"Since the judge bases his decisions almost solely upon the words of these vice-squad-men," Eve continued, "all the women's statements he doubts. She is considered guilty long before it is established — against her constitutional rights. Also, in all other trials evidence must be given by more than one lone policeman before a person can be determined a criminal. — When a girl or woman is brought to court she usually has no counsel, too poor and too ignorant to know one or afford to engage one. Since the laws however say that everyone is entitled to counsel, she is asked on the spot whether she would like one at no cost. She hardly understands what's going on and sometimes says, no. If she says yes, she may be assigned a young man from the Legal Aid Society who may be there. This is largely a formality, for he can give her little or no help as one case is rushed through after another. He knows nothing except what the officer and the woman tell him. And he knows that the weight given the words of the plain-clothes sleuth throw the case against the woman in advance.

"A feature of the accounts to the judge which interests me is how these husky, young men in civilian clothes entice their women so that each often finds himself alone in a room with her disrobed before him — and then every fellow's statement that he immediately showed his badge and arrested her."

Adam sat upright, "I was wondering about that, too. Who knows whether he has sexual relations with her or not? Here he is with the laws and court in back of him, alone in this room with a completely helpless woman, helpless because of her usual smaller size, because he carries firearms, because there are no witnesses and because she is of the lowest caste according to the laws and not protected by them. What is there to stop him?—High character and strong self-control. — If he had these, would he be deceiving all these women, earning his living by this game?"

"I agree, what is there to prevent him? Nothing. He knows that the man customer is considered innocent — that all the evil is in the woman. Why shouldn't he take advantage of her, he thinks?" Eve hesitated then continued, "It is quite clear that at the time of the Seabury investigations, Chile Acuna, who was employed by the police as a stool pigeon, often had intercourse with these women just before he had them arrested. He became a witness for Seabury and wrote all about it in his book.[9] Today these *plain-clothes policemen are the stool pigeons themselves* and there is great likelihood they sometimes act in similar fashion. Being in even a more advantageous position than the man customer they can use these women without paying even a small fee. In such an event the servants of society, the policemen, force intercourse with these women by clear or implied threats, which intimidation constitutes rape, and then these men arrest the women victims."

"An excellent example of what can result from ridiculous double-standard laws." Adam shifted his chair, then stood up and walked across the room. "Yes, these vice-squad fellows represent the citizens. You and I help employ them through our taxes. And when each gives his story in court he speaks for 'the people' — every trial is written up as the "People's case' against Bertha, Agnes or Mabel."

"How true. And if our laws treated men and women alike, with equal restrictions, *there could be no stool pigeons* employed by government, for they would be acting illegally when they encouraged illicit relations, loitered to attract women, talked of passing money for sex relations then went to private rooms with them. The city could do this no more than employ stool pigeons for trapping thieves, engaging a plain-clothes policeman to assist a person in picking the lock of a jewelry store, help him take the finest pieces, then turn on him and bring him to court. People would see the horrible iniquity of that. But in the field of sex with all its skewed and unreasonable views — including the conception of the innocent-man-sinful-woman-union — most people don't know what to think, and accept barbarity."

"You wonder how audiences would react if all this were put into a play. The full horror of the life of just one of these young women could not be presented in drama for the audience couldn't take it, especially if it included the early steps of how she was first led into prostitution —"

"Yes, like Lolita Perez, in that book by Chief Magistrate Murtagh, who was taken when a sixteen year old girl from her poor home in Cuba supposedly to be the bride of this older man, a procurer, who brought her to New York then forced her into prostitution by threat of death and by holding a burning cigar to her bare stomach. — Her whole tragic life could not be presented on the stage any more than Anne Frank's, in the play, 'The Diary of Anne Frank.'[10] The Nazis' treatment of her in their concentration camps and her death there had to be omitted."

"It's something to think about," Adam pondered, "the full truth of human behavior — the churches' treatment of this — the public's knowledge."

236

"Returning to our Women's Court, there are two main types of cases, one in which the policeman is a party to the transaction, as we have mentioned. The other, is where there is a civilian customer who is found with a women and the officer arrests *her*. In this second type the customer often comes to her trial, is put on the witness stand and usually says she spoke to him first, that they had sexual relations and he paid her some fee. That is, he who has participated in an act for which she is arrested and imprisoned, now sits in court accusing her — then leaves as a free man, regarded by the judge and laws as a good citizen. I saw this happen many times," Eve said with disgust. "Pray tell, why does our country act so righteous when this is going on?"

Adam put his hand on her arm as she leafed through her papers, then read from some of her newspaper clippings:

"Sixty men . . . taken into custody in the raids on West Side apartments alleged to have been used for prostitution were questioned . . . and then released.' [11] Most of these men were customers.

"During that investigation by Samuel Seabury and District Attorney Thomas E. Dewey of New York City 'a card catalogue of 200 customers' names was found and then discreetly destroyed." [12]

"This situation is carrying to its extreme the double standard of morals. It is the *reductio ad absurdum* of it all."

"Absolutely! Adam. How refreshing it is to have a man admit it. I should mention here that when these women are arrested and sent to the House of Detention they are given tests for veneral disease. No thought is given to the men customers' possible disease. These women — and I am speaking of those who get arrested, not those successful enough to avoid this — as I said, are poorly educated, from our least privileged families, a large portion are Negroes and many cannot speak English. You should see them brought into court, one at a time in their cheap clothes, some in tears, usually completely bewildered as to what is taking place, no real knowledge of the laws — and, as investigations have brought out, are sometimes arrested because they have disobeyed their pimps or rebelled against their life some way — and as a result someone has tipped off the plain-clothes sleuth to pick them up. — Also these periodic investigations have discovered that these policemen are sometimes part of the ring which extorts money from these prostitutes. We'll talk later of this."

"It's most significant that the net thrown out by the police does not bring to court the more protected prostitutes with many wealthy customers."

"No, you don't see them in court. Someone probably buys off the police officers. — And seldom are any men arrested though there are laws covering owners of houses, pimps, procurers and other henchmen. They arrange to be undetected or buy their way out. And the powerful vice kings who control inter-city chains of houses and relate them to gambling centers and underworld activity are rarely arrested. [13] The last big expensive investigation finally uncovered the vice lord, Lucky Luciano, who controlled and exacted revenue from a syndicate which included most of the houses in New York City. It was found that he extracted an income of some twenty million dollars each year.[14] — Many in authority believe similar powerful rings exist today."

Adam again walked over to the window his hands clasped in back, "Tremendous forces are at work leading underprivileged girls and young women into this game, the demand of millions of customers and the other fellows who take their earnings, besides the girls own need for some money. — You mentioned the case of a procurer who took a girl from her Cuban home on the promise of marriage."

"Yes, this deception is frequently used. These Cuban operators are the most cruel to their girls and the most successful financially. This trick is also used to ensnare young women of our country into prostitution. Or they may be engaged by a night-club, then asked to accommodate customers. Sometimes a man arranges a false marriage cere-

238

mony, has relations with her, then induces her to submit to other men. A girl in trouble, or one sent to a reformatory is apt to be spotted by some crafty fellow who leads her on by making her dependent upon dope or gets control of her some other way. After she is caught in the snare she is often shouldered with debt by her manager or pimp. Most are kept stranded by their pimps, owning only a few clothes and enough to buy their food but little more."

Adam observed under his breath, "Just how can they break away? Where can they get a letter of recommendation for a job? What about the pressures and threats to keep them working as prostitutes?"

"Yes, I should say more about these pimps who play a major part in the racket. Prowling over our country are men, often without the advantages of education, smelling out some easy way to make a living who learn of funds flowing from customers to these needy women who are living with the government against them, secretively and tensely always fearful of detection and arrest. 'Here,' these men say to themselves, 'is a place we can exploit. We simply need to hold in the background the threat of the laws while we take most of the prostitutes' earnings.' These are the pimps who usually live in luxury by keeping their 'stables.' Most every prostitute has her pimp who lives with a far larger income than she does. He has intercourse with all his women and sometimes manages to make them feel he loves and protects them. In their helpless position they often allow this illusion to exist for they have no other friends with any property or power. Everyone is against them except their pimps and some other prostitute friends. However, some pimps control their women through beating and threats of death."

Adam thought they both needed to put their thoughts for a time into fresher air. "It's past one o'clock, Eve, let's have a break. How about listening to the organ recital in the chapel and then getting lunch."

They returned together laughing and ready to pursue their subject further. Adam began, "It seems that some occurrence in this festering situation causes it to occasionally come to the surface. Then a probing into the facts with accounts in the papers shocks the public. A few relatively minor changes are made in an effort to suppress the revealed ring of men who prey upon these women. But soon it all becomes silenced and continues much as before."

"Yes, the basic laws are not altered and the great sham of pretending to suppress prostitution by trials in the Women's Court and the Girls' Term Court continues as before."

"We could call the Court procedure a hoax, a veritable farce used to make the public think the government — the men legislators, to be more exact—disapprove of prostitution and are endeavoring to stop it," Adam added.

"They can say to any inquiring women citizens, 'Look, see all we do to suppress it. Look at that twelve story House of Detention, a maximum security prison, in which are detained over 2,000 prostitutes of New York City each year — arrested by the plain-clothes vice squads. Over 400 of these are sentenced yearly for various periods.[15] We spend loads of money fighting it.'"

"Let's hope some day a group of women interested in the plight of their sisters, joined by some men, will peer under the surface of these answers and see what their tax money carries on."

"Yes, *some day*, Adam, women may be sufficiently liberated in their thinking to study it and bring action toward some solution. — The most sensational revelations of the investigations by Seabury and Dewey we haven't yet mentioned. It was that untold numbers of innocent women who accosted no one, who had no illicit relations, were threatened by policemen if they didn't come across with payments to them. That is, the government was employing hold-up men. Other innocent women were arrested and sent to detention, then given the name of a bondsman from whom they could buy a bond and a lawyer who would defend them in court. The bondsman would often ask for their savings bank book as security. — In one case the book showed $575. The bondsman asked $75., an unreasonable amount for a bond, and the lawyer $500. Then the woman was acquitted, she had paid all her savings to a smoothly operating ring of police, bondsman and lawyer. This is only *one* example of many cases."

"What happened to innocent women who couldn't or wouldn't pass over some money to be divided among the ring members?"

"They were often found guilty by the judge and were railroaded into prison as common prostitutes. The police officers in these cases of course gave perjured evidence to win their convictions. Every case of arrest was velvet for these vice squad men, if a women had money he took it from her directly or he got a split from the ring. If she had no money he got credit for having her judged a prostitute. Some of these innocent women were found in prison during the investigation. The official records and that book by Chile Acuna who himself had formed part of the framing ring give details of many such instances.

"Anna M. Kross, now the courageous Commissioner of Correction of New York City, found cases of frame-ups back in 1912 and they were found still taking place in 1940 and later in 1950. There is great likelihood that although the corrupt bondsmen and lawyers now may be suppressed, some of the vice squad stool pigeons and others may be operating in the same manner as formerly revealed.[16] Also, that large sums are still extracted from prostitution by groups of underworld men who are scarcely touched by our courts. Still, only their tools, the girls and women, are hunted down and imprisoned."

"It means," Adam said while thinking, "that a woman especially if poor should not wait to meet a friend on the street —"

"And it's difficult for a poor woman to look prosperous to aid herself. *Imagine* men being placed in such a precarious position that they couldn't stand or meet a friend on the street. Imagine the government employing women in attractive, civilian clothes to lead men on in conversation then arrest them — or, as found on investigation to threaten arrest unless they buy their way out."

"Of course the men wouldn't dream of passing laws which put themselves in that position."

"Yet, this situation in New York is typical of our other cities and those of most foreign countries. It is the end result of laws which allow one person to enjoy certain actions while another is punished for the same thing. Such illogical, incongruous laws just don't work. They open the door to dishonesty and graft," Eve concluded as she lit a new cigarette.

"They demoralize a society, just as Hitler's methods did." Adam added, "There's yet another part of the racket we must mention, that high government officials themselves have been found to participate in the extortion ring such as, an assistant attorney general, judges and police chiefs. Also local political bosses and groups like Tammany Hall have encouraged and made money from red light districts." [17]

"If any of the customers supporting prostitution get a glimmering of the injustice and cruelty involved, they don't talk or write about it for fear of attacks from their male brotherhood — for men do stand together to uphold their wombless advantages, don't they?"

"Yes, they do. And that's why I'm failing them now when I say these things. You must recognize what may happen to me if we put all this in our book," Adam said looking at her quizzically. She was amused but he was serious.

"You are big and strong enough to take it, Adam Ofeden!"

242

"It's really a challenging subject. What are the main forces which have kept prostitution thriving? What do we think could be done?" Eve asked.

"Well, the most important force is the customer, as we have said. His actions clearly indicate a ravenous appetite for some variety in sex partners and for some available women at all times who may be used," Adam replied.

"Yes, that desire is spread among men, married and single of all stations. They want some sex for sex's sake with no personal relations or feelings toward their partners — and above all without thought of possible resulting children.

"The next influence at work," Eve continued, "is that there are women who desperately need the wherewithal to live. Some are girls of poor families, perhaps orphaned, deserted by their legitimate fathers or their unmarried fathers. And some are married women whose husbands do not support them and their children, perhaps alcoholic husbands, shiftless or just cruel. These two main needs fit themselves together, the customers willing to pay for sex and these poor girls and women."

"A third factor probably is the natural desire of these women for some satisfaction. When they are sexually starved they are surely more apt to be led into the spider's web by these procurers and pimps. Later, I understand, that they regard intercourse with customers as 'work' — that is their own word for it — and only pretend that they are thrilled. Of course there may be a favorite customer here and there whom they enjoy. But it is mainly only in their earliest steps into prostitution that their sexual desires play a part."

"Yes, Adam, that is an influence which helps get them into the spider's web, as you say. — And, as for the fourth powerful force, it is the many men who make money from prostitution whom we have mentioned, those pimps and procurers, those who get income from houses or chains, the vice lords and sometimes those in political machines, policemen, some police chiefs and high government officials."

Adam leaned back in his chair then said, "I agree, these are the four chief forces which keep prostitution going. They all fit into each other. In considering the way out let's take each force along with possible methods of weakening or eradicating it. How about that first one, the demand by thousands of customers for easily available sex relations outside of marriage? That may be the toughest problem."

"Well, we have already talked about men's desire for a variety in mates, also of a kind of boredom or cabin fever that often develops within marriage. And we have accepted the principle that we must honor biological functioning by adapting our ways to the basic facts of nature. The question then is, should men's urge for some change in mates be considered part of their biological structure?"

"I believe to a certain degree we should, Eve, if we view the past millenniums in all honesty. Prostitution is called the oldest profession, you know. Like most appetites this one should be restrained within certain limits. And the limits can be determined by what leads to all-round health of the man—"

"And of his women partners — mental as well as physical health. The question is, how can we accept this male urge for variety at the same time women are not placed in a lower caste or rendered sexual objects in order to satisfy it? We also have touched on this matter. The biology of sex and reproduction makes the man equally responsible with the woman for starting new life and places on him part of his child's care, if he is to live on the same ethical plane as the woman — not be a drone. I have thought of a device which would do wonders in stopping this exploitation of women. It would place men and women in somewhat similar positions in relation to their children. You know, when money is loaned the borrower usually gives the lender a promissory note as evidence. In similar manner when any couple has intercourse out of marriage each could

244

be legally required to pass the other a statement with his name, the time and place, which statements would of course be kept privately, like love letters as tokens of faith in the willingness of each to stand by and help the other in case of conception." [18]

"Ingenious. Let me think, Eve. — This would be part of a new society which does not hypocritically denounce all relations out of marriage and then condemn women alone when they take place and often punish them alone. It would be part of an endeavor through the laws to bring the man's and woman's attitude toward sex relations in harmony with each other."

"That's it. Each child could then know his parents from whom to expect some care, and the courts of this society would demand care from the fathers as well as the mothers. Of course, if the man used reliable contraception there would be small chance of his starting a child. You see, these statements would also make him feel more responsible in the prevention of conception which is equally important."

"Really, you've got something there," Adam laughed. "Bizarre as the dickens. But it simply recognizes the facts of reproduction. The man in intercourse may have loaned his reproductive cells to his mate. If he has a child as the result he may want it.—Sometimes a father decides later he wants his illegitimate child. Or at least he'll know his child."

"As things stand now men pay for sex relations with prostitutes partly to buy off possible future responsibilities for a child. Again we find men struggling with their extensive fertility and again contraception is one humane way to help themselves, not prostitution."

Adam was buried in thought as he refilled his pipe. "Let's stop and think, Eve. As to that device of yours, if one of these women became pregnant these written statements by her partners would have little value if she had been with several."

"Yes, but women really don't want several different men in a short space. *All* women long for sex combined with mutual regard or love, as Caroline Slade so impressively tells in her book.[19] If women were not ensnared or forced into prostitution they would surely restrict themselves to one man for at least a month or two, which would make these statements of value. — That legal requirement would influence men to conjugate only with some women they admire or respect, that is, raise the relationship from an animal to a somewhat human and personal one. It would surely reduce the demand by customers. — We should talk about it more when we consider the unmarried father," Eve said, then rose to stretch herself and gaze out the window. Adam joined her, remarking on the stillness of the air shown by the fluttering snow flakes and the quietness due to the sound-absorbing layer of snow. They stood there studying the peaceful scene.

"Then," Adam returned to the subject, "the second big force leading to prostitution is young women in economic need, usually lacking schooling and families which can assist them. The method of changing this is clear. These women should be provided with adequate training and opportunities to earn a proper living. — The principle of helping to fulfill children's needs for food, warmth and clothing, rather than punishing them if they misbehave in trying to get them, is accepted today. Why not apply this to these underprivileged girls and women?"

"Of course we should! They should not be led through deprivations into receiving funds through promiscuous, impersonal sexual relations. They should be rendered free persons who give themselves only to others whom they choose and when they desire."

"Right, Eve. In most fields of human relations it is recognized that placing individuals in a position to regulate their own lives is the important way of assuring their well-being, that is, for instance, allowing men to be economically independent."

"Then for the third force which plays a part in prostitution, women's natural sexual desire. The fact that our so-

246

ciety is most sex-negating in relation to women we have already brought out. It in effect requires women to deny themselves all sexual satisfaction throughout life except with one man, her husband, who may become tired of her, completely casual, or in love with another woman. Society refuses to acknowledge women's biological and psychological need of a loving partner, not for a few years, but during her entire mature life — in the same manner as most men. Society should recognize these unreasonable restrictions — as it in fact is beginning to do — and be more tolerant of non-commercial relations of a couple based on friendship or love."

"This, I agree, along with various laws to raise all sexual relations to a personal and dignified level including your novel device."

Eve nodded and smiled. "Such legal and social changes would decrease the men customers, as well as lessen women's temptations as they are first inveigled into the web of prostitution."

"And for the last big force that keeps this institution going — the money made by pimps, underworld rings and vice lords — effective laws should be made aimed at restricting *them* instead of our present inadequate legislation.—Also, if the other three forces were reduced profitable operation by these fellows would be difficult."

"This brings us again to the men legislative bodies thinking womblessly, which I say are sadly in need of many more women members to help them see the situation and deal with it according to democratic principles. — If there were a good sized group of women legislators they would work to squash all laws which treat men and women differently for the same offense. This would mean no stool pigeons employed and no customers of prostitutes approved. They'd introduce an entirely new conception of the matter which would probably include recognition of all these four forces we've mentioned. And the question also would be tackled of how to clear out from state and city governments those who are connected with political machines reaping funds from prostitution," Eve added. "You see, I do have confidence in women's interest in social relations and in their courage."

"At least we should give them a chance and see what they'd do."

"I feel sure, Adam, that in time women legislators would come to realize that the millions of dollars spent yearly employing those stool pigeons, running those courts and supporting those prisons could instead be used constructively in helping these girls and women obtain vocational training and find good jobs."

"Prostitution looks like another area where *contradictory* demands are made on women. At the same time men customers are requesting their services, the men in government are making and enforcing laws to punish them, some of the very same men doing both things."

"Absolutely.—It's important to see how attacking each of these forces aids in controlling the others. Something *could* be gained if action were taken on all of them: to limit the men customers' inhuman demands; to make these women economically independent so sex relations are those of a free person only of her choosing, not of a slave; to be more tolerant of relations involving love; and to get after the men grafters, exploiters and thieves who extract large sums from prostitutes." Eve straightened up the papers on her desk, remarking that the room was drafty.

Adam put her sweater over her shoulders and closed the door into the hall. As they sat silently a few minutes the sunshine suddenly appeared and Eve moved her chair to be fully in its glow.

"I was thinking, Adam, there is another approach to the problem. Why don't we stop to consider the reasons which lead us human beings to enter sexual relations?"

The various reasons people enter sexual relations

"All right." Adam felt for his words then said, "Ideally

248

one enters intercourse to express love or regard for his or her partner and incidentally, as usually results in such a relationship, he or she receives real satisfaction himself."

"Yes," Eve replied, "and one of the couple may at times, particularly the woman, consent to intercourse largely to please her mate whom she loves, though her own sexual desire and pleasure is not great. Since the man is not able to participate unless he has a certain amount of desire, he not so often enters conjugation mainly to please her. Relations of this first type, as an expression of love or regard, may be considered generous. That could be our first category."

"Then if we are realistic we should recognize that another category is where the purpose in intercourse is mainly gaining one's own pleasure, disregarding the partner's reaction. Here it is the man who is tempted to conjugate on this basis since he is able to obtain a certain pleasure and release even when his mate finds no satisfaction," Adam observed hesitatingly. "This is a second category. We can't avoid calling it a selfish, self-centered relationship on the part of the man. His thought that his wife owes him this service does not change the situation. — This is something for a man to say, isn't it?"

"It shows you're being honest and unbiased about the subject. I surely congratulate you!"

"Of course there are degrees in the selfishness involved. I believe a husband can usually manage to give his wife pleasure. It is an enormous subject. As we've said, the very structure of marriage with the dependent wife is involved."

"Surely, Adam. — Then there is a third category which includes features of trading. He or she may want to gain some other benefits beside sexual pleasure for himself. That person could be called a prostitute *but* such persons include far more than the poor women brought into our courts. Actually a large portion of men and women within, as well as, outside of marriage often participate in intercourse for some economic return or advantage. — Let me try to illustrate. Tell me if you object.

"We know there are men gigolos who enter intercourse chiefly for financial reasons. And through history there have been men painters, sculptors and writers who with inadequate incomes have been able to carry on through help from some appreciative patron of the arts. These patrons were sometimes women of nobility or property who were in love with their protégés. Perhaps there was grateful love on the men's part and sometimes they may have had intercourse with their patronesses mainly to insure continued aid for their art work, the center of their lives, often making important contributions to posterity. And such relationships exist today — sometimes the man may be an artist and sometimes a worthy person who is in need of financial assistance. The woman may be in love with him, inspired partly by her interest in his art or her deep sympathy with his struggle and society's harsh treatment of him. In her desire to become closer to him whose scale of living is a contrast to her own, she may from her heart want to help him across certain treacherous rivers which threaten to engulf him. Such men could be called prostitutes — but should we condemn them if each of the pair voluntarily gives the other what he desires and which happens to be in his power to give?"

"An incisive question! — There are high-minded women too in similar positions to these men artists — perhaps they are painters or musicians—who have accepted assistance from a wealthy man who admires their work and loves them."

"Oh yes, indeed, Adam. And society is more apt to condemn them than the men artists just because they're women. — And besides these types of relationships with financial return a prominent factor, there are some wives of wealthy men who live in luxury, servants doing the housework, raising no children and giving no work to outside endeavors. They simply keep themselves as attractive as possible to please their husbands. Often they may have

250

relations mainly to continue their own support. Of course, however, they act as hostesses to business friends and sometimes give their husbands real affection and companionship so the situation is mixed—as in most other cases."

"Then this pattern is often found in the reverse we must realize," Adam observed. "Some men marry certain women largely for their money becoming their sexual partners and receiving many economic advantages in return. These husbands as the years pass often have intercourse with their wives mainly to assure continuation of these advantages. — And many other men conjugate with their wives chiefly to assure their continued domestic services in the home, while sexual relations are indulged in for pure pleasure with other women. — There are other situations, within and without marriage, where one's chief desire in sex is to be assured of property or service from the other, and whenever this is so that person could logically be called a prostitute."

"Of course," Eve went on between puffs of her cigarette, "these three types of sexual relationships we have mentioned, according to the purpose of each are not clearly separate, for several purposes are often combined in a person's desire. And sometimes one partner participates purely for love, while the other because he or she wants some favors from the partner. In such a case the relationship would be of the first type for the one in love and of the third type for the one wanting above all some favor."

"I follow you, Eve. Very interesting!" Adam said as he got up to turn over the tape in the sound recorder.

"Isn't there a constant exchange of services and property between men and women — those in love and not in love? Don't we employ each other for hundreds of different services and make gifts to each other of all types?"

"Of course."

"It's surely difficult to draw a circle around a certain kind of exchange of property and call the recipient a prostitute. I think the word should be dropped altogether.

As it is used today it has no definite meaning. If it were used logically it would cover a lot of men and women who'd violently rebel."

"It comes down to being a bad name thrown at certain women whose action is essentially the same as that of many other men and women." Adam hesitated then added, "The bad name seems to be thrown particularly at the poor, relatively uneducated women caught in a snare made betwen customers and managers. *It's filled with prejudice against women and poverty*."

"You've got it there!" Eve gave him an appreciative glance. "And it's filled with that ancient hatred of temptation unreasonably centered upon women and sex."

"I cannot help but mention some other interesting relationships. "You know in some sophisticated, wealthy communities there are temporary exchanges of wives all in fun. Well, in one case a lawyer's wife was encouraged by her husband to continue an affair with a successful industrialist during several years. The lawyer got far more legal business from this industrialist than would have been thrown his way otherwise. This husband and wife reaped clear financial returns through her affair. Question, Eve. Was she a prostitute? And what if she later had an affair with a banker who likewise turned over a lot of business to her husband?"

"Good example of how vague the word is," Eve replied. "Some would say yes—I have heard a woman called a prostitute because she had an affair with a man younger than herself. They were in love and there was no exchange of property. This name was thrown at her because the customary age gradient was not observed. Such messy thinking.—Can't we conclude that the term prostitute as it is used in our laws is far too nebulous to warrant arrest and punishment of the helpless women brought to court! These so-called prostitutes should not be made criminals! Other rational methods such as we have considered should be used to raise sexual relations to those of free persons

252

with regard for each other."

"That's right. I entirely agree, Eve. — Then we come to the question of what should be prohibited in the field of sex. Of course we can't go into this whole question now. But why shouldn't our laws prohibit any sexual action which injures another person — either physically or mentally? For instance, rape is rightfully unlawful, for the girl or woman is at least psychologically hurt at having her body violated against a basic individual right. If pregnancy occurs serious injury is done her."

"And rape in marriage should definitely be made unlawful, too. A principle of law should be that every person's body is his own to use for his own living and to serve others as he choose, be he man or woman." Eve then added, "And deception used by either party proposing sexual relations should be made unlawful in the same manner as deception and fraud regarding shares or bonds being sold. That would include deception regarding one's marital status or promise to marry, and one's willingness to aid in the care of a possible baby shown by a written statement passed the other. Taking advantage of a child or a person of low mentality should be prohibited. To summarize, we think that the use or threat of physical compulsion, trickery or deceit in obtaining intercourse should be banned."

"Yes, Eve, also a person's deprivation should be avoided, especially a woman's, which places her in such a weak position that she cannot avoid others misusing her."

The college chimes struck five o'clock. "We'd better call this enough for today," Adam laughed.

CHAPTER 12

1. This happened in 1936. United States v. One Package, 86 Fed. (2d) 737.
2. *Victory, How Women Won It, prepared* by The National American Woman Suffrage Association, H. W. Wilson Co., 1940, p. 43.
3. Quoted by Manfred S. Guttmacher in article in *Psychoanalytical Review*, October 1956, p. 475.
4. Abraham Myerson, *Social Psychology*, Prentice-Hall Inc., 1934, p. 518.
5. Twelve states regard refusal to submit to marital relations as desertion or abandonment. Nathaniel Fishman, *Marriage, This Business of Living Together*, Liveright Publishing Corp., 1946, p. 164.
   Robert S. Sherwin, *Sex and the Statutory Law, The Personal and Psychological Aspects*, Oceana Publications, New York City, 1949, p. 44.
6. These are the true thoughts and words of a certain man and they represent those of many others, given in book of following footnote, p. 190.
7. McGraw-Hill Book Co., Inc., 1957.
8. Wording from the vagrancy statute Section 887(4) (a) and (c) of the New York State Code of Criminal Procedure.
   Prostitutes in New York City, Their Apprehension, Trial and Treatment, July 1939 - June 1940, by Marguerite Marsh, Welfare Council of New York City.
   Also see *An Inquiry into the Functioning of the Women's Court in Relation to the Problem of Prostitution in New York City*, by Sophia M. Robison of the Welfare Council, 1935.
9. *Women for Sale*, William Godwin, Inc., 1931.
10. Based on her own diary. Dramatized by Frances Goodrich and Albert Hackett.
11. *New York Times*, March 5, 1941.
12. *New York Times*, February 5, 1936.
    Bascom Johnson and George Gould, *Digest of State and Federal Laws Dealing with Prostitution and other Sex Offenses*, Pub. by American Social Hygiene Association, 1942, p. 428.
    The case where the judge proclaims the law does not intend to reach the male customer. People v. Anonymous 161 Misc. 379, 292 NYS 282, 1936 City Magistrate Court of New York.
13. W. C. Waterman, *Prostitution in New York City*, Columbia University Press, 1932, p. 20, 21.
14. *New York Herald Tribune*, June 9, 1936.
15. Figures of City of New York, Department of Correction for 1957.
16. *New York Times*, February 14, 1955, regarding Chief City Magistrate John M. Murtagh's annual report.
    New York Herald Tribune, December 28, 1950. An account of an unlicensed bondsman operating with women charged with prostitution who made some $20,000 a year.
17, The situation was studied in 38 cities of our country. "In over one half the cities, political corruption interfered with proper

law enforcement. The connection between such corruption and the social evil was said to be quite marked. Local bosses were interested in property in the red light district and collected tribute therefrom." High officials, including police chiefs and judges, have subjected themselves to such influence she found. Mildred B. Csontos, Legislative Reference Secretary, N. Y. State Library, "Evolution of Methods used to Repress or Regulate Prostitution in the United States and Foreign Countries," 1937, p. 7 (Available for reference at New York State Library, Albany).

18. I understand that at present girls and women are sometimes required before intercourse with a single man college student to sign a printed form saying that they are doing this of their own free will. The date and place are given. This of course only helps the man in case of future problems.

19. *Sterile Sun*, Vanguard Press, 1936.
    Also see, *Streetwalker*, anonymous, Viking Press, 1960.

CHAPTER 13

Laws Regarding Unmarried Fathers Are Like the Diplodocus

A few days after their last discussion they met again. It was still Christmas vacation, the time to make some progress.

When some men are very young

"When some men are very young," Eve observed, "although they need their fathers desperately they receive no help, sometimes as a result they become sick and die. To put this another way is to say the mortality rate of babies born out of wedlock averages higher than that of those born in wedlock where the father recognizes and helps his infant child. Or we could say that when a man starts a child and later disowns it, as most unmarried fathers do, he places his son's life and care in jeopardy. He refuses to pass on to his own child some of the many services given him by his parents and others. When he repudiates his child he is sliding coldly out of his part in continuing the stream of human life, even in the preservation of his own small section of this living stream."

"He, like an eel, usually wriggles himself quietly and cleverly out of an essential job nature gives him," Adam added with feeling.

"Since our country professes to be interested in basic rights for life our laws should protect these men-when-very-young and their sisters whose fathers disown them."

"— and their mothers whose mates flee from them."

"We have noted that many men rebel at being required to care for all their children and even revolt at arrangements through marriage which connect them with their

256

offspring." Eve smiled to herself as she continued, "Bernard Shaw in 'Man and Superman' tells this so well. Don Juan says 'Well, what place have squalling babies and household cares in this exquisite paradise of the senses and emotions– . . . Invent me a way by which I can have love, beauty, romance, emotion, passion without their wretched penalties, their expenses . . . their illnesses . . . their nurses and doctors and schoolmasters.' Shaw presents the marriage ties and the attempts to connect fathers with their children as imposed entirely by women who seem to be grabbing and clutching at men—while men, poor things, try to escape their grasp. He seems to overlook that this connection between the father and his infant's needs is not made by women but by nature, that the man who tries to avoid this connection is rebelling against the basic features of reproduction, the father's fertilization and the helpless human baby."

"Good Eve, that this rebellion is clearly *unjustified* we don't hear presented anywhere. Many men try to blind themselves to these facts of nature in order to gain their greatly desired sexual freedom. They in their desire to avoid burdens hold that there should be no connection between themselves and their offspring in most relations out of marriage and in prostitution. They refuse to recall their own needs for their fathers' help when they were infants."

"Oh yes, they manage to be oblivious to the fact that their father's assistance was probably more important to their infant lives than the pleasures of sexual freedom is to their adult lives," Eve continued, encouraged by Adam's understanding. "It is civilization clutching at man, civilization which stands against abandoned infants, civilization which limits one's freedom and fun to insure the rights of others, in this case babies' rights. Men are basically irresponsible when they promote customs and laws regarding prostitution and extra-marital relations, which require no clear evidence connecting fathers and their possible or actual children."

"It would be hard to deny that." Adam replied, then added, "Let us consider our legislation objectively, you representing the women, and I, the men; both believing in the sacredness of individuals. — The laws regarding the unmarried father and his child's care surely lumber along like dinosaurs."

Eve's eyes brightened, then she said, "When I lay in bed this morning half awake the thought came to me that these laws could better be compared to the prehistoric animal called the diplodocus. He had a long neck stretching from one end of his body and a long tail from the other. His head is so small you can hardly see it, so when you first look at his stuffed body in the museum you can hardly tell in which direction he walked. — He well represents these laws and the question, are they going forward or backward in building the well-being of women and children?"

"And the character of the unmarried fathers," Adam said, showing he had given the matter considerable thought.

"We know that legislation has been passed in every state tending to make the *mother's* responsibility for her illegitimate child the same as for one born in marriage. Several states forbid separation of mother and child during the early months of the infant's life." Eve looked at one of the papers on her desk saying, "This estimate by the National Office of Vital Statistics shows that more than half of the 200,000 unwed mothers were nineteen years old or younger.[1] Only a small percentage have even high school education. Yet our laws usually place upon this young woman the full task of earning an income for herself and her baby while she must give almost full time to its care — simply a superhuman task. And along with this she is stigmatized by society, often making it difficult to find good employment. Many of these young mothers would die in the attempt to do all this if we didn't come to their rescue through aid to dependent children payments under the Social Security Act and relief by private organizations. But government assistance of course is not a satisfactory alternative to a family with united parents nor does it provide a proper standard of living." [2]

"When relief funds are given these mothers, it amounts to other people assuming the responsibilities the fathers ignore. You and I through our taxes," Adam observed.

"Oh, yes.—And how about the unmarried father? How does our government handle him?"

"Well, that is something again. I know that even the Children's Bureau of the Federal Government held that our legislation is most ineffective in winning some support from him for his child.[3] And these limping laws are also so poorly applied in the courts that the unmarried father is seldom determined. Of course, if he doesn't voluntarily offer to assist his child, the first step is establishing his paternity— and there are many hurdles here. The complicated and expensive task of engaging a lawyer and starting court action to determine the father is usually left to the girl or young woman. If she doesn't win help from him she's spent some of her small resources and is worse off than before. Also," Adam added, "bringing court action provokes the father reducing the chances of obtaining even a little voluntary help."

"Very true. — If she is to become dependent upon public funds the Department of Welfare may bring action in an effort to gain some support from the father and reduce government expenses. But even this is rarely done because these government workers know from experience that there is slight chance they can both determine the father and obtain assistance from him—also his whereabouts is usually unknown.[4] Actually most of these young women are not promiscuous nor are they prostitutes, they have had an affair with a friend usually lasting over several months at least and they *know* who is the father."

"Let's consider a particular case," Adam suggested since he was intrigued by the working of our laws and had visited the courts during such cases. "Mary's family helped in bringing this matter to court. She had had relations only with her fiancé, Bill, expecting they would soon be married. No other man was in the picture. Mary was known to be honest and sincere by her friends and family. Bill earning a fair income was able to give his child some support. I was at the trial. When the case is called in comes Bill with three of his men friends. Bill is put on the witness stand and declares that the father cannot be determined since these other men as well as himself had intercourse with Mary about the same time she became pregnant; also, that she is a girl clearly of low character shown by the very fact she permitted these relations.—Then these other men in turn each state under oath that he had intercourse with Mary during those fateful weeks. It resolved itself into purely a matter of these men's words against Mary's. And since she was regarded as a bad character, a low caste person, by our double-standard society and by the all-powerful judge in his robes, based on the evident facts that she was unmarried and pregnant, he doubts her word. But since the four men who say they have had intercourse with her are not held to be of similar low character, their words are given weight. The fact that these four men have had several mates outside of marriage, or may be starting illegitimate babies in general, is not considered relevant. — Bill, the father stands there — fully as much the parent of this new life as Mary — but separated from it because he doesn't have the nourishing womb—denies any part in its conception and refuses any assistance to his own child or the mother. The judge declares the situation confused, that he can not determine the father and the case is dismissed. Our government in effect pronounces the child fatherless and then places a father's and a mother's job upon the girl's shoulders.—This is a typical court case." Adam looked at Eve who was silent and added, "The principle of law used here is honored with a Latin name *exceptio plurium concubentium.*"

"Can anyone hold that the very idea of the innocent-man-sinful-woman-union and that court's procedures are not the result of the wombless sex taking advantage of those with wombs?"

"I think not." Adam replied as he picked up a printed page. "Here is an announcement I got in the mail recently about a book entitled, 'Disputed Paternity Proceedings.' It starts out with the words 'The *accused* father'. Then it explains what he can do:

'to prove absolutely that he is *not* the father. It shows what steps he can take to cast so much doubt on the issue that he cannot be considered the father . . . The book explains . . . the Blood Test Procedure . . . which *cannot prove* paternity but . . . can *disprove* it. . . . Under cross-examination of the mother (it gives) questions designed to reflect on her character'

It states that this is the book's third edition and that its author has tried over 6,000 paternity cases.[5] — One can wonder if those who make the blood tests which can disprove paternity are always above being bought."

"You'd think there were no real unwed fathers, only accused ones, from the sound of those suggestions instead of at least some two hundred thousand new ones every year with their number rapidly increasing and the rate of illegitimate births also increasing in relation to total births. — We need a book entitled 'The Unmarried Father' with a discussion of the full significance of his refusal to admit paternity and deny proper aid to his mate and child in the light of his future self-confidence and the biological realities — in fact, his approval of exploitation of women and innocent children."

The Satyr

Eve shifted her chair and Adam adjusted the tape in the recorder. Then Eve leaned forward to present a thought which just flashed in her mind. "When I was visiting Italy last year I especially enjoyed the excavated ruins of Pompeii. I could well imagine how the people lived when the entire city was suddenly destroyed by the eruption of Vesuvius. Life was very gay in Pompeii in 79 A.D. with much prostitution. And expressing this gaiety was the statute of a Satyr in the inner court of one of its most

261

beautiful ruined homes. With his arms raised in his carefree dancing, with his tail and his beard — he is a fine symbol of the cheerful, irresponsible male. For centuries back before Pompeii existed, the Satyr was a Greek sylvan deity given to riotous merriment and lasciviousness. — This figure in the ruined court represented to me the many past and present men, refusing to be suppressed or restrained by thoughts of thir possible children." Eve showed Adam a picture of the well-known figure.

They felt its high spirit. "Of course, we must admit wombless man is placed under great temptation to be a Satyr," Adam remarked. "Some have claimed that God expects them to make full use of this freedom. Other men simply see no reason why they shouldn't take full advantage of their womblessness, placing all consequences of their sexual freedom upon women."

"Yes, in fact, the legal acceptance of the double standard results from men's theory that he is entitled to take advantage of his mate. — I sometimes think the key task of society is to induce the Satyr-type man to feel greater responsibility toward human life — not only toward his own children, but toward children of all countries. His attitude toward women is often carried forward toward many groups, foreign peoples and the underprivileged in his own nation."

"I'm sure, Eve, if you talked to the Satyr he would reply to you. 'Why be such a wet blanket on my pleasure? We refuse to restrict ourselves sexually when we don't have to.' "

"And how will we calm him down, how make him more mature?"

"Temptation — this matter of temptation is important," Adam replied. "Since he often hasn't the will power nor the moral strength to properly regard his mate and their possible child we can help him by reducing his temptation through our legal system. In the Lord's Prayer we keep asking not to be led into temptation .We all know it's often suffering to resist it."

262

"That's why a person alone is not usually left in charge of a bank's pile of gold — and why one trying to reduce his weight does not surround himself with frosted cakes and candy."

"So when we consider the Satyr, the question is do our laws reduce his temptations? Or do they add to them?"

"One can't be sure of their net effect. That's why they're like a diplodocus. But, I think they increase his temptation. We'll see later."

Adam puffed on his pipe observing, "In ancient Greek mythology if their sylvan deity, the Satyr, had relations with a maiden in the mountains and she conceived she was not denounced and scorned."

"No, they had more sense than to approve the Satyr and punish her."

Adam in his dreamy mood went on, "I have seen a man wink at another when laws aiming at obtaining the unmarried father's support for his child are discussed. That wink expressed a whole philosophy, a Satyr-like discourse he didn't want to put into words. It silently admitted the fun in their game with women."

"Yes, I've seen it expressed in a smile passed between men which seemed to say, nature, not us, put woman in a trap, made by their sexual desires and possible conception. In fact, it seems most men's fatalistic attitude is—what can be done anyway to improve our legislation? There is no other way to handle the situation. — And yet in the Scandinavian countries, where women have looked into the situation and brought pressure for some logic in treatment of unmarried fathers and mothers, another way *has* been developed, they have boosted men out of their lethargic thinking. In Sweden, for instance, the government, not the unmarried girl, brings court action to determine the father and pays the legal costs. In a case there, similar to the one you presented with Bill and his three friends all claiming to have had intercourse with Mary about the time she conceived, the judge would pronounce all the four men as possible fathers of the unborn child.

"As I mentioned before," Eve continued, "they all, instead of being declared free of any responsibility for the child, would all be made to pay some regular sums into a fund for illegitimate babies. One would be named the father and his payments used for Mary's baby. Money received from the other three men would be used through that fund for other babies who needed more than their unwed fathers could provide. The government would collect the continuous payments from the four men and if payments from the fathers were later delayed the government would provide regular amounts for Mary and the baby out of the fund for such purposes."[6]

"That is a wonderful example of what *can* be done if we exercise our gray matter. What a contrast to the easy treatment of unwed fathers in our country," Adam said enthusiastically, "and those men who come to court to confuse the case."

"The fact that women carry the unborn does not necessarily lead to a double standard of morals. — I'm sure other methods could be devised for protecting mother and child.— To continue noting what happens here, we should realize that in the relatively few cases where the father is determined and the court has ordered him to pay some support, the amounts gained are usually ridiculously small. This recent study shows that half of these fathers paid less than $31 a month. What would that buy for his child, I ask?[7] And such contributions are made usually for only a few years. — Thousands of these mothers know all this from first hand experience.

"In most of our states there is no provision for obtaining support from the father except through ordering a bond and imprisoning him for failure to comply. This process helps but obviously a prison term provides no assistance to mother or child. In Sweden, however, the government agency may in order to collect the support place a lien on the father's wages. There, about 91% of the unwed fathers

264

are established, largely by their acknowledgement and others by court decision and practically all of these were found to be paying support contributions until the child was sixteen. Fathers there who claim to be unable to contribute may be given employment in special institutions. The amount of support usually requested is in accordance with the financial circumstances of the father. It may include funds for the child's university or professional education." [8]

"We should mention that these babies carry as great potentialities for contributions to society as others," Adam observed. "It would be fun to make a list of the hundreds of illegitimate babies who became great leaders through history. Alexander Hamilton, Erasmus, Leonardo da Vinci and William the Conqueror are some.

"I wish we had time to do it," Eve replied as she played with the pencils and pens on her desk. "Another example of Satyr-type men's attitudes towards their children is shown in the expression used by some of our soldiers in the last war. They spoke of leaving behind in Europe some 'souvenirs'. May I say that if a similar number of children were left in other countries by their mothers whom they called 'souvenirs', it would shake the world."

"You bet it would," Adam chuckled.

"This condemning-the-mother-excusing-the-father-attitude has permeated society. Even many social workers hold this attitude. I heard one talking to an eighteen year old penniless, unmarried, expectant mother about the question of whether she keep her baby or let it be adopted. The social worker trying to impress the girl with her important moral duty said, 'Remember, you have to live with yourself,' implying that should she not keep her child she would suffer guilty feelings all her life. — And here is a report by a leading social agency explaining that by insisting the young mother assume this double task she is made 'a sadder and a wiser girl' and will be deterred from future erring. — In this way young forlorn, often lonely girls hungry for some affection are *handed the full task* of controlling men's

sexual urges — and often of seeing through their decep-
tions.

"And what is the effect on the fathers of this common
attitude?" Eve went on, "Does granting the man this sexual
freedom, sowing his wild oats, tolerating him when he
deserts his child make him 'a sadder and a wiser man,' I
ask you? Or do our attitudes and laws encourage his further irresponsibility? Social agencies often find situations
like this: that a certain man was the father of three or
more illegitimate children who had come under its care
by three or more different mothers.[9] — I read the other day
of a man in Holland considered by the police to be the father
of some hundred illegitimate children."

"That surely answers your questions. Methinks I see a
similarity between the legal treatment of the man customer
of prostitutes and that of the unmarried father, and their
similar effects in encouraging prostitution and illegitimacy.
Could the fact that our legislators are mostly womb-free
men have anything to do with it?"

"I wonder," Eve replied smiling. "Here is an interesting
quirk. When men regard women as low caste who venture
outside the restricted path—how should they regard these
women's babies? They have considered them as low caste,
too. It justified the fathers in disregarding their children.
These innocent babies were in fairly recent times in Europe
held as sinful persons even when grown, and excommuni-
cated from the church. We have progressed to the extent
of now commonly holding the child as an 'unfortunate' —
not an outcast — but in practice he is still in a precarious
position and usually denied the care and opportunities of
other children."

"We do become a little more rational about some things
as time moves on. — But the hurdle in obtaining an organized, healthy life for babies and children along with
men's sexual freedom is becoming more and more difficult
for men legislators to arrange. Law-making which incor-
porates both these aims which actually work against each
other *is* tough."

266

"And getting tougher, Adam, all the time. The present way out of this dilemma is by having the government continually support some four hundred thousand illegitimate children. Thus, the married mothers and fathers often struggling to support their own also are forced through taxes to help pay the millions of dollars spent yearly for the support of these. Some day let's hope people will wake up to just what is going on."

"The question is, do we want to encourage a group of drone-bee fathers whose children are government supported? Does your study also show, Eve, how much we pay in taxes for the children of married fathers who after desertion or divorce contribute little or nothing for their children?"

"Yes, the amount that is spent yearly by the branches of government, federal, state and local together, for children of absent fathers has been estimated. Taking together the children whose fathers did not marry their mothers and those whose fathers did marry their mothers but later left their families, we find the government aids in their care to the extent of some 428 million dollars every year." [10]

"Of course that is only a part of what these irresponsible fathers cost us for the expenses resulting from our widespread juvenile delinquency is surely connected with these many fatherless homes," Adam added.

"Besides this amount spent by the government are additional millions paid by private relief organizations to deserted families. — You know these fugitive fathers can cross state boundaries and make the process of detection and enforcement so expensive that often not even the home state government agency can afford to search for him. The great need is for preventive laws which encourage the father to stay with his family and do his part. Some believe that desertion would be cut in half by effective federal legislation." Eve picked up a paper from her desk and read:

"The Family Location Service, Inc., a private agency located in New York City, recommends a Federal family desertion act that will make the abandonment of a minor child and the crossing of a state line a Federal offense similar to the national motor vehicle law. This would give Federal courts, where the deserter is found, jurisdiction to impose orders . . . and would subject offenders to the Federal probation system.[11]

"Seven bills have been introduced into Congress since 1941 to establish a Federal Abandonment Law but all have been buried in committee."

"At present the Family Location Service of New York City, is the only agency which specializes in the location of deserting fathers," Adam said. "Nation-wide location service is strikingly lacking. This private agency is doing an excellent task but can only scratch the surface of our country's problems."

The black market in babies

"Another result of our tolerant treatment of the unmarried father along with scorn for the mother is that there are newly born babies who in effect have no parents. They are little orphans at their most tender age," Eve said with feeling.

"Yes, I see it like this. After a supposedly monogamous man has learned that one of his non-wife women is to bear his child, and has ducked out in alarm and embarrassment, society stands ready to center its condemnation, which could be divided between the two, upon the mother. If she steps forth, bears and keeps this child in the knowledge of all, a ton of bricks will land on her head. Society's punitive attitude, which contains some sadism, focuses on this dramatic revelation of the sinful woman and disgraceful mother," Adam replied, showing real understanding.

"And many intelligent people expect her to step forth and take the wounding blows. Naturally, most naturally, she often does not do it. Then both parents are afraid of the baby and he is often left with none. — Yet he is usually a perfectly good and promising child. — Here then is a place where a shrewd person can step in and make money. He can get the baby for nothing and sell it for from $1,000 to $5,000, in the black market, usually on a cash and carry basis," [12] Eve continued. "One person does not operate alone but usually a group of three or four including a doctor who attends the birth, a lawyer who acts as middle man helping to locate those who will adopt the child and a woman to transport the baby from its birthplace to its new home. One group, however, consisted of nine persons, had two office managers in its two business headquarters. The babies it handled were usually born in Florida and sold in New York State. Most groups operate across state boundaries."

"Yes, they are smoothly functioning big business machines. One manager advertised its babies for sale in Cuba. And of course they go to the highest bidders since they are sold for profit."

"As I look through these clippings, I see one investigated business sometimes paid the mother $50 or $75; another proudly claimed it never paid her a cent from the two thousand or more it received for her baby. I guess she usually receives little or nothing. Often the mothers do not even know that their babies are sold." Eve leafed through her papers. "I see this business unit sold impoverished mothers' babies as well as those of the unmarried. — What a fine example of how our customs and laws often expect the impossible from a wife and mother. Here so much is demanded of the poverty-stricken mother that she acts against her deepest instinct. — Of course we know children have been, and are still being sold in other countries. But we like to think of ours as a leader in civilized ways."

"These babies are handled like simple commodities, in the same manner as a chair or sofa."

"And what about this, Adam? We have laws which force a woman to carry an accidental pregnancy to full term and bear the child even when she thinks it unwise. That is, the minute fertilized cell is held to be so sacred by our laws that her judgment as to the management of her own body is denied her. Then when this life has matured into a baby and is born its value to society descends to such a level that it is treated like an inanimate commodity."

"I admit such ridiculousness comes from the complex of legislation," Adam said while gazing at the ceiling "which does not recognize woman's position in reproduction."

"Yes, it overlooks the vitality-absorbing task of pregnancy and childbirth, also the true value of a baby. It is the result of men's restricted vision from their easy part in creating new life, of their wombless thinking. — We must mention here while talking of the black market that there are approved social agencies, public and private, which help unmarried mothers. And sometimes they arrange for the adoption of their babies in homes which after investigation they think will give them good care. A trial period is provided for the adopting parents before the adoption is finally legalized. That is, the well-being of the child is the major consideration in placing him — not the price paid for him. —But these agencies are not sufficiently staffed to handle all the babies needing placement. Also, they usually insist that the unmarried mother care for her baby six months according to most laws and often do their best to persuade her to permanently keep him. That is, the agonizing position of the young mother — her choice between the devil and the deep blue sea — is made twice as difficult."

"I suppose the devil is giving him away, and the deep blue sea is keeping him while being drowned by society," Adam said. "Yes, that puts it well."

"Then, if an unmarried mother accepts help from one of these social agencies and allows her baby to be adopted there is some danger in some states that information kept in files open to several may be spread in the community. Therefore the methods and attitudes of social agencies is part of the question. These agencies and their workers, forced to fit into our double-standard laws and attitudes, often do not fully recognize the truly tragic question the young mother faces. The workers often speak of the most approved method in counselling the mother, as keeping themselves aloof and recognizing that it is *her* problem and *she* alone must decide what to do with the baby, as if it weren't equally the father's; and that of our state legislatures' which keep all these laws, all these rules of the game. And perhaps the girl's own parents did not, or could not, provide the young mother with the affection and security she needed. — But the social worker is led to regard her as solely responsible and belittle her well-nigh impossible task if she keeps the baby, probably leading an essentially lonely life with no spouse-companion, on a low income while she performs this heavy double job; as is evidenced by some of their remarks in one of their reports, which says: we must help her 'to be a parent to her fullest capacity', to 'regain a sounder sense of values' to 'recreate her own life', to 'rebuild her self-respect and integrity' and 'to know herself better'." [13]

Adam smiled to himself as he asked, "Perhaps the unwed father should be asked to acknowledge his child and care for it alone, or place it in a foster home paying for his care and 'rebuild his self-respect'? It would be easier for him than for the unwed mother. He probably earns more, nor would he suffer from such a social stigma as the mother."

"We must stop and think before we criticize the mother's willingness to let the baby be adopted. I would say that society places her in the most traumatic position possible. She is forced to struggle between her great love for her baby leading her to keep it, and the probable consequences if she rears it with little or no help from his father. She feels it is her own and wants to care for it — if his father and others would help. — Only those who have experienced the tremendous mother love for a new baby can comprehend her ordeal." Since Eve had a child of her own she knew this overwhelming love. "This situation where the mother is tempted to give away her child is also of course the result of the double standard and the accompanying man-made rules of the game."

Adam walked toward the window saying, "We must

271

recognize that there is another angle, that is, the many sterile couples wanting a baby to adopt. Some may think that the whole situation is quite all right since they obtain their babies this way. What do you say to that?"

"Well, I'd say this is a cruel process by which these babies are nurtured, born and then passed to others. After the young mother has been deserted, gone through the nine months of pregnancy and the long hours of child birth, and perhaps cuddled and nursed her child she sees him carried off never to lay eyes on him again or know what becomes of him."

"I grant you, Eve, it is not humane. — Sterile couples should be given extensive assistance toward having their own babies."

"At least it should be conceded that a woman's body is her own — not something open to trickery or seduction, then if conception occurs forced to grow a new life which others take away — If sterile couples want babies there are many children in need of loving care whose mothers or both parents have died, or are unable to give it themselves. Such children offer opportunity for adoption which helps all concerned.'

Dark clouds suddenly spread over the sky. Eve joined Adam at the window to see the saffron light which shone low from the west below the layer of gray clouds. They talked together of the strange effect on the campus scene.

Then Adam got back on the subject, "Looking at this illegitimate family from a bird's eye view we find the feature which most shocks people is selling babies like commodities and many attack the situation here. Yet this is the result, the end of a chain of events. We need to focus on the causes. Of course the beginning of the chain is conception along with a disappearing father or his inability to raise his child. So we could say, carelessness or lack of conscience by the man regarding contraceptive measures is usually the starting point."

"Yes, and you are right when you say contraceptive measures by the *man* for that is the least he should do when exposing a single woman to the tragic experience of conception. — If anything is to be done about selling babies it should be centered on this starting point," Eve replied.

"Yes, we could put it this way. — Since a man is connected biologically with his child he should also be attached to him by human laws. The effects of this would be; first, to induce precautions; second, to lead him to have relations only with a woman whom he would like to mother his child in case contraceptives failed.—And here I see again that written statements passed between an unmarried couple would influence him in these directions. — I didn't realize I was coming to that again," Adam chuckled. "That requirement would help in many ways."

"It looks that way. I didn't realize it myself until we got into these discussions."

"That device of required statements passed between a pair will seem laughable to most—just as Henry Ford's first 'horseless carriage' was thought a big joke by most people of his day. But your idea is, I think, a sociological invention which should be experimented with just as Ford's first car underwent further experimentation and development," Adam then concluded.

Treatment of unmarried fathers illuminates our marriage institution

After a pause Eve observed, "But to return to the big matter which touches all of us, the marrriage institution, I would say our treatment of the unmarried father reveals that the flesh-and-blood baby completely dependent upon adults' care is not the chief feature which determines the relationship between its parents. — It *would* be possible for a society to regard the parents of a child as bound together at least for its care. Then the child would constitute the main factor in their relationship — and the child is something important enough to assume such a connecting link between those whose inheritance it carries."

273

"Eve, you are right. But let's see where this reasoning of yours would take us. It would mean that an unmarried father financially responsible for his out-of-marriage child might also have children in marriage. He might have too heavy a load."

"Of course, so he should be careful to prevent this. Don't present laws allow him to recognize only part of his children?"

"It surely looks that way."

"We find then that it is not the *living baby* which binds its parents together, or the father to his child, in our society today as would be reasonable and beneficial for all. Instead of this what do we have? It is really quite shocking when you analyze it." Eve hesitated, "It's hard to put it in the right words, but — our present legislation quite clearly states that a woman can expect her mate to be responsible toward his possible or living child only if she become his possession sexually, lives in his home and assumes other restrictions and tasks placed upon her."

Adam thought that over, "I believe that's right, those are the essentials, for a common law marriage exists when a couple have sexual relations over a period and live in a common domicile. Also, we have noted that the two clear grounds for breaking a marriage are the wife's unfaithfulness to her husband and refusal to live in the domicile he chooses."

"That's right. If a woman does not accept this position in relation to a mate the law in effect says she should not expect him to be a responsible father. And this may sound radical but it's a fact. In this way every woman is denied the essential functioning for which her body is created and toward which her urges center, sexual satisfaction and reproduction, unless she steps under the power and control of some one man, called her husband. *Our society does not allow a woman to function as a woman with a mate as an equal.* She is legally prohibited this while she maintains entire possession of her own person, chooses her vocation,

274

gains economic independence, while sharing with her mate the care and support of her children. — Do you follow me? Most husbands don't realize this, nor do most wives. Only when a man becomes tired of his wife or takes some sexual freedom, does he begin to discover what advantages the marriage laws give him and the wife discover in what a weak position she is placed."

"I admit it is hard to picture a woman with such freedom — so different from what she has now. — But we must expect change in customs even at a faster rate than in the past—as science and atomic energy come more and more to our service."

"I believe, Adam, that the people living in the year 2200 will look back at our present times and will smile condescendingly at the way women lived today, at their round of household chores if they are mothers, their general lack of real opportunity for adventure or specialization in some chosen area, and in the restrictions on their social life especially with men."

"Or perhaps they'll think us all rather blind, deaf and dumb to submit to the old patterns and restrictions.— You've led me to see this," Adam laughed to himself. "Perhaps I shouldn't admit it."

"Why say that? You've simply given time to dig into all this and have now moved ahead of other men. Honestly, most men are like ten year old children when it comes to thinking in this area. Just one reaction occurs to most of them if a woman speaks of enjoying greater opportunities. It is regarding their own corresponding loss of authority over them. One word comes into their minds, 'feminist,' with its implied dislike and unpopularity. As if that were all there is to the problem. Most have never glimpsed the fact that they themselves would live a richer, deeper life if their women companions had a fuller one—"

"— And if their mothers had had a greater security and opportunity to give their sons what they wanted to."

"I know many will laugh at you when they read what you

have said but I kiss you for it," and Eve placed a big kiss on the top of his head, taking him quite off his feet.

Then she took his hand, saying, "Thousands, millions of other women will want to kiss you too! You don't begin to guess what an appeal is made to them by the *combination of a man's strong body with an understanding heart* — as compared to the combination of his strong body and an essentially self-centered mind. Women go mad with love when they find that first combination."

Adam blushed, them composed himself fussing with his pipe again.

Eve went on, "I was thinking when we spoke of looking at the present from the year 2200 that we could correspondingly glance back to our country's women some two hundred years ago, see them cooking over burning logs in a fireplace, weaving sheets on hand looms, usually not able to write or read, bearing eight or ten babies each, losing several in infancy, and themselves dying in large numbers during their reproductive years.

"They meekly accepted all this, thought it was ordained by nature and by God. If any woman had dared to write that she imagined in the 1960's large numbers would be students at colleges, voting at elections, running automobiles and weighing the laws she'd have been considered a mental case."

A footstep at the door, a rap and John de Dios moved in like a breeze, "Hello friends, you're working too hard. I've brought the makings of some highballs. Won't you join me?"

Adam got up to greet him and help mix the drinks. "Just the right moment, John. How did you know it?"

"Oh, I'm good. I could feel the seriousness flowing out of that office and thought, that's enough for today."

They chatted about families and friends and their latest subjects of discussion while enjoying the highballs. Then Eve, feeling a little silly, asked John, "Now phrase for me the average men's thoughts about our sexual customs and their own behavior. Then I'll give you the average woman's thoughts."

"OK. I'll try." He calmed himself and looked intent, then said, "They claim to approve the single-standard ideal and hold that they are in spirit steadfast and faithful lovers to their wives. But particular, overwhelming circumstances sometimes make them swerve from their ideal course. Wives face no such temptations."

"Go on, John. And what are those overwhelming circumstances?" Adam asked.

"'My wife doesn't love me any more.' Haven't you heard those words?"

"Oh yes, from many sides."

"And the thoughts, 'She no longer cares for intercourse;' 'She is always nagging me;' 'The baby is her chief interest and I'm now left in the cold.' You've heard those thoughts, too, Adam."

He nodded agreement. "But there's another side to the overwhelming circumstances. Out with it."

"Sure, sure. This man knows Betty. She's single, pretty and she's playing up to him. Her eyes tell him too much, and he shouts within himself, 'Why shouldn't I give her what she wants.'"

Adam and Eve laughed and Eve broke forth, "Now for the women. Their thoughts are not so familiar. They hold strict faithfulness to a husband as their ideal. But they also sometimes face overwhelming circumstances but don't explain these temptations even in confidences. — Someday soon however their inner feelings may break forth and sweep across us like ocean tides."

"Will we drown, Eve?"

"I don't know, John. Not if you've got some sense. — You will hear, 'My husband doesn't seem to love me any more. At least he takes no time to express his love.'—'He comes to me in the most matter of fact manner as if I were always ready and waiting. — I want a real lover!'"

Eve paused to see their reactions, while each took another swallow from his glass, then went on, "'Since I do the heavy work in reproduction, why shouldn't I have at least some of the loving sexual satisfaction I desire.' The boldest of the wives I'm sure will say — 'I want a real lover!' "

John and Adam were enjoying this, were quiet so as not to break the spell.

"And other wives will say, 'My husband seems to have aged before me' or 'He has affairs with other women, thinks I don't know it — thinks I should be as eager for him as if he were a faithful husband. — I want a lover!' "

Eve looked into her glass then replied in a strong, stern, manlike voice, " 'Impossible,' you wombless men will shout, 'You might have an illegitimate child,' and you'd think confidently you had spoken the profound, all-encompassing truth."

John and Adam looked at each other but were still silent.

Eve pulled out a book from the shelf saying, "Havelock Ellis puts it well." Then she read:

> " 'There is no sphere which we regard as so peculiarly women's sphere as that of love. Yet there is no sphere which in civilization women have so far had so small a part in regulating. Their deepest feelings, their modesty, their maternity, their devotion . . . were used . . . to mould a moral world for their habitation which they would not themselves have moulded . . .' [14]

He put it very gently but very truly."

"That passage presents it well," Adam agreed.

"But, Eve, those remarks you put in the mouths of future wives are so selfish. Women are the guardians of the hearth, they won't ever have such thoughts," John blurted out.

"Of course you don't think so. You imagine women's submissive, quiet nature is born in them — that they are born to want to sit by the hearth while their husbands are gallivanting around.—I prophesy many will reveal this is not so. Some will speak out, not only for their own sakes, but for the sake of their daughters and granddaughters. They will speak in favor of regulating, according to some carefully thought out considerations, the revitalizing powers of sex for the mental and physical health of women—and of men."

"Maybe you've got something there," John said feeling too gay to argue further. He put his arm around Eve and kissed her. Adam did the same not to be left out of the fun.

CHAPTER 13

1. Estimate of illegitimate live births for 1956 is 193,500. More than half of the mothers of these births were 19 years old or younger, 149,900. The rate of illegitimate births of 16.3 per 1,000 total live births in 1951 had increased to 19 in 1956. *U.S. Census*, National Office of Vital Statistics, May 1958.
   Sara B. Edlin, *The Unmarried Mother in Our Society*, Farrar, Straus & Young, 1954.
2. The average payment for public assistance to families with children who were dependent because of death, disability or absence of a parent was $26.90 for each recipient per month in 1957. "Contributions of Public Assistance to Family Life in the United States," Helen E. Martz, Public Welfare Advisor, Bureau of Public Assistance, Social Security Administration, Department of Health, Education and Welfare. Article in *Marriage and Family Living*, August 1958, pp. 213, 218. Most recent study.
3. U.S. Children's Bureau, "Paternity Laws, Analysis and Tabular Summary of State Laws Relating to Paternity and Support of Children Born out of Wedlock" in effect January 1, 1938. According to a letter from this Bureau in 1958, it has not made a more recent study of these laws.
4. A study by the U.S. Department of Health, Education and Welfare found that 308,800 illegitimate children were receiving aid to dependent children. In 89% of their families no contribution was made by the father in spite of efforts by government authorities. The fathers' whereabouts was unknown in 61% of these families. Saul Kaplan, "Support from Absent Fathers in Aid to Dependent Children," *Social Security Bulletin*, February 1958. For present laws see Helen Clark, *Social Legislation*, D. Appleton-Century, 1957, pp. 336-339.
   We have no figures on the large number of unwed fathers who give no contribution toward the support of their children, whose children receive *no* government aid. Instead their mothers alone and her relatives support them or they are adopted by others or sold in the black market.
5. The italics in the quotation are mine. Sidney B. Schatkin, Assistant Corporation Counsel of the City of New York, Matthew Bender & Co., Inc. Albany, New York, 1953.
   Blood tests in paternity cases are being used only to disprove paternity of a particular man. If a test indicates that a man *may* be the father, that is, gives an inconclusive result, it is not allowed to be given in court as evidence of any kind.
   A positive result, proof that a man *is* the father may be ob-

tained by a series of blood tests but no state at present allows this result to be introduced as evidence in court.

6. *Social Sweden,* published by the Social Welfare Board of the Country, 1952, pp. 214-220. Norway and Denmark have similar provisions.

   Social Services for Children and Young People in Sweden, a pamphlet, Swedish Institute for Cultural Relations, Stockholm, 1948, p. 15.

7. See study mentioned in footnote 4 above.

   Eight states have shocking laws to protect the unwed father by setting the maximum payment which he may be required to make for support of his child. These maximum payments which a court may order range from $8.30 a month to $15 a month. U.S. Children's Bureau study mentioned in footnote 3.

   Chester G. Vernier, *American Family Laws,* Stanford University Press, California, 1931-1938, Vol. IV, pp. 213, 214.

   Some states are attempting to improve legislation requiring the father's assistance including Minnesota and Wisconsin. Helen Clark, op. cit., pp. 322-332.

8. *Social Sweden,* op. cit.

9. Ruth Reed, *The Illegitimate Family in New York City,* pub. by The Welfare Council of New York City, 1934, p. 162.

10. About 57% of Aid to Dependent Children is to families with fathers living but absent. Shown in a study of August 1957 made by U.S. Department of Health, Education, and Welfare, Social Security Administration, Bureau of Public Assistance. Printed July 1958, table #8.

11. From remarks by Hon. Emanuel Celler of New York in the House of Representatives, July 8, 1947. Published in the Congressional Record.

    At present all the states are aiding eachother under uniform support laws and in location efforts under reciprocal state agreements.

    Jacob T. Zukerman, Executive Director of Family Location Service, Inc. 31 Union Sq., New York City. Annual Reports 1957, 1958.

    Joseph E. Steigman, "The Deserted Family," in *Social Casework,* April, 1957.

12. *New York Herald Tribune,* November 2, 1951, an account tells of a ring run by Marcus S. Siegel, a lawyer, and four doctors operating from Massachusetts to Florida. They and others were indicted. Issue of December 6, 1949, an account tells of Irwin Slater and others who advertised in two newspapers in Cuba to place some of the babies.

    New York Times, July 10, 1958, an article gives Charlton G. Blair's story of how he ran his business.

13. From an article in a social agencies publication, reprinted and sent to me by the U.S. Children's Bureau.

14. *On Life and Sex: Essays of Love and Virtue,* Garden City Publishing Co., 1937.

CHAPTER 14

Human Justice Demands Improved Abortion Laws

Christmas vacation was over. Adam and Eve were thrown into the busy examination period, so Eve alone during some evenings wrote the following chapter: —

Nature unguided clearly leads us to produce more children than we can properly raise. This is so for most couples as well as all nations. Methods of conception control are still not entirely reliable. When an accidental pregnancy occurs should a country extend its authority to the minute fertilized cell within the woman's body disregarding her wishes or her health? The most basic of all freedoms is the right to control the functioning of one's own body. Most countries are now well—or over-populated.

A blot on our country's culture

Our legal dinosaurs seem blind to reason regarding interruption of pregnancies. Even if a girl is forcibly raped, the laws say she must carry her illegitimate child to term and bear it. The English and Scandinavians are one step ahead of us in a humane attitude toward a raped woman. At a conference the late Dr. Robert L. Dickinson brought up the incisive question of the ethics in compelling a girl who has been violently raped to carry on the pregnancy. He reported the case of a fourteen year old English girl who was raped by some of the Royal Horse Guards and made pregnant. Dr. Alex W. Bourne felt the injustice of the British laws which even in this situation made abortion illegal. He, therefore, although he risked a prison sentence, performed the operation in an endeavor to win an enlightened legal decision. At the trial he was exonerated.[1] In England there is now an "Abortion Law Reform Association" with prominent people on its board.

This incident presents the weak and exposed position of the womb-sex, the risk of having her body cruelly misused by the combination of the man's greater physical strength, his frequent lack of sensitivity toward her and the laws he makes regarding new life he may start within her womb.

Before we go further, we should stop to recognize the different types of abortion. The two main divisions cover first, the unintentional or "spontaneous" and second, the intentional or "induced" abortions. *Unintentional* abortions are usually caused by a severe accident or some physiological condition of the mother or the embryo. Lately it has been discovered that an imperfect male or female reproductive cell may be the cause of abortion. Another discovery is that a normal mother may have an Rh-minus blood condition and the fetus an Rh-plus blood condition inherited from the father, a situation which may cause unintentional abortion.[2] Some of these abortions are also now believed to be due to the mother's inadequate nutrition since recent successful therapy by supplementary foods have caused an end to many a woman's habitual abortions. Also a high rate of unintentional abortions among some employed industrial workers has been found, where they are exposed to certain poisons.[3] Since no registration of unintentional abortions during early months of pregnancy is required we only can estimate their extent. Most studies conclude that about 10% of pregnancies end this way.[4]

Then there are *intentional* abortions, ones that are brought on with the purpose of terminating a pregnancy. These again can be divided into those which are done within the limits of our present laws, called "therapeutic," and those which are illegal.

Relatively few intentional abortions are legal, perhaps only 5% are performed on a doctor's decision in a hospital, usually after consultation, that they are necessary to *save the mother's life.* The narrow, short-sighted legislation of most states which allows doctors to interrupt pregnancies only on the basis of probable early death of the mother if the pregnancy continues,[5] are perhaps the best example of sluggishness in law-making and a society dominated by those who do not bear children. Should not preservation of the mother's *health* be ground for legal interruptions? What society would be so foolish as to make illegal all operations except those deemed necessary to save a person's life? The laws evidently do not consider that women's opportunities for health should be the same as others.

At the 1942 conference on abortion and the later conference of 1955, some doctors stated that interruption of pregnancy can be done with a high degree of safety by trained physicians having good technical facilities.[6] The record of practically no loss of life by patients of skilled "abortionists" who operate only in the early stages of pregnancy demonstrates what is possible. There is also a similar record in the Scandinavian countries where more enlightened laws allow more abortions to be performed for reasons of health in hospitals under good conditions. Likewise, there is almost no sterility resulting from these well-handled interruptions of pregnancy.

While our country's legislation reduces legal, therapeutic abortions to a tiny percent of the total, the women of higher income families are more likely to obtain these than are those with smaller incomes. The fact that the wealthier can pay more for their care enters this picture. The laws can always be interpreted, narrowly or broadly. If a woman or her doctor knows personally a staff doctor of a hospital a broad interpretation, including even the need of preserving mental health, may be made. If she can afford to engage a psychiatrist to consider her entire position, that in relation to her children, her husband and the economic facilities available, and he finds an abortion necessary to preserve her future health, she may with the aid of his recommendation obtain a legal abortion in a hospital.[7]

The several studies presented at the last conference on abortion in the United States were summarized in a courageous statement by Dr. Sophia Kleegman:

"Indications for therapeutic abortions should be similarly interpreted and applied to *all* economic levels. Medical indications for therapeutic abortions are now reduced to an insignificant number. Psychiatric indications for therapeutic abortions are likewise insignificant in number in municipal services but high in private practice, for 80 per cent or more of therapeutic abortions in private practice are performed for psychiatric indications. The figures speak for themselves. An unwanted, undesirable, or harmful pregnancy is a burden. A profession dedicated to service must be helpful to poor and rich alike. Undoubtedly there is need to make it easier for the poor woman to get a therapeutic abortion, always, of course, under the direction of reliable auspices. In our society there is room for more consideration of humanitarian reasons as an additional indication for abortion for all women, and particularly for the poor woman . . ." [8]

For *most* women the laws are interrupted narrowly and abortion is not allowed on the ground that the parents lack sufficient income or strength to raise an additional child. That is, economic and social grounds are not recognized. Therefore perhaps a million women each year arrange for abortions outside our restrictive legislation. One of the first of our country's leading students of abortion, Dr. Frederick J. Taussig states, "So powerful and universal is the instinct for motherhood, that when a woman is compelled to do away with the child within her body, we may feel sure that the fault lies primarily with the special conditions under which she is living . . . economic distress is the root of the largest number of abortions." [9] The majority of the illegal intentional abortions are had by mothers who are already raising children. [10]

A good cartoon could be sketched of an austere man in the dress of Uncle Sam sitting on a judge's bench looking down upon a frail woman. She would be telling her story: "I have to earn to help support my three children. My husband is not strong. I can hardly get

enough to keep us going. Now I am pregnant. After I
have this child I won't have time to earn anything.
What will happen to my family them?"

He would look bored upon hearing her words and reply "Don't you know, lady, our laws are clear—we think
nothing should be done to help you — I mean you must
have your baby. After that if things are very bad you
may be given public relief."

As a result of our legislation many a woman of poor and
moderate circumstances who is determined not to bear a
child whom she cannot properly rear goes into what amounts
to the underworld; a world where some men and women
without medical training perform operations, where non-
sterile methods and dangerous practices may be used, and
puts her life in the hands of these people. It is a world
where the abortionist often has no space to keep the patient
until she can safely travel home; and a world where perhaps
a half of those operated upon are not even pregnant.[11] If
one can pay enough however, she can find experts using
great skill and care in their illegal abortions.

When women are "over-due," if not able to raise another
child, they naturally are upset over possible pregnancy.
Simple inexpensive tests can quite definitely determine pregnancy when ten days "over-due," (the urine tests such as
the Friedman or the A-Z tests). Such women could, if they
knew these tests existed, determine their state. Many illegal
operations where no pregnancy existed would be avoided by
simply bringing to women at low cost the use of these
tests.[12] Dr. Regine K. Stix suggests that such availability
might be part of a public health service.

Since illegal action is always surreptitious, illegal abortions are beyond the regulation of all branches of the government and medical groups. No examination can be required to determine satisfactory training or experience of
the persons who perform such operations. Nor can we know
how many take place; only very rough estimates may be
made. Nor can we learn the later effects of these abortions
upon the women.

Thus, abortion is the *only* operation which is prohibited

doctors unless the patient faces imminent death and the only operation concerning which skilled knowledge by widely experienced doctors cannot be given to other doctors. That is, the high degree of skill developed by some "abortionists" is not being passed to the general doctor for use in legal therapeutic cases to save the mother's life. Under our rigid laws, if general doctors learned the best techniques from expert "abortionists" or studied the after-effects on women they might be regarded as "participating in the crime." (Some have been told this.) This restriction on the spread of valuable medical knowledge is about the best example of an existing irrational taboo in medicine.

It is a hush-hush subject which is sadly in need of being brought to light and considered. Its present treatment is similar to that of venereal disease some forty years ago which was then not discussed scientifically in most books and magazines. Little progress will be made in abortion problems until the full facts are boldly presented.

The great social problem of unwanted pregnancies is untouched

Among most primitive people it is recognized by both the men and women that more pregnancies occur than children are desired, and therefore custom seldom prohibits abortion and other methods to restrict the numbers of children they endeavor to raise.[13] The ancient Greeks, including Plato and Aristotle, recognized the frequent need for abortion and therefore tolerated it. Lysias held that abortion could not be considered homicide because life in the uterus was not a person and had no separate existence. The early Romans held similar views. The Oriental religions in general have recognized its frequent necessity on the clear grounds that parents are often unable to feed all the children conceived. According to Shintoism the infant does not have a spirit until it has seen the light. In Japan today with great population pressure abortion is not held morally wrong nor is it legally prohibited. Then, if we turn to the enlightened Scandinavian countries and Finland, we find a far more liberal and understanding attitude toward abortion than our own. They recognize it as a social and humanitarian problem, with consent granted on several grounds. In short, only a relatively small portion of the world's population at present considers abortion a criminal offense (except in extreme circumstances to save the mother's life) as do our laws. And if we include the peoples of the past this portion becomes much smaller. Then if we recognize the millions of men and women today who take part in arranging abortions prohibited by their governments, we are left with an extremely tiny fraction of mankind who hold it in general to be a crime.

Christianity made it a sin in its early years about 300 or 400 A.D., in its mystical thinking regarding it murder to interrupt the life of the tiny invisible joined cells. And today its denominations still vaguely or absolutely hold this view. We who live in the Christian countries whose laws almost entirely prohibit it often erroneously think this attitude is universal and existing among most people back through history.

This unreasonable restriction of pregnancy interruption in our country amounts to the womb-free male society burying its head in the sand, ostrich fashion, and leaving the individual women to struggle in secret with the tormenting realities of the contradiction between nature's lavish fecundity and parents' limited strength and resources for raising children. Since the wombs of the race are part of women, *they* cannot escape the problems of preserving their own health and limiting their children to the number they can tend and feed. In individual cases some men have helped their wives and partners find a solution, but the important social problem of unwanted pregnancies in our country has been left practically untouched to this day.

At the 1942 abortion conference one doctor said that when an unmarried girl became pregnant, as frequently happened during this last war, she seemed to have less psychological trauma by undergoing an interruption than by bearing a baby and then letting it be adopted.[14] Does our legislation prohibit the less traumatic course of interruption because it desires to punish her severely for not restraining the father? It seems so. After men have instituted a double standard, to cap the climax they demand through the laws that the fertilized cell they have caused should be carried to term by the women persuaded to satisfy them.

True, understanding of conception control would greatly reduce the problem. Nevertheless a large portion of our population is still kept from satisfactory knowledge. To reduce abortion all state health departments should assume the responsibility of giving mothers the knowledge to control conception during the mother's postpartum care as is done by some of them today.[15] Efforts clearly should be made to reduce undesired pregnancies and thus the number of abortions. The operation, although it may be done skillfully and cause no ill effects, is still an operation, and returns the glandular balance to that of the non-pregnant woman.

The web of inter-relationships between some legitimate doctors who refer patients to "abortionists," certain members of the police force and departments of justice who accept abortionists' protection money is a subject filled with fire. Socially-conscious doctors, lawyers and legislators to whom are given responsibility for public health, for legislation and administration should courageously clear up this situation. But it may be that women themselves will have to take up the problem and fight against hundreds of obstacles and vested interests, as they did in the case of the birth control laws.

The whole question of pregnancy interruption has been intelligently considered in Sweden. Briefly its present legislation allows a theraptutic abortion: (1.) on account of a woman's disease, bodily defect or physical weakness for which childbirth would endanger her life or *health*. The Scandinavians have a term "the worn-out mother" indicating a real understanding of some mothers' jobs, and the provision here of a mother's weakness would include that of the worn-out or generally run down mother. Also it is permitted (2.) for humanitarian reasons, such as when a girl or woman is impregnated in a case of rape or other criminal coercion; and (3.) for a eugenic indication, such as, when it is expected that the child would carry an inherited mental disease, deficiency or serious defect; and (4.) when the *future* effects on the life of the mother are considered and the mother's physical and mental strength would be seriously reduced by the birth and care of the child considering her conditions of life and circumstances. That is, her life and health, not only during pregnancy and childbirth, but in the following years may be considered in making a decision.[16]

What facing of reality, and what recognition of the mother's position and child-care tasks do we find here! It is like a fresh breeze on human endeavors to guide its affairs in the light of wisdom, understanding and kindness.

All these legal abortions in Sweden are approved by one of the special committees of the Royal Medical Board, of which there are three for the different regions. These committees are made up of a physician, usually an obstetrician and a layman, preferably a woman, both appointed by the government; and thirdly, the chief of the Bureau of Social Psychiatry of the Royal Medical Board. All approved interruptions must be carried out before the twentieth week of gestation except under some exceptional circumstances.

Turning to the United States again, it is estimated that some million abortions are performed every year outside of the laws but of course no one knows the number.[17]

When the extent of illegal abortion is discussed in our country it is usually in the spirit of being shocked, grieved and mortified that so many women would do such a thing, overlooking the fact that everyone of these unwanted conceptions involved a man. That is, every abortion is usually the result of difficult social and economic circumstances surrounding the father as well as his mate. Especially when

289

one speaks of a single woman's abortion, it is generally regarded as purely her affair and her crime. Men generally seem to be quite knocked over at the extent of illegal interruptions, as shown in a recent article where we find, "The totally unexpected facts revealed in the report will undoubtedly arouse a great deal of moral indignation. . . . Most readers have doubtless found the figures . . . shockingly high." This big surprise to men is the result of course of their putting their heads in the sand, their lack of recognition that contraceptives even when used are not 100% efficient, that our laws are unreasonable and other important matters.

A certain amount of injury, sterility and death results from some of the poorly managed illegal abortions in the United States. Our rigid legislation is being obeyed about as well as the old prohibition laws and is encouraging all of the evils which accompanied those unenforceable regulations. The successful bootlegger corresponds to the successful "abortionist" today.

Most of the conscientious, enlightened doctors of our country recognize that their hands are tied in this sphere of abortion, preventing them from using their own best judgment to preserve the health of their patients according to the Hippocratic Oath they take on entering their profession.[18]

The unscientific manner in which the subject is usually presented is significant. The problem is befuddled and women are made to believe that intentional interruption of pregnancy is a fearful thing, that it is *necessarily* a criminal affair, that the risks to life and health are *necessarily* great. This method of presentation must be regarded as one of the present methods of controlling women's minds and, as a result, their bodies. *The rational way of presenting the subject would be by first considering the laws' part in making most abortions a furtive and sometimes a risky matter and then the wisdom and ethics of our laws.* Above all we need more humane legislation which will allow this side of medicine to be developed according to our best thinking about health preservation.

If we used the words, "interruption of pregnancy" instead of "abortion," with all its fearful connotations; and the words, "against our backward laws," instead of "criminal" or "illegal," we would begin to see the light. The public would then realize that our problem is mainly one of laws lagging far behind public opinion and scientific knowledge rather than one of suppressing so called, "criminal abortions." During the later days of the prohibition laws people realized that the problem consisted of unreasonable statutes rather than one of suppressing illegal traffic in liquor.

Our popular magazine articles which often tell of risks in abortion usually do not explain that this is largely the result of legislation which surrounds "abortionists" with difficulties while it places them beyond all regulations.

Present attitudes incorporated in our legal regulations provide an important part of the pattern which endeavors to place women's contribution in reproduction beyond her own control. Refusal to give all women the best scientific knowledge regarding contraception and the so-called legal "wifely duty" provides another part of this pattern. Then we must recognize the fact that the mother's reproductive services do not entitle her to any economic return proportionate to the number of her children from either husband or society. That is, her facilities to feed and care for her children are usually not extended as the number of children increase. Such a combination of pressures has entrapped and baffled most mothers and brought mental and physical illness and early death to many.

Men can refuse to work if their wages and conditions of work are not satisfactory. They can bargain this way for their food and security. But women are on the whole not allowed to bargain and gain security through their unique contribution in reproduction and child care, since this is more or less forced by these various laws and regarded as their sacred duty.

The most fundamental of all freedoms

We talk of freedom of speech, freedom of worship, freedom from want and fear, but the most fundamental freedom is that to control one's own bodily functioning. This means freedom to eat or not, to sleep or remain awake, to grow a child within one's body or not, according to one's desire.

Most nations, including our own, have held that the need for a growing population justifies the denial of this freedom to women, *but* most countries are now well populated when future natural resources are considered. Without realizing it, we are still refusing woman her basic freedom. We are denying her liberty to control her own biological destiny. We often make her a reproductive slave of the state. Our laws suggest that if women were to bear only wanted babies, insufficient numbers would be born. Shall we continue to force their reproduction, or shall we make conditions such that women will *want* the children needed to maintain a desired population size? The basic principle of civilization is that one should not be forced to work against his will or without just compensation.

Even if we hold that mothers should sacrifice self and be strong enough to adjust to any difficult situation, what about the babies? We grant it is not healthy and often impossible for a tender baby to adjust to insufficient food and warmth. All the theories regarding the nation's need of population and the precepts on the virtues of self-sacrifice will not help these babies. We are not so foolish as to say to a baby, "Dear child, you must realize that your self-sacrifice is for God and the good of the country. If you haven't enough food you must bear it stoically. We need lots of babies even if we don't give them all proper care." But we are foolish enough to hold such sentiments regarding the need of mothers' self-sacrifice.

Men's bodily functioning has been free of corresponding restrictive laws. Men in general would not tolerate laws which meant for them the strain, physical depletion and incidence of death prevalent among many underprivileged mothers. We like to think that we have outgrown the theory that the "legal existence of the woman is suspended during the marriage or at least is incorporated or consolidated into that of the husband." [19] Yet wives' reproductive organs have been and still are in effect largely owned by their husbands and by society.

Many women will be cool or frigid in their sexual lives as long as we leave many ignorant of effective contraception, keep this legislation on "wifely duty" and abortion tending to produce unwanted children. If in having sexual relations men ran the same risks as women do in our present culture, I am afraid many would find themselves usually impotent.

As we note the seriousness of women's position when unplanned conception takes place, we might turn again to womb-free men's frequent light attitude toward the same occurrence. We have all heard humorous stories centered around women's susceptibility to accidental pregnancy. The unplanned conception in marriage is considered lightly by some men. The slip which starts a child out of marriage, though taken seriously by some, is winked at by others and often fled from; while that which causes pregnancy in a prostitute is trivial, usually of no concern whatever to men.

A high degree of sexual satisfaction cannot be enjoyed by most women until they feel that men, not only as individuals but as a group, are seriously seeking women's welfare. Would not men like such laws that they could say to their mates: "I value you as I value myself. I grant you opportunity to try to determine the course of your life as I do mine. You will never be forced against your will to bear a child. I will do my part to prevent an unwanted pregnancy. If this should happen accidentally you still will have your fundamental freedom and, if you desire, the most skilled medical care. We men have done all we can to free you from worry and to allow you to rest confidently in our arms."

Women would respond with new confidence and delight

to men's passionate embraces upon such practical evidence that they have tried to understand and help. Though such a realization looks into the future, shouldn't we consider the question and chart some course?

Parents should determine the sacredness of their fertilized cells

Let us consider how much sacredness should be attributed to the different stages of the growing reproductive cells. How sacred are the living male cells which initiate new growth? We must remember that enough sperm are produced by each man to fertilize every woman on earth. Each man has some 4,000 ejaculations during his life and each of these contains between 200 and 600 million sperm. Here nature's wastefulness is almost beyond our grasp. Should the law of supply and demand operate, these sperms would have little value.

From the individual male's point of view only the sperm needed to assure his desired children seem important. That is, *their value is determined mainly by the individual man and his wishes.* He may value these relatively few sperm he uses for reproduction highly because of their power to continue his life through posterity. (The innate potentialities of every minute sperm could be held as of inestimable value, for some might produce great geniuses, but *every* sperm cannot be valued according to these innate possibilities, for he could not possibly raise all the children he is able to start.)

From the country's viewpoint also not all these spermatozoa are valuable, for should they be used to the maximum of women's capacity almost every woman would bear some fifteen or twenty children. Yet most countries want sufficient sperm used to insure continuity of their present populations. A country should therefore concern itself only with insuring each healthy male opportunity to produce the offspring he desires and is able to raise. It can encourage those with better inheritance to at least replace themselves, but its people do not want the offspring of any one particular man or group of men to dominate future populations while others' opportunity to have children is greatly limited.

Nature likewise provides that each woman produce in her life some 350 ripened ova. What individual and national value shall be assigned to these? Approximately the same as allotted the sperm, though they carry more value since they are fewer in number, especially those which ripen during her best years for reproduction. *The ovum's chief value is also determined by the individual woman and her wishes.* Here also the country should therefore concern itself only with insuring each healthy woman opportunity to produce the offspring she desires and is able to carefully raise, to continue her line and for the satisfactions of child raising.

We seem thus to concede that the main value of reproductive cells before they meet *is to the individual.* We allow persons to remain unmarried and waste all their reproductive cells. Likewise we permit married couples to waste most of them. *But*—and this is striking—we are inconsistent and illogical when we hold that the main value of these reproductive cells is not to the individual the instant after fertilization occurs. From that instant on the wishes of the parent are pushed aside, our country steps in saying through its laws prohibiting abortion, "This fertilized cell belongs to the people of the country."

Yet since parents, and mothers particularly, assume the main task of raising their children they want to determine their number. Most think they should be able to control not only their unfertilized but to a degree their fertilized reproductive cells.

The question becomes where should the line be drawn when the new life in the womb no longer belongs to the mother but is considered property of the government. Some groups have held that it should be drawn at twelve weeks after conception, others at twenty weeks. Many religious and other groups have considered that the new life is the mother's and should be largely under her control as long as it is part of her body and has no independent being.

At the 1942 conference on abortion Mr. Algernon Black of the Society of Ethical Culture went to the core of things when he said:

"We have a deep religious feeling of the sacredness of all life upon a philosophical . . . basis, and particularly a sense of the sacredness of the human personality. But does that mean that we do not destroy the fly, the insects, the bacteria? . . . No! So we make a choice . . . The embryo, . . . especially in the early months, has not the selfhood, . . . or the consciousness of human personality — save potentiality. . . . My own sense is that the law should be liberalized in this matter and that the medical profession should broaden its interpretation of therapeutic abortion to include other indications —" [20]

Most scientists support this view. The fertilized cell invisible to the naked eye and the subsequent early embryo are regarded by them as mere unrealized potentialities, mingled proteins and lipides. Biologists have seen through the microscope the gradual growth of the brain, nerves and other organs. Most believe that the spirit and the body thus slowly develop together from these earliest stages until the baby gains an independent life and then self-consciousness.

Should we not try to be enlightened beings as we form our abortion laws? Couldn't we consider whether the mother's wishes as to her bodily functioning should determine the continuation or not of this new life potentiality? We might decide that if the mother is given full opportunity to make this decision and has allowed the fetus to grow for twenty weeks that society could step in to preserve its life. But it could do this without denying her all basic human rights only if it insured the mother facilities for her proper food and rest during pregnancy, good medical care at birth and provision for her and her baby's health during the following year at least. Even this renders her a reproductive slave of the state after the twentieth week, if she should decide she could not carry the heavy prenatal and later baby-raising tasks, and wanted to interrupt the new life. But allowing her to make the decision up to the twentieth week and giving her assurances of facilities for life and health lifts her from the position of a badly exploited slave to one of a slave treated with some consideration. If our law makers went as far as this, giving the mother power over her own bodily functioning up to the twentieth week, we should congratulate them, but they probably won't do even this for a long, long time.

If parents choose to preserve the mother's strength and be assured of healthy children, rather than to raise a large number of possibly less healthy, less educated children, should they not be free to do so? Cannot they judge their own affairs more wisely than can sweeping legal regulations aimed at higher fertility than parents choose? If they wish to waste a fertilized cell because pregnancy has occurred when the mother is physically depleted or ill, should the parents not be free to legally arrange this, and when they later see fit start another child? Why such heavy penalty for accidental conception?

All in all it now seems unjust for any country through its laws to sanctify and to take control of the fertilized cell with no regard for the mother's or the parents' wishes. As long as billions of separate reproductive cells are going to waste, a country cannot reasonably seize upon the life of every minute embryo and say it cannot be touched. If the mother and father hold it as precious, it is then sacred and they should be allowed to nourish and develop it.

The Roman Catholic Church in particular attaches mystical value to the united sperm and ovum but strangely holds them of little value before they have joined. This is evidenced by the celibacy which it requires of its consecrated members, the priests, monks and nuns. Rationality is especially lacking here where supposedly valueless reproductive cells the second after they meet become so sacred, that their value is held to be even greater than the mother's own life. The encyclical of Pope Pius XI says, " . . . however much we may pity the mother whose health and even life is gravely imperiled in the performance of the duty allotted to her by nature, nevertheless what could ever be a sufficient reason for excusing in any way the direct murder of the innocent?" [21] referring to the fertilized cell.

We might ask whether society should hold such power over the invisible cell within the mother's body when it will later expect her to raise the resulting baby whether she has the strength or not to do so and whether her whole family will suffer by having too many mouths to feed. Clearly the economic position of each member of the family decreases as the number of children increase, which means less basic facilities for each child in the middle and lower income families. The extensive Beveridge studies in England found that one of the two chief causes for families with serious economic needs was a large number of children in relation to family income. Since our society expects every parent to use his and her own judgment and efforts in raising his family in our private enterprise system, should it restrict their opportunities to determine the size of their task?

Most all countries are now reconsidering their past policies on contraception, recognizing that their population must be balanced with their land resources. They will in time reconsider their policies on abortion and not be so rabidly anxious to preserve every fertilized cell. The Roman Catholic Church, however, is not so definitely faced with the danger of having too many people in relation to the resources of one country, for its people are spread over many countries. Its organization is in a position *par excellence* to be a dominant world power through increase in its numbers.

Parents have difficult reproductive problems

Parents must make decisions on reproduction while unable to foresee the circumstances which will influence the lives of their children, such as their own ability to support them or even their own continued life. They must move in the dark and hope. The young mother is in the period when she can best bear babies yet the young husband is often unable to support them. He may want to prepare for a profession after marriage. Why complicate parents' problems still more by denying them full knowledge of birth control and prohibiting the interruption of a rare accidental conception?

If when a mother of three children is ill a pregnancy is interrupted, and later, when better, another child is conceived and born, should she condemn herself for preventing the growth of the earlier one? We should recognize that had the earlier child been born the later one might never have been started. Which is more valuable to society: the mother whose health was impaired by the birth of the earlier one and the child who, due to prenatal conditions, was also under par, or the well mother and the well child born some years later?

As parents watch the stream of events they recognize how the element of pure chance enters to make each child what he is. One couple may realize how John was welcomed as their first when they were ready with open arms; how Peter, who was accidentally conceived when his mother had influenza and born less than a year after their third child, was a weak, anemic baby and never did get hold of life. Most parents recognize that these small helpless beings are often tossed about, not only by uncontrolled features of fate, but by the features which could and should be controlled. We adults, so important to ourselves and others, are to a fair extent only the end results of these chance circumstances. Each of us feels his own development should not have been thwarted by avoidable traumatic influences. And yet little is done compared to what is possible to prevent the children of today from being born at times inauspicious for their later opportunities.

Instead of clinging to the old folklore about the supposed benefits of dubious, confused theories let us recognize the facts and work out a plan for reproduction which does credit to the human mind and ideals. As Erich Fromm states, in humanistic ethics the good is the "affirmation of life, the unfolding of man's powers. Virtue is responsibility toward his (the human race's) own existence" [22]—physical, mental and spiritual.

CHAPTER 14

1. *New York Herald Tribune,* July 20, 1938.
   Abortion in the United States, reports of a doctors' conference sponsored by Planned Parenthood Federation of America and the New York Academy of Medicine. Ed. by Mary S. Calderone. Paul B. Hoeber, Inc., medical book department of Harper & Bros., 1958, p. 193. Conference was held in 1955.
2. *The Abortion Problem,* Proceedings of the Conference held under the auspices of the National Committee on Maternal Health, Inc., June, 1942. The Williams and Wilkins Co., Baltimore, 1944.
   George L. Streeter, "Embryological Defects and Their Relation to Spontaneous Abortion," ibid., pp. 60-66.
   Phillip Levine, "Serological Factors of Possible Causes in Spontaneous Abortions," ibid., pp. 74-89.
3. Charlotte Silverman, "Maternity Policies in Industry" *The Child,* August 1943, prepared by U.S. Children's Bureau.
   George Gellhorn, "Influence of Industry on Health of Women Workers", *The Nations Health,* March 1925.
4. Dorothy G. Wiehl, "A Summary of Data on Reported Incidence of Abortion". *The Milbank Memorial Fund Quarterly,* January 1938, p. 7.
5. *Abortion in the United States,* op. cit., pp. 187-192. In 45 of the 48 states abortion is criminal except when performed to save the mother's life. In Colorado and New Mexico it is also allowed "to prevent serious or permanent bodily injury". In Alabama, Oregon and District of Columbia it is allowed if her health is in peril.
6. Ibid. Figures show extremely small loss of life from abortions when performed under good conditions, p. 66. In Sweden, Denmark and Finland, pp. 29, 105, 209. Regarding almost no sterility from abortion, pp. 61, 62.
   The Abortion Problem, op. cit., p. 170.
7. *Abortion in the United States,* op. cit., pp. 78-80, 90-92, 101, 111, 183, 146-147, 183. If a woman threatens to commit suicide it is possible that a therapeutic abortion can be arranged through a psychiatrist to save her life.
8. Ibid. p. 115.
9. Frederick J. Taussig, *Abortion, Spontaneous and Induced,* Mosby & Co., St. Louis, Mo., 1936.
10. Alan F. Guttmacher, "Selective Pregnancy," *Human Fertility,* April 1941, p 35.
    Studies show "a marked rise in illegal abortion with increasing

order of pregnancy." That is, its incidence is much higher with mothers who have three or four children or more. Dr. Regina K. Stix, "Abortion and the Public Health," *American Journal of Public Health*, American Public Health Association, May 1938, p. 623.

P.K. Whelpton and Clyde V. Kiser, "Social and Psychological Factors Affecting Fertility," *Milbank Memorial Fund Quarterly*, April 1948, p. 312.

11. John Harlan Amen, Assistant Attorney General of the State of New York who was in charge of the Kings County Investigation said, "Our evidence showed that almost 50 percent of the abor-tions performed by illegal abortionists were cases where the woman was not pregnant at all." *The Abortion Problem*, op. cit., p. 173.

12. The Margaret Sanger Research Bureau, 17 West 16 Street, New York City, and other maternal health centers offer this service at little cost.

Dr. Stix made this suggestion during part of the discussion at the conference, reported in *"The Abortion Problem,"* op. cit., p. 171.

13. G. Devereux, A *Study of Abortion in Primitive Societies*, The Julian Press, Inc., 1955.

14. *The Abortion Problem*, op. cit., p. 56.

15. *Abortion in the United States*, op. cit., p. 155.

16. Ibid., pp. 25-32

17 Ibid., pp. 110, 171, 180.

19. Ibid., pp. 167, 181-184.

19. Sir William Blackstone, *Commentaries on the Laws of England*, G.T. Bisel Co., Philadelphia, 1922.

20. Algeron D. Black, "Influence of Moral and Cultural Patterns," *The Abortion Problem*, op. cit., p. 101.

21. Encyclical on Marriage, Pope Pius XI, in *New York Times*, January 9, 1931.

22. Erich Fromm, *Man For Himself*, Rinehart and Co., Inc., 1947, p. 20.

CHAPTER 15

Some Possible Social Patterns

Adam and Eve came into the room, their skates hung over their shoulders, their cheeks red and cold from the stiff wind. He helped her take off her coat and scarf then lit the logs in the fireplace while she prepared coffee on a near-by table. Most students were home this week-end between semesters, so they could enjoy the comforts of the dormitory lounge alone. The warm sun from the wide windows and the heat from the flaming logs soon began to sink into their bodies.

They chatted about the thrilling lightness when they were blown across the smooth ice. Then Adam said with amusement, "Well, we've got to bring this discussion to an end. How will we do it?"

"We could go on and on. Many subjects we've only touched. But I suppose we should further consider the future."

"Yes, people would like us to present a plan which would bring deeper satisfactions between the sexes and heart-warming relationships throughout life."

"I agree, Adam. I know this can be done. I just noticed in the newspaper the picture of a leading citizen seventy-one years old who has just remarried a most attractive woman his junior by many years. He has the self-confident and brilliant smile of a young bridegroom. Look at this picture! [1]— Most think that the lost emptiness of the later years is destined — that it is an inevitable condition. Yet I have seen certain older persons who sparkle as in their youth, whose faces reveal a still-smoldering fire. And I believe this is usually due to their close companionship, body and soul with another. — We think that emptiness and weariness is physiological, never guessing it may be mainly loneliness and this the result of our customs which often demand it, especially of women."

"What plan would allow the happiness shown in that

bridegroom's face to many other older persons?"

Theories justifying women's restrictions need analysis

"Well, we must first admit that women's present suppression means men's confusion and uneasiness. So often the thwarting of others hurts oneself as well. — Many women now have a vague, confused feeling of dissatisfaction with their present opportunities. There's much talk about it in magazines and books usually without any analysis. Their restrictions are well camouflaged under theories we've considered. Around their heads float gaily painted balloons representing the precepts that they should happily submit to the double standard, and cheerfully accept the theory that they do not own and control their own bodies. And many other lavender and pink balloons saying, that a mother can well raise her children alone when her husband has deserted or died and can do other superhuman things."

"We hope we'll help them pierce these balloons and see just what's inside. Recognition that many of their restrictions are unnecessary is the first step in building a new pattern," Adam reflected while filling his pipe.

"I should add a balloon painted with silver clouds representing the thought that women are very well off, well supported, doing pleasant, easy work but they don't know it. And of a gilded one saying women's interests are *identical* with men's so meek submission is best for them."

"Actually those theories are similar to those floated over the heads of the Egyptian slaves and the mediaeval serfs, aren't they?"

"Remarkably so." Eve rose to look out on the sparkling trees, each twig encased in ice, all crackling and creaking in the breeze. Adam joined her, pointed out a red headed woodpecker pounding on a near-by trunk. They watched him a while, then a rabbit bounding over the drifts leaving a perfect chain of footprints.

She placed her chair so she could watch the scene. "We shouldn't be surprised that women are confused by all these theories, for they have been presented by the most learned and imposing leaders, ministers and priests in their robes, professors in lecture halls and male writers of authoritative tomes. The women have been so busy keeping their men fed and clean, pleasing them and raising their children, they have had slight opportunity to study and question their theories. If some get a glimmer of the truth they don't dare express it or act upon it. And we understand why. It might lead to their being divorced by their husbands, disinherited by their fathers or ostracized by their friends. They must become enlightened in large numbers, then support each other as they move along into greater opportunities."

"I think you have rare empathy for women, for the many who have not been entirely fortunate."

"Actually I've been interested in women's problems since I was thirteen or so. I think it started from watching my mother's great submission to my father. He required her to serve his every thought and wish, and to voice a sweet echo to all his views. Yet I felt her intuitive understanding of most family problems and her children's needs, including my own, were far better than his. She was sensitive and her mind supple, while father's was ruled by over-self-confidence and a certain rigidity—acting woodenly. But he was the one who made all the important decisions concerning our up-bringing, education and social life. It never occurred to him that he might not have been placed by God as the head and judge over his wife and children. — It was his mother who struggled to keep her children fed when his father deserted for a period; and she who helped him get his college education which his father opposed; then his wife who raised three sons and two daughters while serving him over fifty years without restraint or complaint; and in his last feeble years when his wife, my mother, had died it was his sister and his daughters who read to him, fed him and led him while his eyesight failed — all women who had sustained him, kept him alive and in comfort. Yet to him women still had an evil, inferior streak not usually found in men. So insidious are the ancient myths and the strength of desire to feel superior."

Adam looked at Eve with new understanding and felt he would love to hear more of her girlhood. He puffed on his pipe then commented solemnly, "If our readers want us to present details of a social structure which would bring more joyful living between the sexes they ask an impossibility. Progress here will inch along depending upon many factors, especially what is done with our new slaughtering weapons."

"But we could give some thought to possible choices as to patterns of sexual life since our book centers on this subject. *It seems to me there are only three possible patterns for us to live under, besides today's double standard. —One is a single-standard society with strict laws prohibiting both men and women any sexual relations outside of marriage. Another is a single standard which is somewhat flexible and allows some controlled freedom to both. And a third is one which seems unimaginable, but is possible, a pattern which puts men in a strait jacket sexually while allowing women considerable freedom. It would be our double standard in reverse.*"

Adam cleared his throat and sat up, not knowing just what to say. Then remarked, "That last possibility would be fun to picture."

"But we should consider the others first. Of course that of our present privileged men and restricted women we have discussed at length. We needn't say more here. — Let's think about a society with one standard for men and women, absolutely no relations allowed either before marriage, only with one's spouse when married, and absolutely none if separated or widowed."

A society with a single standard, laws prohibiting any relations outside of marriage

"All right, Eve, I'll begin. To enforce these laws every

person would be required to carry an identification card with his picture, fingerprints, a certified statement as to whether married and a picture of his or her spouse. This card would be shown whenever one registered in a hotel, boarded a cruise ship, entered a night club, or airplane or was found in a parked car at a lonely spot. — Of course policemen in plain clothes would be circulating in all these places. Plain-clothes women police also, young women sometimes dressed in bare-shouldered evening dresses would be on cruises and in night clubs. They would take the part of stool pigeons to trap the men. Men who 'accosted' them would be arrested.

"Police records in central offices would be kept on each person with the suspicious places he had been seen. His whereabouts could be traced in the same manner as that of a banded bird, with a numbered ring around one leg. You know, each time a banded bird is caught the record of the time and place with its number is sent to Washington."

Eve caught her breath, "That is something to imagine! There would probably be no question as to who was the unwed father if a conception occurred. He would be as definitely known as the expectant mother. And of course he couldn't flee to escape responsibilities. — How about these young blades in our colleges? They'd have to be watched especially carefully."

"Yes, the boy and girl students would be segregated of course in different colleges, which would be placed out in the country or in very small towns, as are some of the exclusive girls' preparatory schools today. Autos not allowed."

"Widowers, separated or divorced men would be spied on continuously to assure their lonely celibacy. Their friends would also watch them, as friends and neighbors now watch women left alone —"

"— To help keep them in the straight and narrow. Every single man would guard his every move to prevent suspicion." Adam adjusted the tape on the recorder while he mulled this over, then continued, "Punishments for men's stepping aside would be much more than a levied fine. Prison sentences, such as are given prostitutes today, would be necessary. Yes, these and houses of detention and work houses would be numerous and all filled, but the government would approve these large expenditures."

"And one more thing we should mention. The sale of contraceptives would be permitted only to married persons upon showing their identification cards."

"Surely, Eve, we should also mention the institutions for the mentally ill, those men and women who were strained and torn by frustrating situations and also deprived of any solace derived from friendships with the opposite sex." They looked at each other as much as to say, "What a world of turmoil that would be."

"A very good point for I agree that some satisfying relations keep most of us from becoming really depressed at times, also from breaking down. Nature has made our bodies to rely on some relief, some lift at intervals," Eve said slowly and seriously as she heated water for some more coffee and Adam laid a fresh log on the fire.

They sat quietly watching the spreading flames buried in thought. At length Adam observed, "We must recognize that our country doesn't have legislation which restricts women as severely as that which we have just pictured for men and women."

"That's right. Actually our government depends upon other means of restricting them. It relies mainly on the fact that a woman may become pregnant — that she has the womb — to keep her in line. This, along with the plight in which society places her if conception out of marriage occurs."

"And more, as you have mentioned, Eve, the fact she may become pregnant is used as a reason why she must control the men, as well as herself.—The men are regarded as more or less irresponsible beings entitled to proposition all the girls and young women they wish, leaving it to them to make the big decisions. That is, young women are asked to hold the throttle controlling most all the extensive temptations and needs for some sexual life outside of marriage!"

"Some burden for them to carry, isn't it?—I do believe a society such as we imagined with its strict law enforcement operations *would* be necessary to compel men to live within such a rigid pattern. Most people would agree, I think."

"To realize the strength of the sexual drive we need only notice what has happened during past milleniums and goes on at present in other societies. I have here George Murdock's book, 'Social Structure', which we have referred to. After his study of various societies as to their customs and regulations he concluded that practically all have allowed some variation and freedom beyond marital intercourse." Adam leafed the pages and added, "He writes that, from available evidence, it looks as though a general prohibition of sexual relations outside of marriage occurs in only about 5% of the peoples of the earth."[2]

"But men's sexual freedom is always held within some bounds."

"Yes, that is emphasized by Murdock. In addition to men's permission to have more than one wife at a time in about 83% of the societies on which he had information, a majority of these societies allowed a man to conjugate with certain prescribed women besides his wife or wives. As we noted before, sisters-in-law are frequently allowed him and cousins sometimes. Also, a number of societies sanction either general sexual license or a definite slackening of usual restrictions on the occasions of certain festivals and religious ceremonies. Since most of the women who are allowed the men on these occasions are married, as well as the allowed sisters-in-law and cousins, it means that wives were usually permitted also some variation in mates."[3]

"There are many other anthropological studies which tell the same story, aren't there? — Let's turn to the next possible pattern which our country might develop. How about a society with a single standard, but instead of this being a strict, confining one, it were somewhat flexible, allowing certain freedoms?"

A single standard but flexible society

"All right. We should make clear first we don't mean complete license but rather some permissive variations under certain circumstances," Adam emphasized.

"Yes, and the basis of all allowed relationships would be mutual respect for each other. Such a society would necessarily be one with a higher degree of ethics than we have today, one where men recognized the justification of women's rounded, healthy life as well as their own. — In fact, such a society could not develop unless these things were so."

"Yes, and Eve, here every married couple would largely lay out its own pattern. Many would probably agree to restrict themselves entirely to each other for a good part of their life together, and the unusually well mated, all their lives. Also those couples where each of the pair was centered on certain projects or interests he might simplify his life by being entirely faithful to his spouse. — It is interesting to run over in one's mind the couples he knows. A man often learns of the freedoms his friends take."

"Don't think a single woman doesn't know also! Most all her men friends, married and single, feel her out and proposition her. I believe she may know the general situation better than the men."

"Perhaps she does; she is in a good position to know," Adam nodded.

They rested, again taking in the winter scene, watching the drifting snow and lacy shadow patterns of the swaying branches. Then Eve murmured, "You know, picturing this possible society seems painfully radical. I wonder if we should do it." She gazed at Adam for his response.

"Well, we can't stop here in our discussion between you and me, anyway. In fact, Alfred Kinsey and his associates in their extensive research have said a good part of what we could say here.[4] They have presented what takes place

309

largely by figures — in the most prosaic manner possible. If that material were presented as personal accounts by these thousands of women, telling the circumstances, reasons and satisfactions from their stepping aside, we'd have something far more enlightening and interesting."

"But all that would make several volumes in place of each one of their books." Eve added, "I'm sure that if each misstep were presented with the full, surrounding situations the reader would often regard it as justified— even a rigid Puritan. An insightful reader would realize that some affairs had undoubtedly kept a woman from serious depression. — What of the devastating experience of a husband's desertion of his children and his wife leaving her to carry a burden twice as large as he had borne and found too heavy? — I am convinced some of these mothers have been mentally saved through the companionship and consoling satisfactions with an understanding friend. It would have been too much to bear and adjust to in complete loneliness and sexual deprivation. — We must realize that these overwhelming experiences by mothers when their husbands decide to leave their families are usually accompanied by his attempted self-justification which includes severe criticism of her for this and that. Most of it is untrue, exaggerated or based on unreasonable expectations from her, as we have discussed. He often explains her supposed faults to their children, who are inclined to believe them since they have insufficient experience and knowledge to form a correct opinion of their own. The mother in this strained position naturally may be nervous and cross, which tends to verify the husband's critical remarks."

Eve paused as she lit a cigarette then went on, "When her half-grown children turn on her with accusations while expecting her continued care and affection as her husband goes freely off to a new honeymoon — believe me, she needs a friend. The loss of her children's appreciation and love is the last straw in tearing from her the regard of her family to which she has given her adult years and which

has constituted her world. It is the bitterest cup of gall! —
I have known well several instances like this."

"I have, too. Many men who stay on the boat with their
first families, often denying themselves certain novelties
recognize the ruthlessness of some of these divorcing husbands."

"I'm glad to hear that. — Of course such mothers on the
verge of collapse constitute only one group of women who
have misstepped. We must consider the many widowed
women. Here is part of a letter I received from a friend
which indicates what our present laws and customs, which
she obeyed, asked of her:

" 'After twenty years of warm closeness, sleeping together, our bodies against each other part of every
night, with his arms around my waist on occasion every
day, gaining fresh encouragement and sympathy
through his glances — I suddenly pass into the cold-
ness, strangeness of life without him. He is not there
for me to tend, to touch, to feed, to express his thoughts
or listen to mine.

Now, no arm ever rests around my waist, no warmth
of body ever touches me day or night. The indescribable
strength one feels from contact with a companion is
lacking day after day.

I keep asking myself, why should I do this just for
myself? It's not worth doing. Why should I dress this
evening? No one will see me. Why prepare a decent
meal for myself alone?

I snuggle my little six year old nephew to me. But
his mother gives me a cold look, as much as to say,
"Don't do that, it's not natural, not good for him. Don't
transfer to him the outgoing love your body longs to
give."

I may want to hug and kiss a woman friend so I
might only feel the warmth of an understanding human
body and obtain the fleeting shadow of the strength and
vitality I received daily from my husband. But all society would frown and think homosexuality, though
no sex would be involved.

My childhood beau, now married?—No. I must not
even feel the warmth of his hand except for a second
when I formally shake it.

The young man friend of my son's whom I have helped for years, who seems bursting with life and a certain appreciative love for me. Oh no, all say, 'Try not even be in the same room alone with him. You might give him a swift kiss.'

The sign, *Don't Touch*, seems to hang out everywhere. I'm like an Untouchable of India. I'll contaminate others. And why? Because I am starving for love, both to give and receive. Because I want to hold some breathing body to me, to share his breathing, his heart beat — just to feel less isolated from all other life for a few minutes—not the enfolding embrace of sex—only something to help me endure the days without it. And how many days will they be?

Perhaps all those in the next thirty or more years.' "

They sat silently when Eve had finished reading. Then Adam rose and strode across the room. "We do ask an awful lot from some women!" he remarked as he partially closed the window curtains since they were now too warm.

"I believe," Eve went on, "there is another group of wives made up of those who have accepted a lover while their husbands were gone for periods of months or years, and were taking their own freedom.—And still another group, I think, are those women of couples long married where both husband and wife have found sexual relations completely monotonous, where each knew the other's thoughts before he spoke. The husband had found he sometimes was not interested in intercourse when she was, and vice versa. It had surprised them both—this situation compared to their first years together. So he had decided to gain some new lift through a cautious affair with a lonely widowed friend. And he, having a sense of fair play, had agreed his wife could also enjoy a change. Some of such wives of course were beyond their reproductive period."

"Yes, and we haven't mentioned the young women before marriage — nor the engaged young women in Kinsey's study, who learned something of this field before they were in it for life with one exclusive partner. — We'd find other groups if we knew all the circumstances of the misstepping."

"Who can say, Adam, that an engaged couple are better

312

off if they remain sexual strangers until after marriage? Or that each can best know whether he is going to bind himself to the most congenial mate he can find, while he remains ignorant of that person's attitudes toward the core of their future life together?"

"I gather that all the situations must have been surrounded with deep emotions which led these women to revolt while threatened with ostracism and other dangers." Adam continued, "In the single-standard society we are now imagining, people would view with understanding the true position of these women —"

"Instead of hanging a sword over them for finding some relief, they would recognize them as human beings needing to keep poised while they carry on their tasks in good spirit," Eve added. "And as to possible conception out of marriage, we must realize that scientists will soon develop a more effective contraceptive. Since they have created other wonders they'll surely make this before long. Some shudder at the thought of such a development. But they are really shuddering at relieving women from bearing unplanned babies. — Not something to shiver over. We will come to recognize that a condition which means only planned and wanted babies is devoutly to be desired."

"All these thoughts do sound radical, particularly to those who imagine that our present regulations are generally observed. In fact, many seem to feel that if they turn their heads from the present facts, the facts won't exist. Also, that if they refuse to inquire into the reasons why our rigid regulations are not completely bowed to, they will be better obeyed."

"Exactly, Adam. And most adults seem to believe that the wise policy is not to give boys and girls at sea in our confused society any thought as to what might be a dignified ethical pattern of life which also recognizes their vital needs."

"We should mention here again your idea of each passing the other a love-letter or statement if he has relations out of marriage to express his mutual regard and trust. — I believe that such a pattern would avoid the hypocrisy and frequent exploitation in our present society which eats at the roots of all ethical and religious thinking. Just as an example, I know a judge who sat in his robes and determined a prison sentence for a young woman with whom he had had illicit relations. He confessed it to me.—We need a new tone in our living, one of freshness, honestly, aboveboard behavior, especially in this area," Adam concluded as he watched the changing reds and purples in the fire.

"And there's another consideration we haven't mentioned. This single-standard society would, I think, do wonders in the matter of preventing the horrible disillusionment most women now experience some time in their lives. One can't deny that our girls are taught to expect their husbands' exclusive, life-long partnership. Doesn't the bridegroom promise this? — And then about one wife out of every three or four is deserted or divorced and most of the others must endure his unfaithfulness. Shouldn't education aim to give the truth, to prepare young women for what they may encounter? In this imagined society women could be prepared and would be allowed to help themselves. They might lose some of their delightful dreams of their husbands' exclusiveness, but they'd be saved from the later devastating depths of disillusionment." They mulled over this. Then Eve glanced at the clock. "Let's have a good lunch at the Corner House."

They climbed into Adam's car, turned their minds to other things while eating and shopping. When they returned Adam laid a new fire, observing, "This is our last session for the tape — an important one."

"Yes, indeed. We hope those interested will read between the lines — will regard many of our statements like strokes of a brush in impressionistic painting, only suggestive of our full thoughts. — I was thinking that if we knew the full story of the great men of Old Greece, the philosophers, sculptors and writers, we would find they were sustained and inspired by the women they loved, not one and only one through the life of each, but several who filled their needs

314

at different periods. The same is true, I think, of most the sculptors and artists of the Renaissance; then those of the later ages, the leading writers in all tongues as well as most creative leaders. I should not attempt to give the names of all those where we know this is true. They have as a rule refused to be deadened by the loneliness of a celibate life, to have their imaginations withered by the frustrations of a relationship whose inspiration had passed. They, being men, could violently break from the walls which society has at times tried to place around them. They were able to continue to make their contributions in the face of criticism, often poverty and sometimes persecution by gaining some sustenance, some encouragement, from the close companionship of a lover."

Eve then sought the right words as she continued. "It is to be marvelled that any woman has made any leading contribution in the arts or sciences when we realize that not only has she usually struggled with frequent pregnancies and childbirth but has handled most of the mechanics of family living, while often forced to continue a relationship which has lost all its glow, or to live with no lover for large portions, or her entire life. She has often existed in essential loneliness, in the deadening adjustments to unsatisfactory sexual companionship, or its denial, all under surrounding fears that she could be ruined by evil tales if only she made a gesture showing her deep hungers. Where has she gained the necessary sustenance to carry her along through the difficulties in steadfast persistence, basic to making any mental contribution? Yet some women have made great creative offerings, and their number is large considering the very few who have been allowed some time for concentration, some opportunity for flights of the imagination."

"True, quite true, Eve. — Also, when we study the lives of these leading men we find that they usually gained the many, uninterrupted hours for their work by passing to their mates most of the child-raising work, as deserting fathers, as unwed fathers and also as fathers who stayed with their families. It would be fun to gather together these features of their lives. — They had the stimulation of sexual companions while often freeing themselves largely or completely even from child support."

"And now, as to the present," Eve said with feeling, "as our race actually teeters on the brink of destruction, it calls for sufficient concern for human life to keep in bounds our lethal weapons. — Women's greater influence is essential to our salvation. Let us at last liberate them. Let's allow their full vitalities to grow. Let their imaginations soar, their ingenuity with human relations be put to work for some solutions to our present, painful state. This can be done only by taking them out of their strait jackets, allowing them blocks of time for concentration and a full and rounded, natural life. Such a society as we are now imagining would allow them these far more than at present."

Adam and Eve seemed to silently carry on this direction in their thoughts. Only the crackling fire could be heard. Adam moved closer to the flames stretching out his hands to feel their warmth, and smiled to himself. "Shouldn't we now glimpse the next possible pattern of life between the sexes — that one with two standards of morals, one giving the women considerable freedom, the other forbidding the man all sexual relations except with his wife. It seems impossible. But it could come about through some catastrophic circumstances, such as—," Adam reflected, "—a deadly plague following a war which attacked a large portion of men. A disease, like hemophilia, to which only men were subject, might carry off great numbers of them, while those who survived were left in a weak state. During the following centuries women would be forced to shoulder the leadership of society. The government positions now occupied by men and those in business and trade would be given to the women."

"And they would regard the men, Adam, as very precious helpers and mates, concluding their place was best in the shelter of their homes. Wives might also feel it risky to

316

allow their husbands association with other women out in the business world."

A society with a double standard in reverse

"The men would probably keep busy cleaning and cooking while they tended the children. Since their wives would bring in the money income, the men and children would be financially dependent upon them and women doubtless would become the legal family heads." Eve paused, "You know, many men will think our picturing such a society is a vicious thing, that it reveals my personal discontent—that we should not stoop to such outlandish thoughts."

"Oh, yes, but this is not the first shocking thing we've done in our discussions. We might as well throw them all out together."

"Well, we'll hold each other up. I'll go on. — After some decades during which the roles were largely reversed women would have found it all quite pleasant. They would gain real self-confidence and learn through their extensive responsibilities. I believe they'd find stimulation in receiving an income which was somewhat in proportion to their ability and the complexity of their jobs. This would be envigorating for them, I'm sure—a contrast to their former situation where most mothers were passed some of their husband's earnings, the amount they received having no relationship to their efficiency in the home, or the size of their jobs. — The husbands in this reversed society who did the most difficult dollar-stretching in running the home would be those whose personal economic rewards were the lowest, were in kind, that is received in the form of food, housing and clothes — and these of the scantiest and poorest quality."

Adam always interested in family economics added, "And the husband who cared for six children might well have only $3,000 yearly available for running the home while a house-husband raising two might have $30,000 yearly.— Men had never realized these unreasonable relationships until they did the house work."

"And even the women when they lived in our present setup had not fully recognized this. Those who had felt the full brunt of heavy jobs and insufficient funds had been buried in tense confusion — told to pray for patience and strength."

Sudden loud footsteps were in the hall, then a voice calling. "Eve Beaupomme, where are you—and Adam I've looked in your office. I hear your voices."

"It's John," Adam said as he went to the door and called out to him, "We're in the lounge, come on in."

John entered with a flourish. "So here you are, cuddled around the fire. You felt out the choice place. May I join you?"

"Take off your coat," Adam said and pulled up another chair.

"Where are you now — in the moon, on Mars or living a thousand years in the future?" John inquired, making himself at home.

They explained that his last guess was closest and told him of their imagined society after a calamitous war.

"Well, that's fun to consider. Glad I dropped in to help. — Did you bring out how hard the women would work if they were out in the world earning the living, the stiff competition, the slack periods?"

"It would be tough at times," Eve replied, "but I think almost none of these young earning women would want to return to the former restricted life in the home — no more than most men today are willing to take on their wives' housekeeping rounds."

"My guess is, you're right." Adam continued with thought. "The women would build up a mountain of reasons why most the cooking and cleaning should be done by their husbands. In fact, if any men complained or tried to break away from the pattern they'd soon find they were far better off if they happily adjusted themselves to their assigned role."

"Here are some of the thoughts which would be spread among the house-husbands who might write or struggle for more independence." Eve read a passage from a book reversing the sexes:

> "They are 'unsexed men, unsexed in mind, all of them propounding the doctrine that they should be allowed to step out of their appropriate sphere to the neglect of their duties which both human and divine law have assigned them. . . . Man's power comes through a self-sacrificing spirit ready to offer up all his hopes, upon the shrine of his wife's wishes." [5]

John sneered. "Well, for the like of that! What nerve! We'd be expected to exist wholly to please our wives."

"Yes, that might well become the theory. You might work not only for your wife's business success, but also to help her enjoy her hobbies, her dogs, her fine clothes or her collection of house plants — to save her *valuable* time," Eve added with a twinkle. "You'd do it without complaint, too, or your wife might become estranged — find another man friend who better played up to her.'

"I'd be damned if she would!"

Adam and Eve chuckled. "You haven't thought carefully enough about it all yet. What could you do to stop her?" Adam asked, "If you had almost no property of your own and were attached to the children to whom you were giving daily care would you risk her becoming estranged — and perhaps leaving you for a new husband?"

"Your explosive attitude, John, toward a wife who expected so much and who had the power to readily put you in the soup with your children is because you haven't been properly conditioned to such a role. — As new generations of men came along they'd be better and better adjusted. Some marriage counselors and psychoanalysts would be continually advising their calm acceptance of their role." Eve continued, "Remember John, the culture on all sides would value the men who sweetly accepted their place, who made a peaceful, settled atmosphere in their homes and it would be filled with criticism and prophecy of failure for the men who rejected it."

Adam took the ball and went on, "I believe the women would enjoy many friends made in their business life, eating lunch with them, taking business trips and going to night clubs — and more — with them when out of town."

"And you musn't omit the ever-present young man secretary at each business woman's beck and call who'd never dare give her any back-talk, as her husband might sometimes. This well-dressed young fellow would respectfully look up to his superior for orders," Eve paused. "When she came to the office after a self-deflating family argument in which her adolescent children entered, this pleasant, obedient secretary would give her just the lift she wanted. — She might even fall in love with him."

Eve glanced at John, who seemed to be bewildered as he shifted in his chair, then straightened up and said, "Yes, I've heard of more than one husband who left his family to marry his secretary. I guess the business wives in your society might do it, too. — You don't mind my saying that this supposed arrangement of things doesn't go down well with us men. — It makes me feel a little nauseated." John looked at Adam for sympathy.

"You're right, John, it gives me that feeling and more. I keep thinking, *impossible* for me to be in that position and closing my mind to it. — But then, I've entered this job of analyzing our present pattern and I know there's no better way of seeing all sides than stretching my mind, by imagining myself in the position of others. So I force myself to do it. I can't refuse to carry on at this point."

"Well, you're brave. Don't know if I can follow you."

"Try to a little more. It's good mental exercise, John. — Your wife in this reversed society would have the routine of office work performed by her men secretaries and clerks, while the routine of her home would be carried on by you. She would be free for administrative work, decision-making or some kind of challenging mental activity — all of which would bring her a good income. It might well give her a feeling of superiority." Adam poked together the unburned pieces of wood in the fireplace.

"Many men, I am afraid, would feel restless, find it hard to believe what they were told, that their tasks were as stimulating and challenging as the women's. Their basic uneasiness might be that they were not using their mental and creative capacities. This would come over some of them during the tenth or fifteenth year of pounding the type-writer, or the twentieth year of washing dishes." Eve glanced out the window as she thought. "They'd probably find some relief from home chores by joining groups of house-husbands, rolling bandages, sewing for Red Cross, helping with rummage sales."

John sneered again, "A big relief, a great change for them!"

"You see the situation, John. Good! — Most husbands would be irritated also over their economic dependence and their resulting weak position. Their wives would constantly reward or punish them for their compliance to their wishes, passing them more or less of their salary, making them gifts or not," Eve went on, "taking them out to dinner or not, and even sometimes threatening divorce. Some inde-pendent husbands might think that a basic principle of democracy is that no person is wise enough — or should have the power to so completely rule over another's life."

Adam looked at John, "We haven't yet pictured the half of it! Here are some Tums for your stomach. Perhaps you should also take some tranquilizing pills. — In this society you, as a young man, would have to cover up your excited feelings toward a particular girl. Would you dress strikingly to win her attention, risking her thinking you loud, or would you dress modestly, hoping she'd figure you'd make a good home-loving father?"

"You think this is fun. I don't! My mind refuses to work. —Sorry I dropped in, but now I'm here, I'll stay." John mumbled slouched in a blue fog.

Eve was sympathetic. "You needn't answer him. We are not imagining this to upset you, John, remember. We are simply trying to illuminate the features of our present pattern — hoping to thaw out some men's minds which are in a deep freeze. They have been frozen for ages thinking women's role, as they require it, is the role women entirely wish for thmselves and would adopt if they were free."

"Don't feel bad," Adam added. "You react to this only as most men would. In fact most would leave the room right now — and you are staying with a partially open mind. Some Greek poet wrote, 'Wisdom is supple; folly keeps in a groove.'"

Eve nodded her approval. "We'll go on with our picture, if you don't mind, John. — Of course the woman would decide on which man she'd propose to. There'd be marked psychological effects on the man as he waited patiently, tried to keep up his hopes, to look happy, while he longed for a girl friend to ask him out, to invite him to a dance, to telephone. Some would see all the women they liked gradually marry, they themselves being left out — and getting older, soon too old to be in demand. If they then took more initiative toward women their uneasy or desperate state would be evident and the women would avoid them still more. — Such forward men might chase the women away, for all these women would want to keep in the lead."

"Of course we should mention the private life in bed of the married couple. Most of what we've noted would probably take place in reverse," Adam observed, now putting himself in this aggravating position rather than John. "The double standard would require me, if I were in that society, not only to restrict myself sexually to my wife but restrict all my goings-out and comings-in with other women, my conversations, my roving eyes, so that I would not disturb her. — And all this, even if my wife seemed to be having an affair and was away from home weeks at a time on 'business trips'."

"You nevertheless would try your best, Adam, to enjoy sexual relations with your philandering wife, and if you didn't succeed you might *pretend* you were taken to the heights of satisfaction to please and stimulate her. It would be hard, but your bread and butter might be dependent on doing it, and also that of your children. You'd probably be eating out of her hands and would act accordingly. At least this pretense might be necessary to preserve the united family. — That fatal downward spiral of affection you'd realize must be avoided, for if your wife felt your sexual interest in her was waning, that you were cool, she'd find further ground for her outside affairs."

Adam and Eve mentioned further incidents which would occur and the many husbands who would endure long periods of quiet frustration.

John, to show that he was recovering his equanimity, or to rest his mind, called attention to the sunset, the lavender light showing over the snow drifts. They rested while drinking it in and Adam refilled his pipe.

"Now tell me, Eve, why do you think that the women in this society would support the double standard in favor of themselves and would make the men dependent house-husbands? Perhaps they'd develop a more democratic set-up?"

"A good question, John. I do think that women generally have more insight into human relations, greater sensitivity to others' feelings. Psychologists recognize this quality in women. So the roles of the sexes might not be exactly reversed. In our imagined society the women might remember their previous caged-in feelings and allow men a broader life. I think they'd not expect them to raise such large families of children. But human nature, especially as to the effects of power on the personality, is fairly similar in men and women. Since these women would hold extensive power, I believe, we should expect that the same impulses which led men to develop the pattern of our present society might lead women to arrange a society with things largely reversed.—Of course I may be wrong.—We must remember that we are trying mainly to *feel* the full impact of our present social customs and laws upon women."

"Well, Eve, I must admit you've made me feel it. You've

made me very uncomfortable. I see too much. — How will we ever get a setup that is really democratic, that allows both men and women basic freedoms and opportunities," John asked.

"I wager the guess, it can be developed only as men and women come to have some equality of power — so that neither sex can center upon his own advantages, but is forced to cooperate as a partner with the other. Then I believe they can work along together a step at a time, experimenting, weighing results and experimenting some more."

"Actually, in our society today women are gradually gaining more power," Adam interposed. "In a prosperous country like ours property flows over to women from their parents as gifts and inheritance and from wealthy husbands, also numerous job openings allow larger and larger numbers of women to earn. Opportunity to vote and their higher education are important factors. If women are conscious of what is taking place and of what they want, they can influence current changes."

The telephone ringing in the hall interrupted, and John went out to answer. Returning he explained, "It's Dorothy. She says a friend has dropped in to see me, I must go home. If you're going to make more real that society of walled-in men, I'm glad I'm leaving."

They laughed as John bade them good-bye. Adam and Eve wandered to the window to feel more a part of the sparkling scene. They stood there quietly. Adam called her attention to the slow rhythm of the swaying ice-covered branches.

"This eerie light part from the moon, part from the reflected sun all mirrored about from ice and snow is appropriate to our efforts at glancing into the future," Eve observed as they settled back on the divan Adam's hand holding hers.

A new ethics for survival

At length Eve reflected, "It may well be that as mankind gains more and more ability to cripple the whole human race or to kill it off, he will be forced to face social problems, to organize his thoughts and to figure what should be done in order to survive. When he comes to this he will turn his mind to methods of assuring health and well-being, not for the fortunate, but for all, those of all classes and of all nations."

"This common aim will bring together peoples' thinking. They will see that in order to stop international anarchy they must move toward a rule of world law and negotiate their differences."

"Oh, yes. And people will realize even better than today— though it has been evident since written history — that one's holding extensive power over another individual or group is likely to lead to his demoralization, for 'power tends to corrupt, absolute power corrupts absolutely.'"

"To build a balanced, peaceful society," Adam added, "pressure, constant pressure, will be brought upon the dominant groups to limit their acquisition of power and property."

"Yes, *if* we pass into this stage of planning a healthy society, it will involve a difficult-to-come-by recognition of certain basic truths by the various groups with the reins. They will finally be persuaded and convinced that if they wish to live with others in an interdependent community — and they will realize this cannot be avoided — their desires must conform to the realities of such a society. And their desires for personal property which often increase without limit: for luxuries and evidences of their wealth; for the enjoyment of many mates; for the pleasures of wielding authority will be curbed in order to be an integral part of that on-going community upon which they depend for their existence. They will recognize that using another person while disregarding the other's own needs for autonomy and growth cannot be continually done even if the other has the womb. The dominant groups in short will find the necessary conditions of successful association.

"To put it concretely I think of that model in the Metropolitan Museum of Art in New York.[6] It presents so vividly the life of an Egyptian noble about 2000 B.C. The small wooden model was found in his grave along with others, which were placed there to assure his taking his slaves and luxuries into his life after death. It shows the figure of Meket-Ré, the nobleman, sitting in his boat under a canopy as his servants row him down the Nile. This model shows that all his senses are being catered to; as he enjoys the passing scenes along the river; listens to a kneeling servant who sings, another who plays the harp for him; as his body is cooled by a palm leaf fan waved over him; and to please his sense of smell a man holds a lotus blossom to his nose, while the odors of cooking are kept at a distance in a separate tender which follows where women servants grind wheat and bake his food. He rests in the thought of his stores of oil, wine and grain tended by still other slaves; of his faithful wife and harem of submissive, beautiful girls; of his life in the hereafter well provided for by the models and jewels to be arranged in the tomb of his pyramid.

"All this while the large majority of Egyptian people, as serfs and slaves, lived in small huts constantly in fear of not pleasing their superiors and of not having sufficient food.—Tyranny with many in servitude is the natural and easy form of government.

"I claim," Eve continued, "that the contrast today in the position of our business tycoons and head officers of large corporations, compared to that of many mothers is as great. Here is a notice of an annual shareholders' meeting of a big company. An officer receives $100,000 in yearly salary and $50,000 in the year's bonus, has rights to buy his company's shares below the market, of course gets an additional income from his other investments, deducts most of his entertainment expenses from his income tax and when he retires will receive a pension of $35,000 a year. The woman who cleans his office is of retirement age and has raised by herself five children. One of her sons was killed in combat resulting from action which saved the lives of his platoon, another received a medal for distinguished service. But our society says through its remuneration to her in the past and present that she has done practically nothing for our country. It is not only the skimpy amount of property which is allowed her but denial of health-giving thoughts and activities, sufficient rest, sexual satisfactions, respect from others and freedom from worry, which build up the great contrast in their lives."

"A good illustration of basic injustice. It illustrates the present often illogical distribution of honor and property, similar through history. We perceive it in other countries but it is hard to recognize in our own. The question is, how far should each person limit his personal gratifications in order to help develop a sounder pattern?" Adam leaned back in his chair, then observed, "There's much preaching by the wealthy, such as that workers should be willing to move their homes about in order to find jobs, like good hunting dogs; that mothers should gladly work ten or twelve hours daily at a double job to raise their children — with no thought of how these preachers might limit their own gratifications for society's good. Doesn't their affluent living spark the whole elbowing about, the squeezing of each other financially, the centering upon personal property?"

"Oh, yes, our religion today with its vague ethics does not seem to be inspiring many government officials and business leaders with the sacredness of their jobs. I've just been reading about some high federal officials' misuse of their responsibilities. Could a religion based on building a worthy future for our race inspire them — a religion that instills the realization that we are all setting examples to children?

"I believe," Eve went on haltingly, "we need a new religion or new emphasis in our old one — a new ethical philosophy which includes at its base the wise bearing and raising of those who carry on our life. We need a philosophy which is concerned with the present, which recognizes the foolishness of trying to save one's own soul by formalities while he ignores nearby neighbors sick with worry or downcast over a son's leaving school to help earn, and distant neighbors half-nourished, wanting more education. Instead of patting each other on the back for our high standard of living and imagining that we are leaders in the world, we need to recognize our responsibilities through our wealth, not gained entirely by our own work but partly because we occupy this land of rich natural resources. We should vision the possibility of establishing the basic conditions of a good life for all humanity. That is, sufficient food and proper housing, to liberate the mind for study and for thought, allowing it freedom to plan for the future and to believe as reason and conscience prompt."

"You've got it," Adam said like an amen as he again poked the slowly burning logs. "The big challenge of the age is to develop the concept of a higher loyalty—loyalty to the human community."

"To re-discover our moral strength and re-direct our energies. Biologists say that each group in animal life tends to realize all its inherent possibilities and then becomes stabilized, incapable of major advance. Could male society be there — incapable of breaking away from international competition backed by weapons of massive retaliation? It might. It's salvation may be found by calling forth a somewhat different social group, the women, and asking their help." Eve paused. "We should come to recognize the importance of women's minds, their drives toward nurturing human life, and call them into government council chambers to help break the impasse of threatened destruction and to help map a new orientation of our lives. God created woman's body and also her mind. Men have not yet really recognized this."

"Not in general. I agree, we need their help. And this new ideology or thought-organization should recognize the constant change in our knowledge, the basic fact of evolution in all things, and continually restate its ethical standards in

328

the light of new conditions. We should not be solely concerned with general persuasion from the pulpits of churches that people follow an ethics laid down 2,000 to 4,000 years ago. We must move beyond the magic pattern of primitive, tribal thought and the supernatural centering of medieval religion into an ideology based on what we now know and sense in the various sciences and the concept of human progress recognizing that we may be misled if we misuse and kill our brothers for some *abstract* purpose, such as the honor of God or the honor of a particular nation and become buried in emotional clouds of anger and fear. In past wars the nations on both sides have claimed they were killing their enemies for the honor of their God."

"How true, Adam. A religion for survival cannot use other-worldly morality, soul-saving prayers, songs and formalities as a pretext for evading the questions of morality among living people. All these religious ceremonies are rightfully only a means to the end of leading us to be one with our fellow beings. Yet many make these means the end. — And I believe a newly oriented religion," Eve continued in her modulated voice, "should hold up to its followers a policy which most are able to carry out, not one which asks such self-sacrifice that none observe its full teaching. Complete self-sacrifice even unto death may be the highest service if one has no children, but it cannot be so universally. At least one of the ideal men held forth in such a religion would be an admirable father, giving men greater inspiration in their parental tasks. And of course it would give an equally elevated position to the admirable mother."

"I understand, Eve, what you are saying with caution. Go on, don't let me interrupt."

"Our ethical pattern, our religion of today, is largely man-made, belittling the extensive tasks of parents; belittling woman's importance, her tremendous contributions, her fine abilities and judgment, especially in the crucial matters of human relations."

"What an argument could be started on each of those features," Adam exclaimed. "At present we are gaining in our control of everything except ourselves."

"Yes, we dream and stare at the satellites we have shot into space while our race may be moving toward its own doom. More women than men wonder if these may not be men's flaunting and flourishing of his new power while he looks away from the more difficult job of controlling himself — of preventing the careless using up of our natural resources, of preventing the too rapid increase of the mouths to be fed while preparing for a nuclear war, the most senseless and lunatic act which could take place. Some of the billions upon billions now used for war devices would be turned to the care of our children under this new religion. A child's opportunity would not be left to chance, in the hands of a widowed mother or a family with an alcoholic or invalid father. A mother's energies would not be considered indefinitely extendable. Men, as well as women, would recognize that, 'The future of the race marches forward on the feet of little children.' The father would be expected to give far more thought and time to his children and to children in general, than he gives today."

"And the pattern of allowed sexual relations would be one which considers children's opportunities. A man, married or single, would not be allowed to act disregarding possible conception of his child. You have convinced me of the importance of that," Adam added smiling.

"Thanks, my dear. I do believe it's fundamental. Of course this all sounds so simple, so naive — planning around children—but actually it has never been done, not even in family laws, for the council chambers have been occupied by men, the religious thinking formulated by groups of men, such as the Essenes of 100 B.C., whose manuscripts have been recently found. Most were not married. Children were regarded as of little importance and they thought God was soon bringing human life to an inevitable end. The women were kept out of their walled religious center, away from their sacred baths, from the libraries of manuscripts and the discussions on morality and the future. Evidently women were regarded as a disturbance to their profound thought and the saving of their souls.

"In similar fashion women today are excluded from the conferences which direct the spending of some two thirds of our national government's income in preparation for war and which judge the morality of other nations and our own. — Was the masculine thought of the Essenes and is that of our military groups on the wrong track? — At present our councils of military men are making decisions on how much strontium-90 is thrown into the air by nuclear bomb testing, absorbed into our bodies, stored in our bones emitting rays affecting our blood corpuscles—also influencing our sensitive reproductive cells so that, 'Generation after generation, for centuries to come will witness the birth of an ever-increasing number of children with mental and physical defects, as the medical doctor and philosopher Dr. Albert Schweitzer states.[7] Are our military heads corrupted by the power in their hands?"

Adam knocked burned tobacco from his pipe. "Our dream of a new society planning for survival may never occur. Man may be unable to change his course. The animal drive toward combat, toward domination of others may continue, leading certain groups in most countries to keep or gain vast power, threaten and bomb each other until the lethal end."

"All this, while that half of our race most concerned with raising and preserving life is held down with strong hands and rigid laws, thought too soft to help govern national and international events."

Adam put his arm around Eve's shoulder. "Lincoln said it well, 'The dogmas of the quiet past are inadequate for the stormy present. We must think anew, we must act anew, we must disenthrall ourselves.' "

"And part of our disenthrallment, of shaking ourselves from the servitude of past theories is the necessity for men and women to combine their thinking as you and I are doing, to mutually honor and help each other so we may be able to take steps toward this new society."

Eve gave Adam a warm kiss expressing her deep appreciation of his understanding and of her love for him. He took her in his arms.

CHAPTER 15

1. *New York Times*, September 13, 1957.
2. George P. Murdock, *Social Structure*, Macmillan Co., 1949, pp. 24, 263, 264.
3. Ibid., p. 28, 267, 268. Also Chapter 9.
4. Alfred C. Kinsey et al, *Sexual Behavior in the Human Female*, W.B. Saunders Co., Philadelphia and London, 1953.
5. *Victory, How Women Won It*, prepared by the National American Woman Suffrage Association, H.W. Wilson Co., 1940, pp. 35, 11. Said by a man opponent.
6. Egyptian Collection, The Metropolitan Museum of Art, New York City, Models of Meket-Ré.
7. Albert Schweitzer, "An Obligation to Tomorrow," *Saturday Review of Literature*, May 24, 1958.